ON THE ROAD TO PERDITION

BOOK 3: DETOUR

writer
MAX ALLAN COLLINS

penciller
JOSÉ LUIS GARCÍA-LÓPEZ

inker
STEVE LIEBER

letterer
ROB LEIGH

PARADOX PRESS  NEW YORK, NEW YORK

Paradox Press / DC Comics
DAN DiDIO, VP-Editorial · JOAN HILTY, Editor
HARVEY RICHARDS, Assistant Editor · AMIE BROCKWAY-METCALF, Art Director
PAUL LEVITZ President & Publisher · GEORG BREWER VP-Design & Retail Product Development
RICHARD BRUNING Sr. VP-Creative Director · PATRICK CALDON Sr. VP-Finance & Operations
CHRIS CARAMALIS VP-Finance · TERRI CUNNINGHAM VP-Managing Editor
ALISON GILL VP-Manufacturing · RICH JOHNSON VP-Book Trade Sales
HANK KANALZ VP-General Manager, WildStorm · LILLIAN LASERSON Sr. VP & General Counsel
JIM LEE Editorial Director-WildStorm · DAVID McKILLIPS VP-Advertising & Custom Publishing
JOHN NEE VP-Business Development · GREGORY NOVECK Sr. VP-Creative Affairs
CHERYL RUBIN VP-Brand Management · BOB WAYNE VP-Sales & Marketing

❖

❖

Cover artist: STEVE LIEBER
Cover colors and separations: DAVE McCAIG

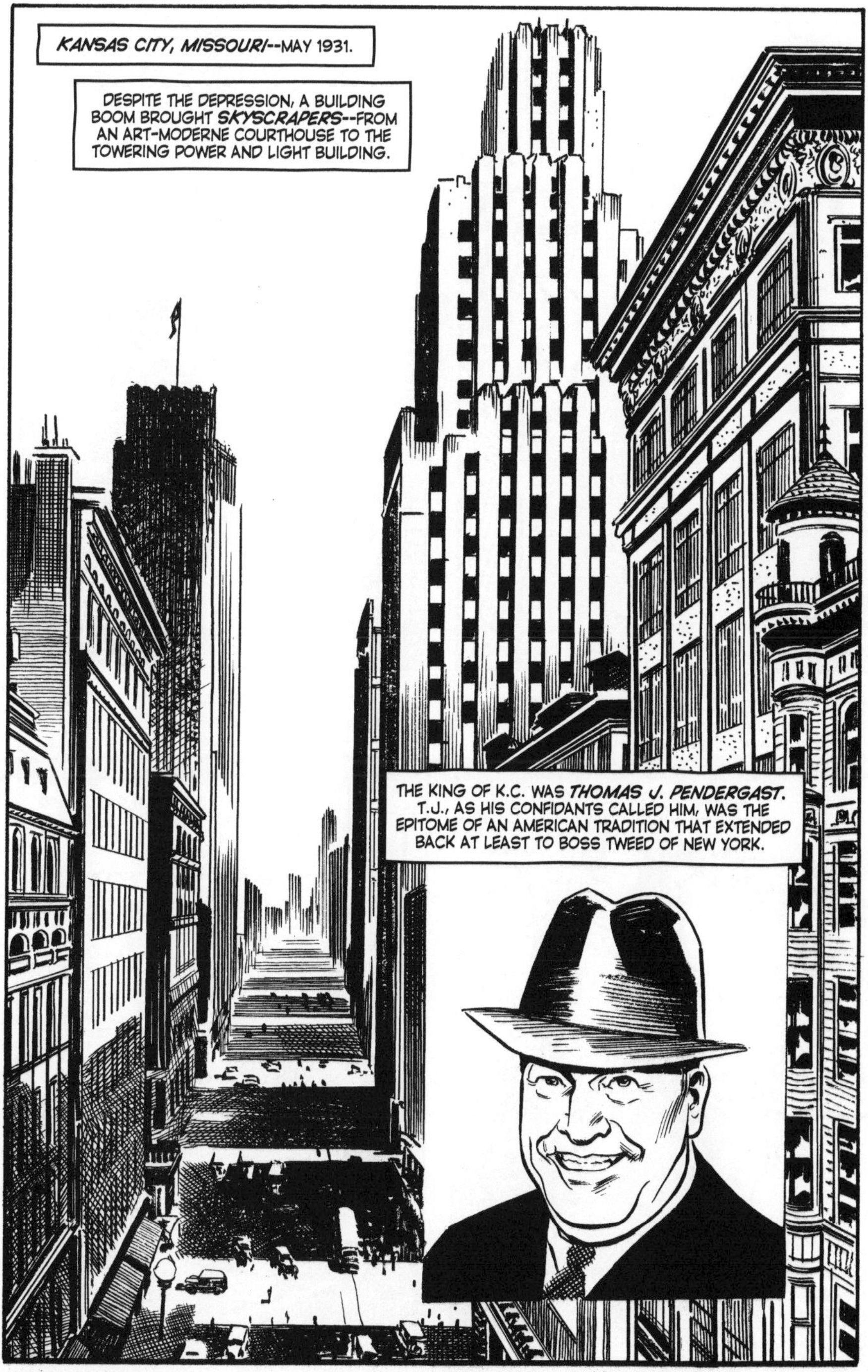
KANSAS CITY, MISSOURI--MAY 1931.
DESPITE THE DEPRESSION, A BUILDING BOOM BROUGHT SKYSCRAPERS--FROM AN ART-MODERNE COURTHOUSE TO THE TOWERING POWER AND LIGHT BUILDING.
THE KING OF K.C. WAS THOMAS J. PENDERGAST. T.J., AS HIS CONFIDANTS CALLED HIM, WAS THE EPITOME OF AN AMERICAN TRADITION THAT EXTENDED BACK AT LEAST TO BOSS TWEED OF NEW YORK.

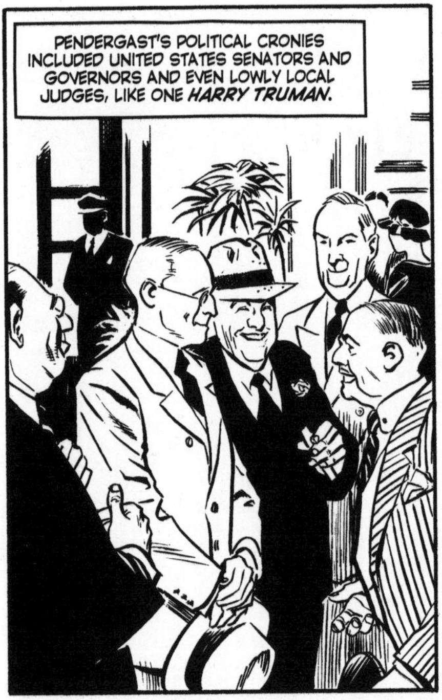
PENDERGAST'S POLITICAL CRONIES INCLUDED UNITED STATES SENATORS AND GOVERNORS AND EVEN LOWLY LOCAL JUDGES, LIKE ONE HARRY TRUMAN.

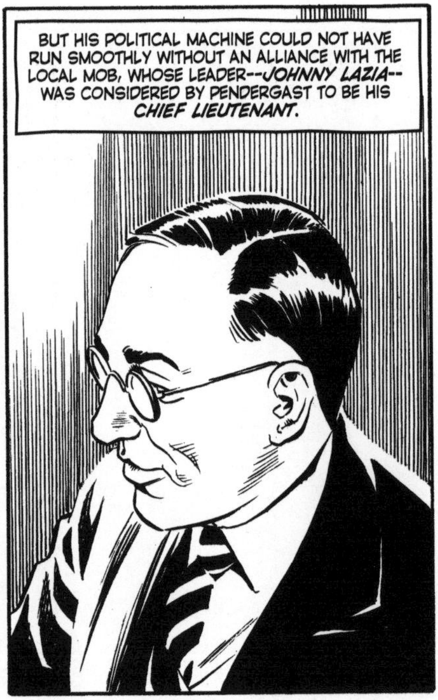
BUT HIS POLITICAL MACHINE COULD NOT HAVE RUN SMOOTHLY WITHOUT AN ALLIANCE WITH THE LOCAL MOB, WHOSE LEADER--JOHNNY LAZIA--WAS CONSIDERED BY PENDERGAST TO BE HIS CHIEF LIEUTENANT.

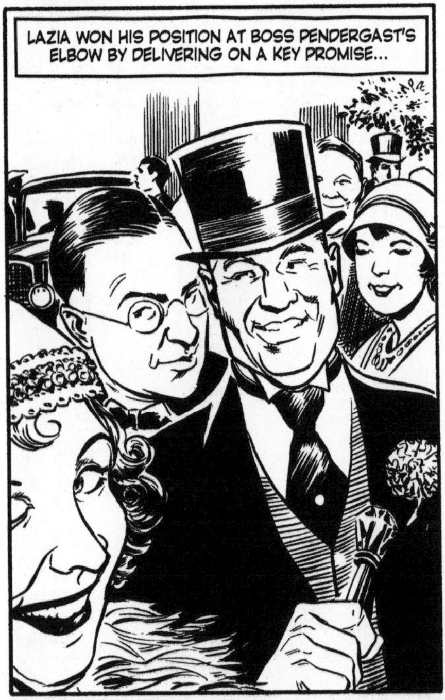
LAZIA WON HIS POSITION AT BOSS PENDERGAST'S ELBOW BY DELIVERING ON A KEY PROMISE...

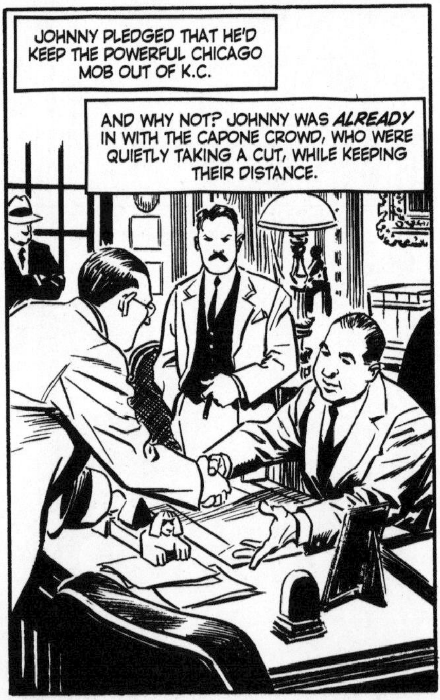
JOHNNY PLEDGED THAT HE'D KEEP THE POWERFUL CHICAGO MOB OUT OF K.C.
AND WHY NOT? JOHNNY WAS ALREADY IN WITH THE CAPONE CROWD, WHO WERE QUIETLY TAKING A CUT, WHILE KEEPING THEIR DISTANCE.

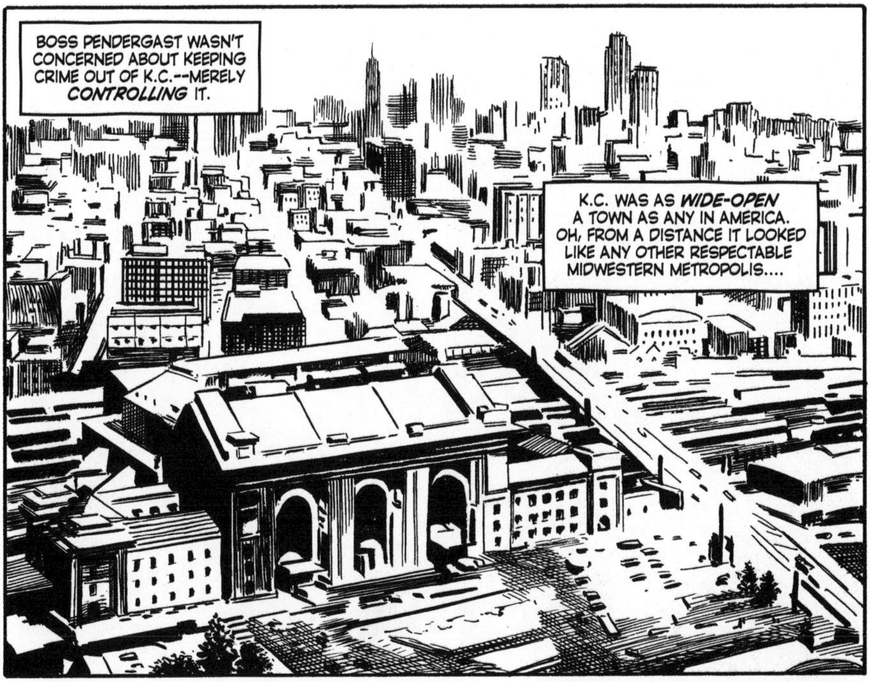
BOSS PENDERGAST WASN'T CONCERNED ABOUT KEEPING CRIME OUT OF K.C.--MERELY ***CONTROLLING*** IT.
K.C. WAS AS ***WIDE-OPEN*** A TOWN AS ANY IN AMERICA. OH, FROM A DISTANCE IT LOOKED LIKE ANY OTHER RESPECTABLE MIDWESTERN METROPOLIS....

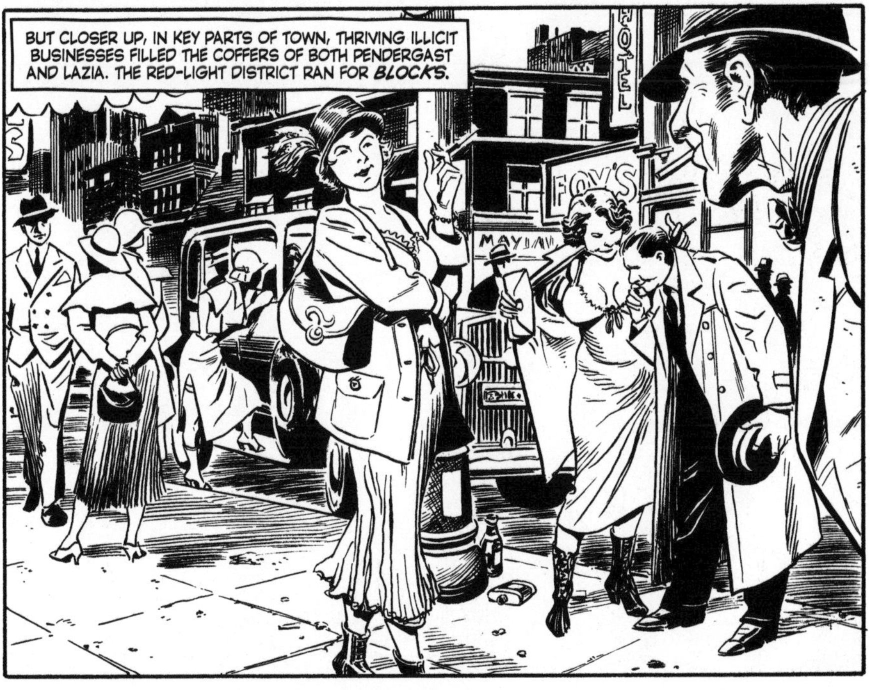
BUT CLOSER UP, IN KEY PARTS OF TOWN, THRIVING ILLICIT BUSINESSES FILLED THE COFFERS OF BOTH PENDERGAST AND LAZIA. THE RED-LIGHT DISTRICT RAN FOR ***BLOCKS***.
HOTEL
FOY'S

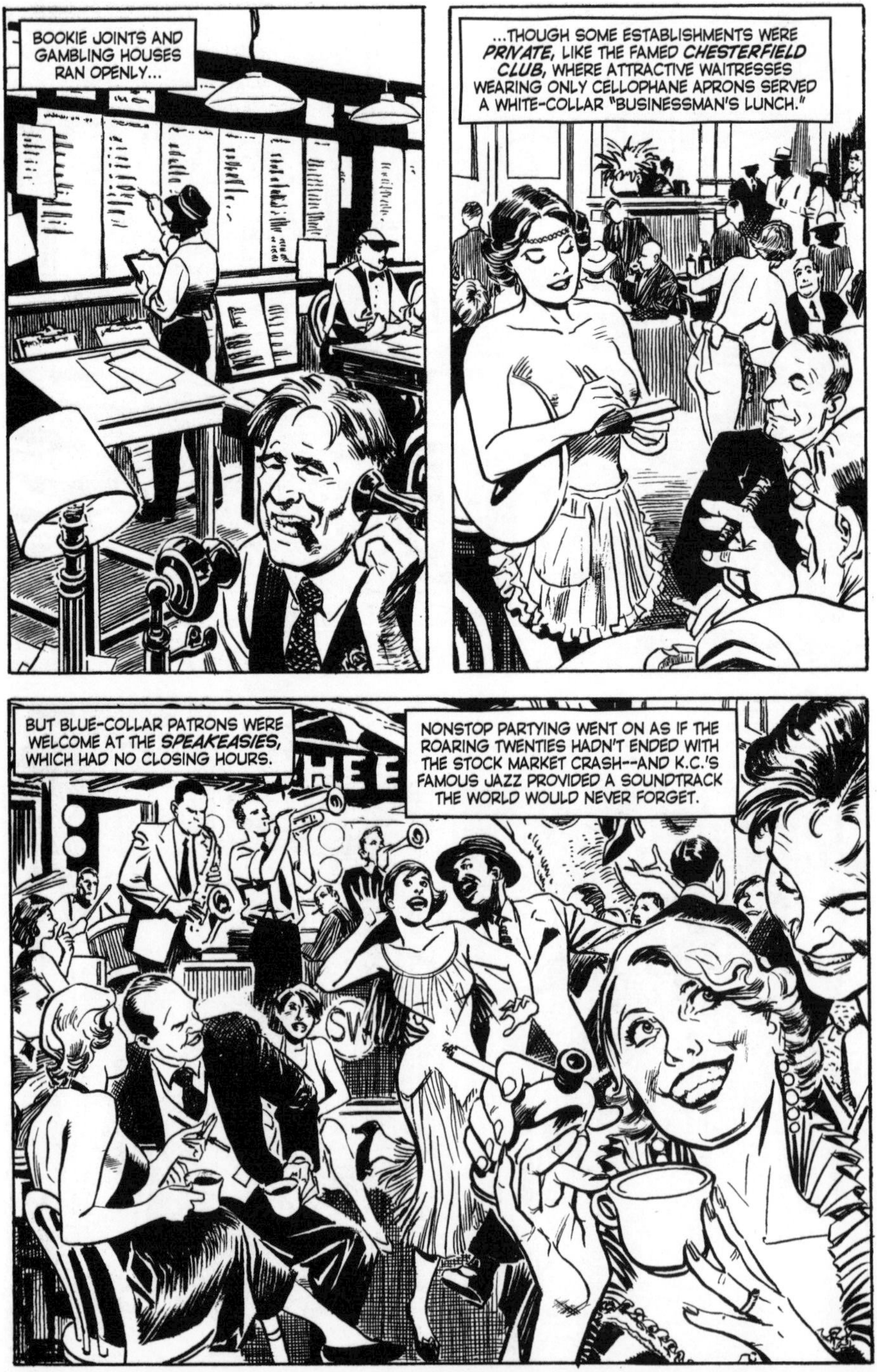
BOOKIE JOINTS AND GAMBLING HOUSES RAN OPENLY...
...THOUGH SOME ESTABLISHMENTS WERE PRIVATE, LIKE THE FAMED CHESTERFIELD CLUB, WHERE ATTRACTIVE WAITRESSES WEARING ONLY CELLOPHANE APRONS SERVED A WHITE-COLLAR "BUSINESSMAN'S LUNCH."
BUT BLUE-COLLAR PATRONS WERE WELCOME AT THE SPEAKEASIES, WHICH HAD NO CLOSING HOURS.
NONSTOP PARTYING WENT ON AS IF THE ROARING TWENTIES HADN'T ENDED WITH THE STOCK MARKET CRASH--AND K.C.'S FAMOUS JAZZ PROVIDED A SOUNDTRACK THE WORLD WOULD NEVER FORGET.

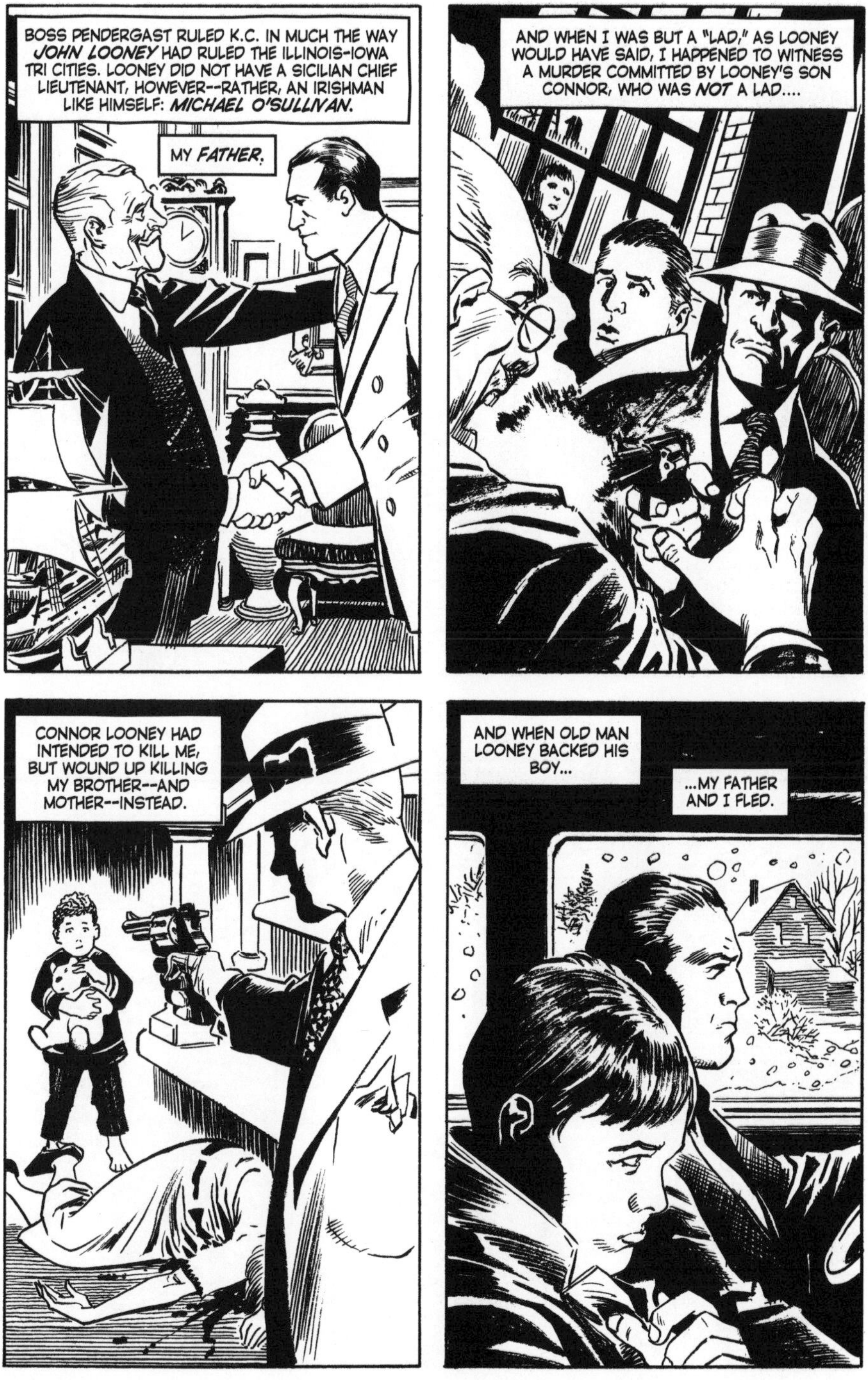
BOSS PENDERGAST RULED K.C. IN MUCH THE WAY JOHN LOONEY HAD RULED THE ILLINOIS-IOWA TRI CITIES. LOONEY DID NOT HAVE A SICILIAN CHIEF LIEUTENANT, HOWEVER--RATHER, AN IRISHMAN LIKE HIMSELF: MICHAEL O'SULLIVAN.
MY FATHER.
AND WHEN I WAS BUT A "LAD," AS LOONEY WOULD HAVE SAID, I HAPPENED TO WITNESS A MURDER COMMITTED BY LOONEY'S SON CONNOR, WHO WAS NOT A LAD....
CONNOR LOONEY HAD INTENDED TO KILL ME, BUT WOUND UP KILLING MY BROTHER--AND MOTHER--INSTEAD.
AND WHEN OLD MAN LOONEY BACKED HIS BOY...
...MY FATHER AND I FLED.

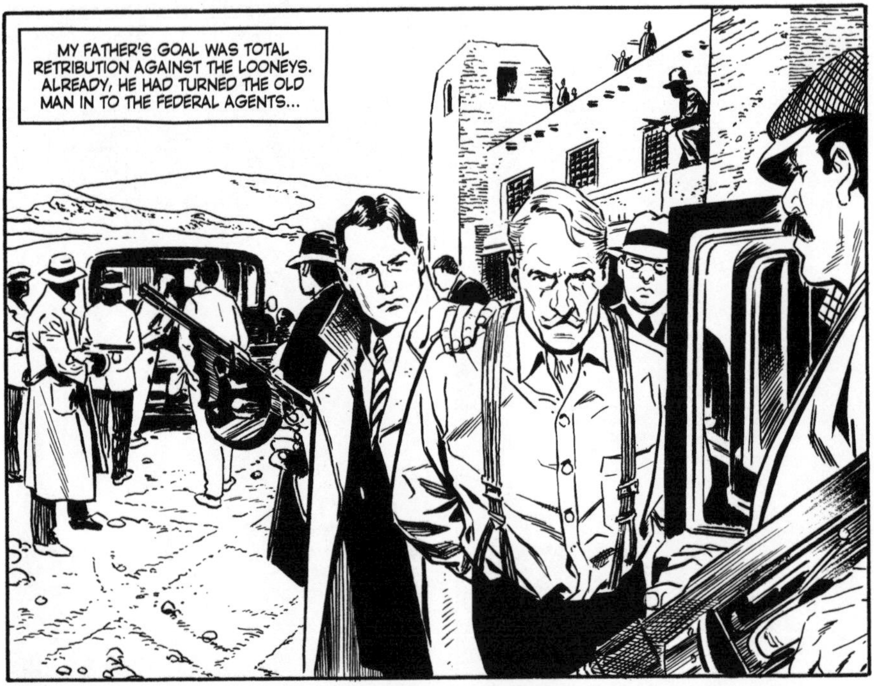
MY FATHER'S GOAL WAS TOTAL RETRIBUTION AGAINST THE LOONEYS. ALREADY, HE HAD TURNED THE OLD MAN IN TO THE FEDERAL AGENTS...

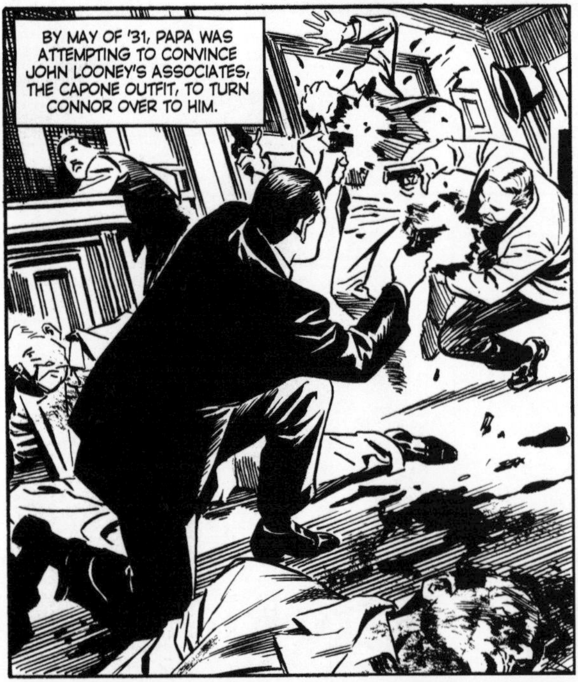
BY MAY OF '31, PAPA WAS ATTEMPTING TO CONVINCE JOHN LOONEY'S ASSOCIATES, THE CAPONE OUTFIT, TO TURN CONNOR OVER TO HIM.

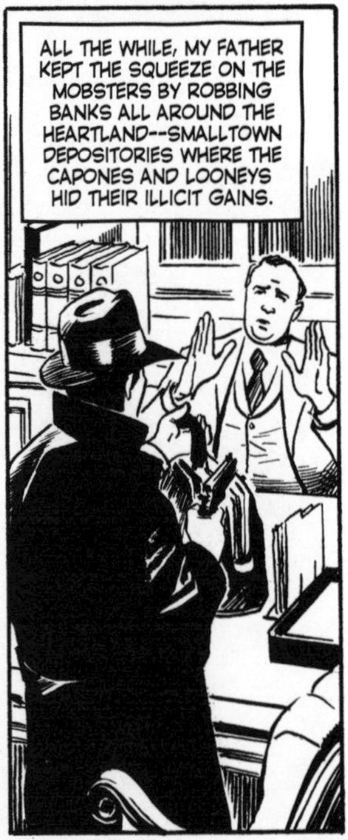
ALL THE WHILE, MY FATHER KEPT THE SQUEEZE ON THE MOBSTERS BY ROBBING BANKS ALL AROUND THE HEARTLAND--SMALLTOWN DEPOSITORIES WHERE THE CAPONES AND LOONEYS HID THEIR ILLICIT GAINS.

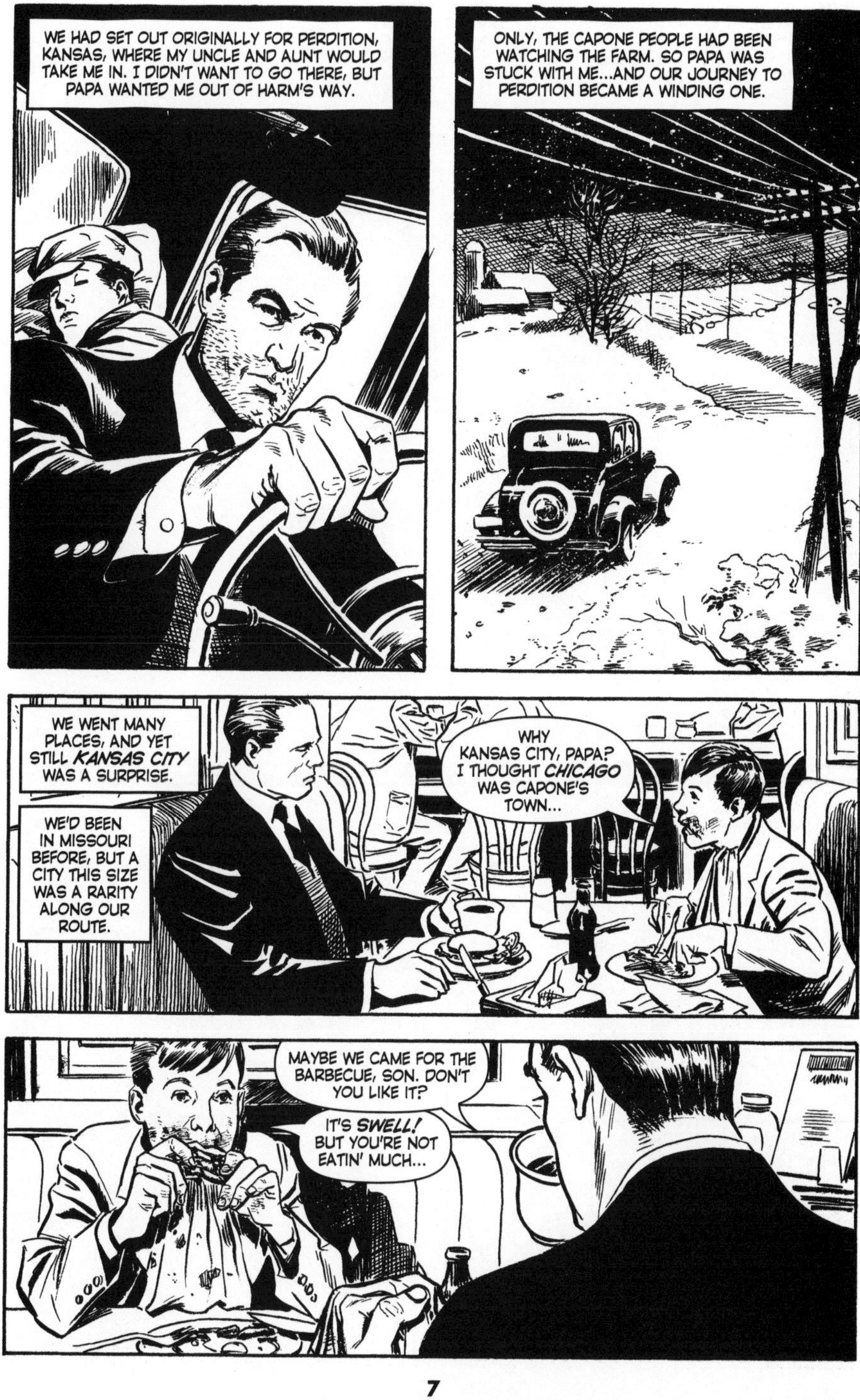
WE HAD SET OUT ORIGINALLY FOR PERDITION, KANSAS, WHERE MY UNCLE AND AUNT WOULD TAKE ME IN. I DIDN'T WANT TO GO THERE, BUT PAPA WANTED ME OUT OF HARM'S WAY.
ONLY, THE CAPONE PEOPLE HAD BEEN WATCHING THE FARM. SO PAPA WAS STUCK WITH ME...AND OUR JOURNEY TO PERDITION BECAME A WINDING ONE.
WE WENT MANY PLACES, AND YET STILL *KANSAS CITY* WAS A SURPRISE.
WE'D BEEN IN MISSOURI BEFORE, BUT A CITY THIS SIZE WAS A RARITY ALONG OUR ROUTE.
WHY KANSAS CITY, PAPA? I THOUGHT *CHICAGO* WAS CAPONE'S TOWN...
MAYBE WE CAME FOR THE BARBECUE, SON. DON'T YOU LIKE IT?
IT'S ***SWELL!*** BUT YOU'RE NOT EATIN' MUCH...

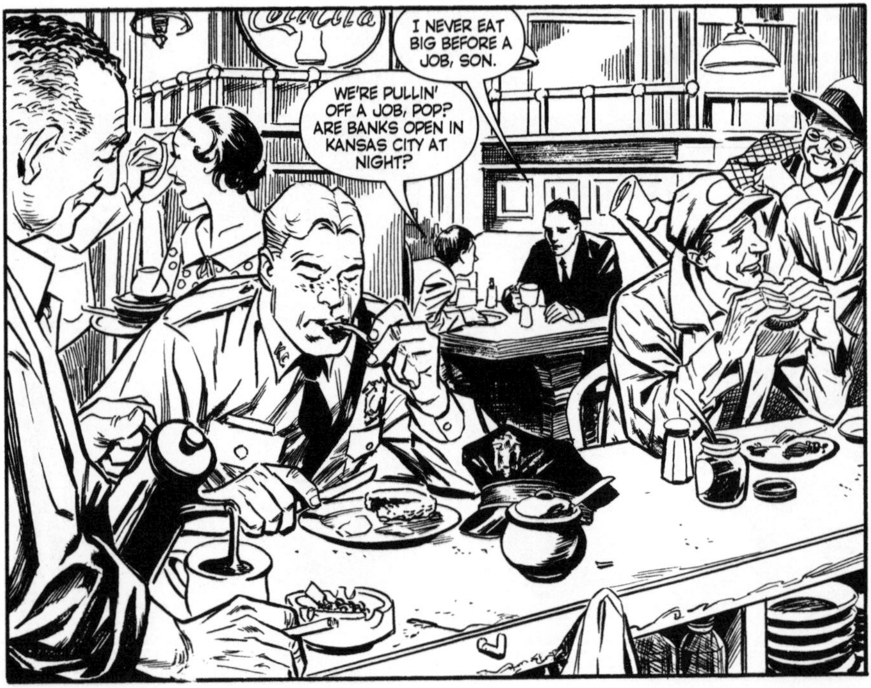
WE'RE PULLIN' OFF A JOB, POP? ARE BANKS OPEN IN KANSAS CITY AT NIGHT?
I NEVER EAT BIG BEFORE A JOB, SON.

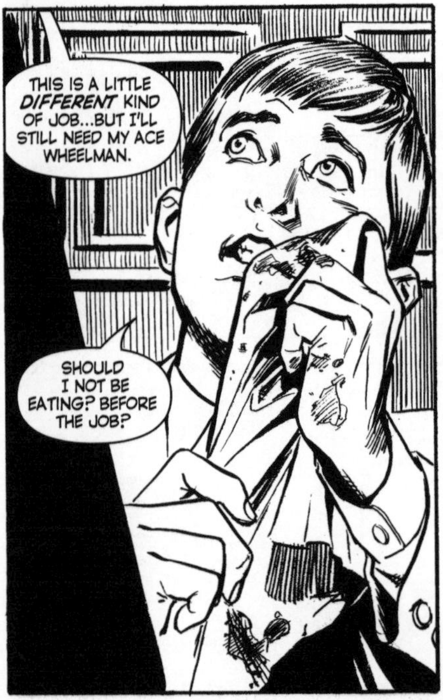
THIS IS A LITTLE *DIFFERENT* KIND OF JOB...BUT I'LL STILL NEED MY ACE WHEELMAN.
SHOULD I NOT BE EATING? BEFORE THE JOB?

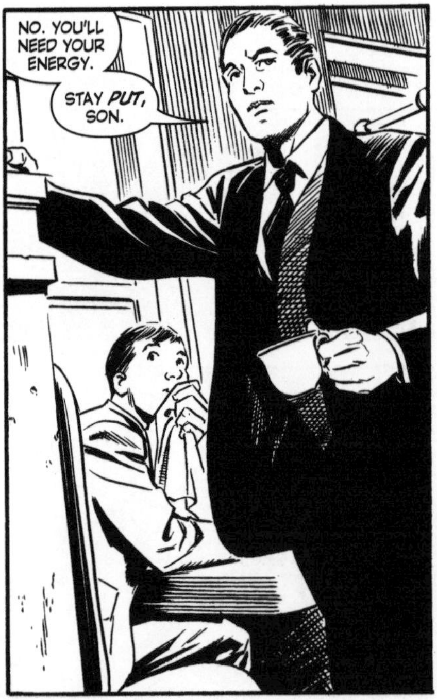
NO. YOU'LL NEED YOUR ENERGY.
STAY *PUT*, SON.

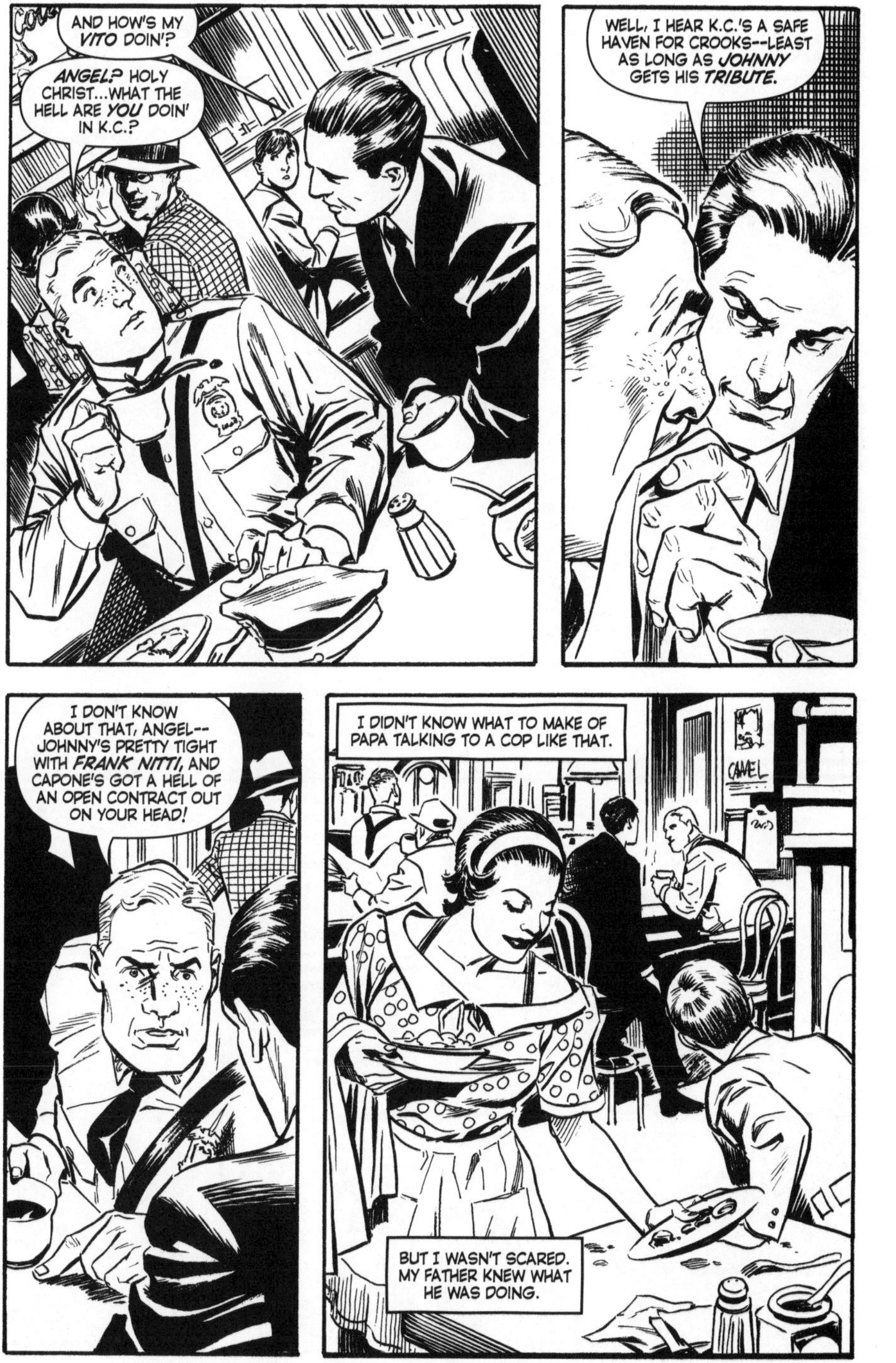
AND HOW'S MY VITO DOIN'?
ANGEL? HOLY CHRIST...WHAT THE HELL ARE YOU DOIN' IN K.C.?
WELL, I HEAR K.C.'S A SAFE HAVEN FOR CROOKS--LEAST AS LONG AS JOHNNY GETS HIS TRIBUTE.
I DON'T KNOW ABOUT THAT, ANGEL-- JOHNNY'S PRETTY TIGHT WITH FRANK NITTI, AND CAPONE'S GOT A HELL OF AN OPEN CONTRACT OUT ON YOUR HEAD!
I DIDN'T KNOW WHAT TO MAKE OF PAPA TALKING TO A COP LIKE THAT.
CAMEL
BUT I WASN'T SCARED. MY FATHER KNEW WHAT HE WAS DOING.

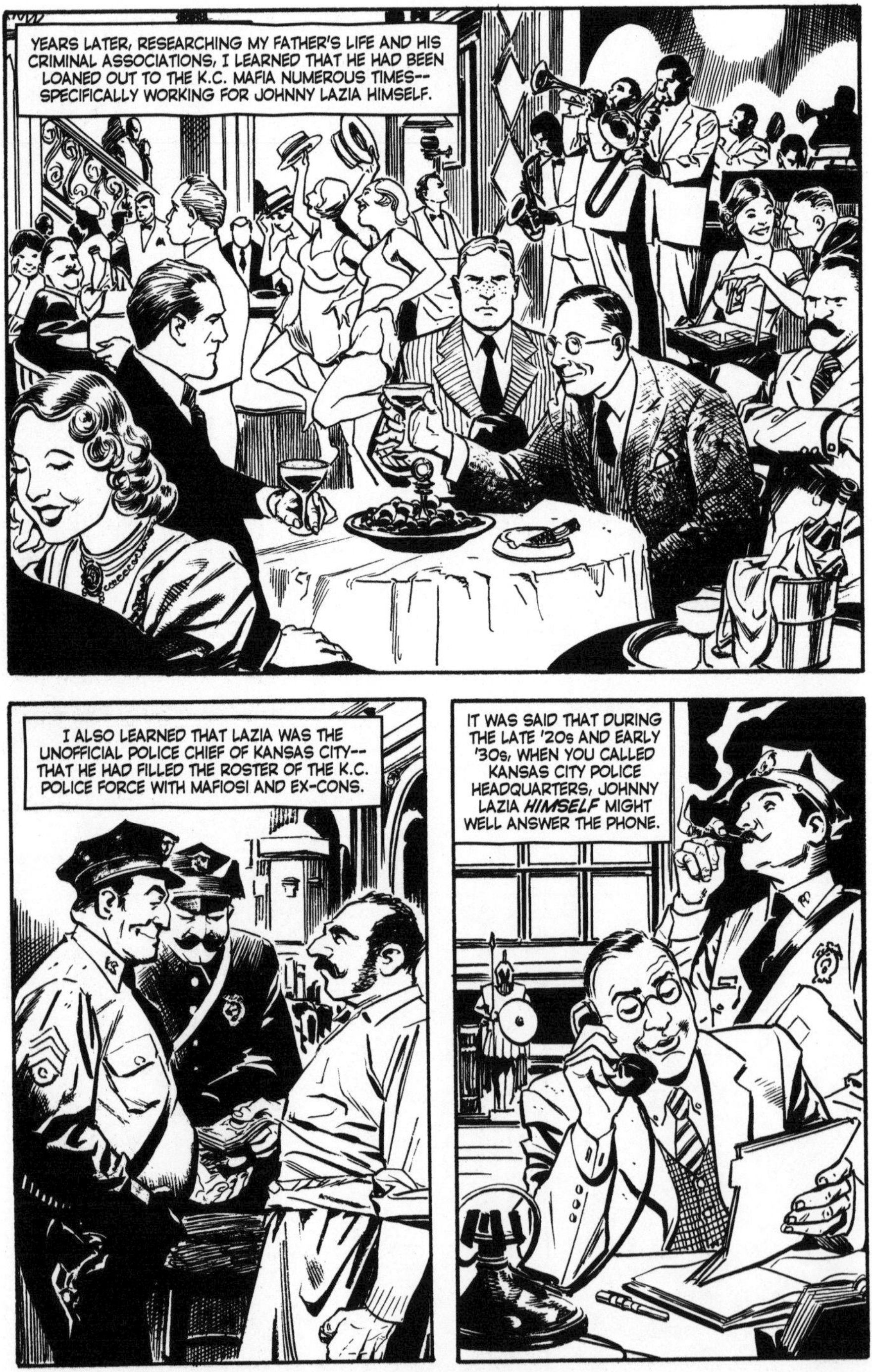
YEARS LATER, RESEARCHING MY FATHER'S LIFE AND HIS CRIMINAL ASSOCIATIONS, I LEARNED THAT HE HAD BEEN LOANED OUT TO THE K.C. MAFIA NUMEROUS TIMES-- SPECIFICALLY WORKING FOR JOHNNY LAZIA HIMSELF.
I ALSO LEARNED THAT LAZIA WAS THE UNOFFICIAL POLICE CHIEF OF KANSAS CITY-- THAT HE HAD FILLED THE ROSTER OF THE K.C. POLICE FORCE WITH MAFIOSI AND EX-CONS.
IT WAS SAID THAT DURING THE LATE '20s AND EARLY '30s, WHEN YOU CALLED KANSAS CITY POLICE HEADQUARTERS, JOHNNY LAZIA *HIMSELF* MIGHT WELL ANSWER THE PHONE.

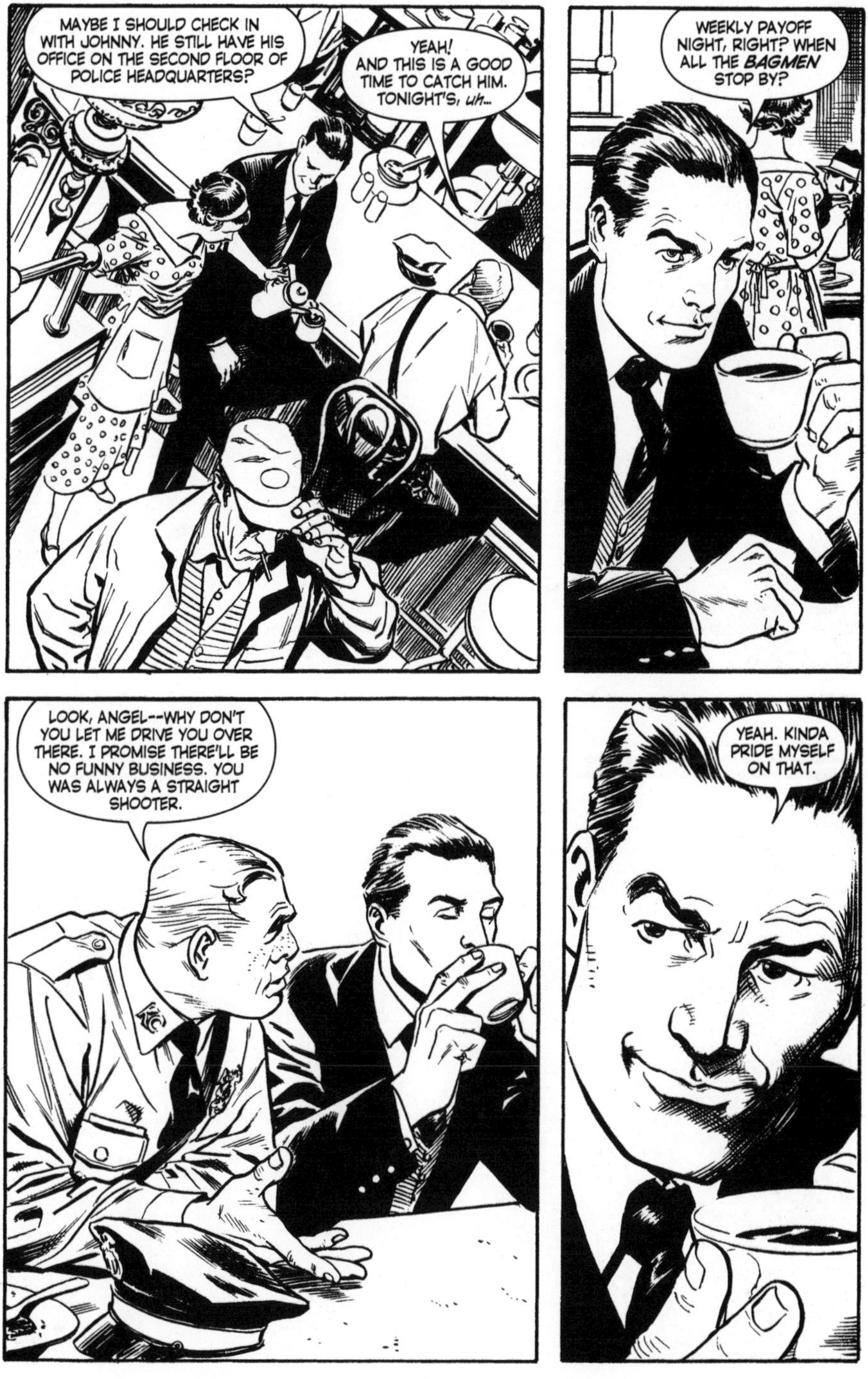
MAYBE I SHOULD CHECK IN WITH JOHNNY. HE STILL HAVE HIS OFFICE ON THE SECOND FLOOR OF POLICE HEADQUARTERS?
YEAH! AND THIS IS A GOOD TIME TO CATCH HIM. TONIGHT'S, *uh...*
WEEKLY PAYOFF NIGHT, RIGHT? WHEN ALL THE ***BAGMEN*** STOP BY?
LOOK, ANGEL--WHY DON'T YOU LET ME DRIVE YOU OVER THERE. I PROMISE THERE'LL BE NO FUNNY BUSINESS. YOU WAS ALWAYS A STRAIGHT SHOOTER.
YEAH. KINDA PRIDE MYSELF ON THAT.

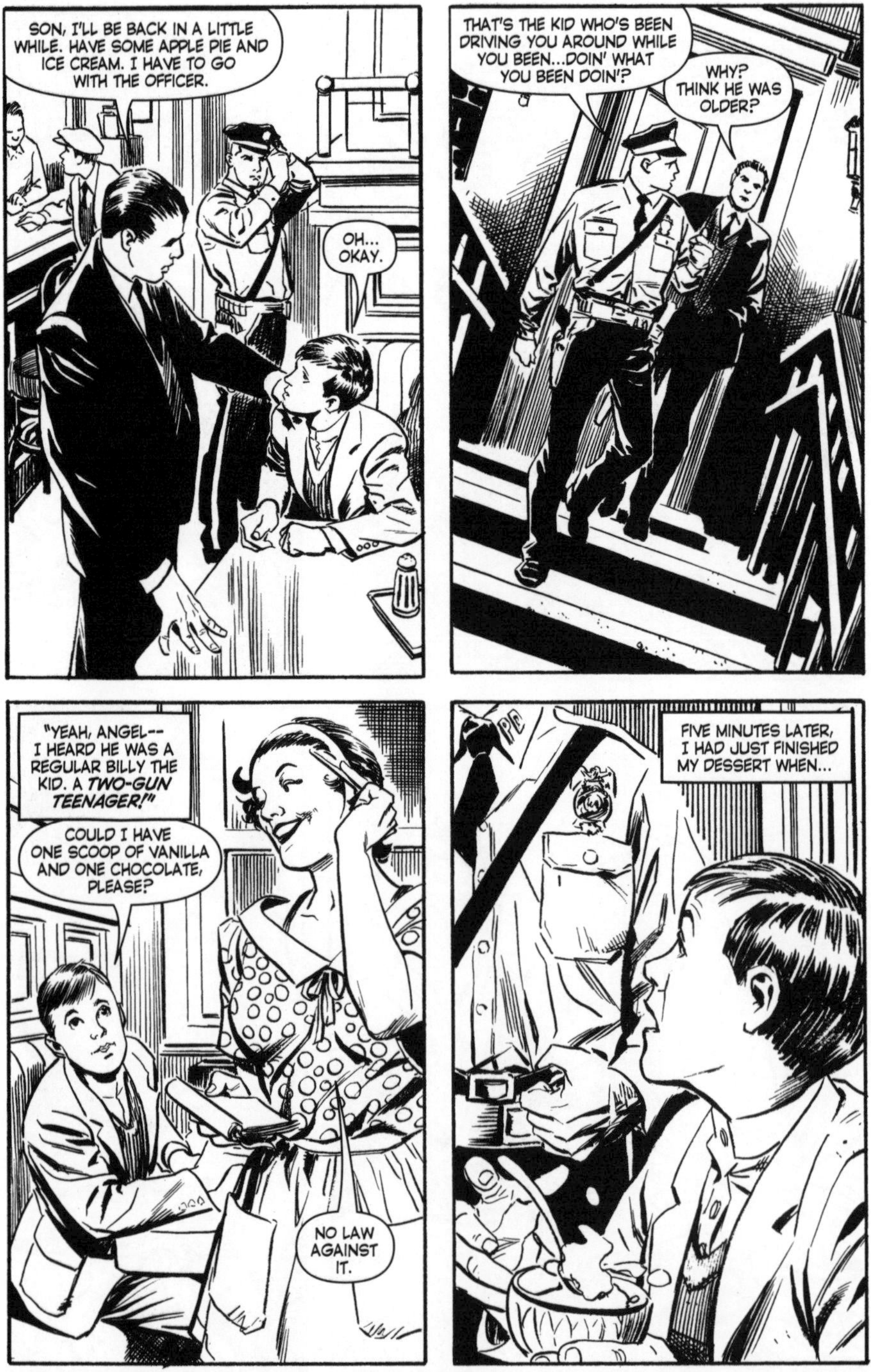
SON, I'LL BE BACK IN A LITTLE WHILE. HAVE SOME APPLE PIE AND ICE CREAM. I HAVE TO GO WITH THE OFFICER.
OH... OKAY.
THAT'S THE KID WHO'S BEEN DRIVING YOU AROUND WHILE YOU BEEN...DOIN' WHAT YOU BEEN DOIN'?
WHY? THINK HE WAS OLDER?
"YEAH, ANGEL-- I HEARD HE WAS A REGULAR BILLY THE KID. A *TWO-GUN TEENAGER!*"
COULD I HAVE ONE SCOOP OF VANILLA AND ONE CHOCOLATE, PLEASE?
NO LAW AGAINST IT.
FIVE MINUTES LATER, I HAD JUST FINISHED MY DESSERT WHEN...

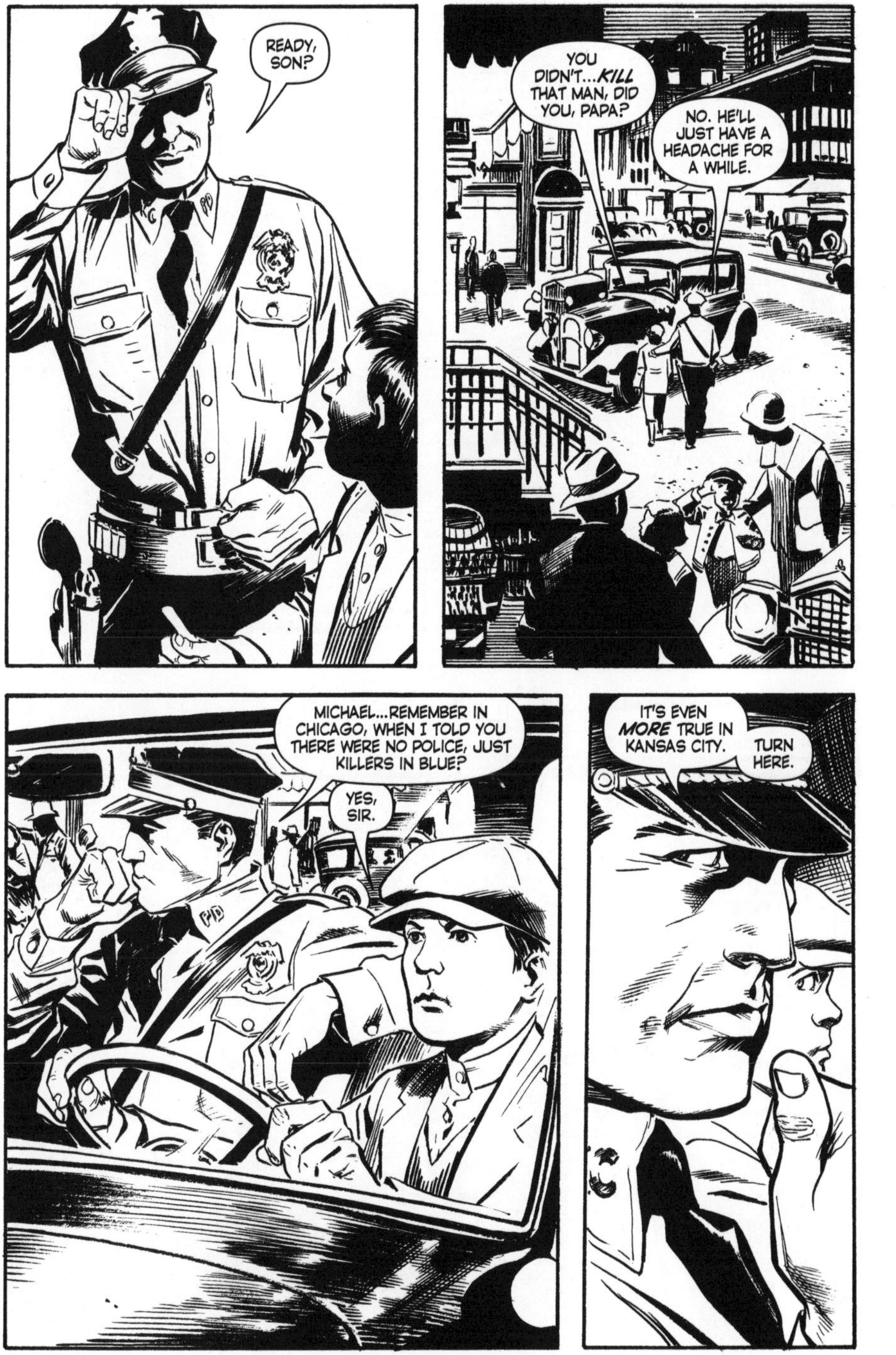
READY, SON?
YOU DIDN'T...KILL THAT MAN, DID YOU, PAPA?
NO. HE'LL JUST HAVE A HEADACHE FOR A WHILE.
MICHAEL...REMEMBER IN CHICAGO, WHEN I TOLD YOU THERE WERE NO POLICE, JUST KILLERS IN BLUE?
YES, SIR.
IT'S EVEN MORE TRUE IN KANSAS CITY.
TURN HERE.

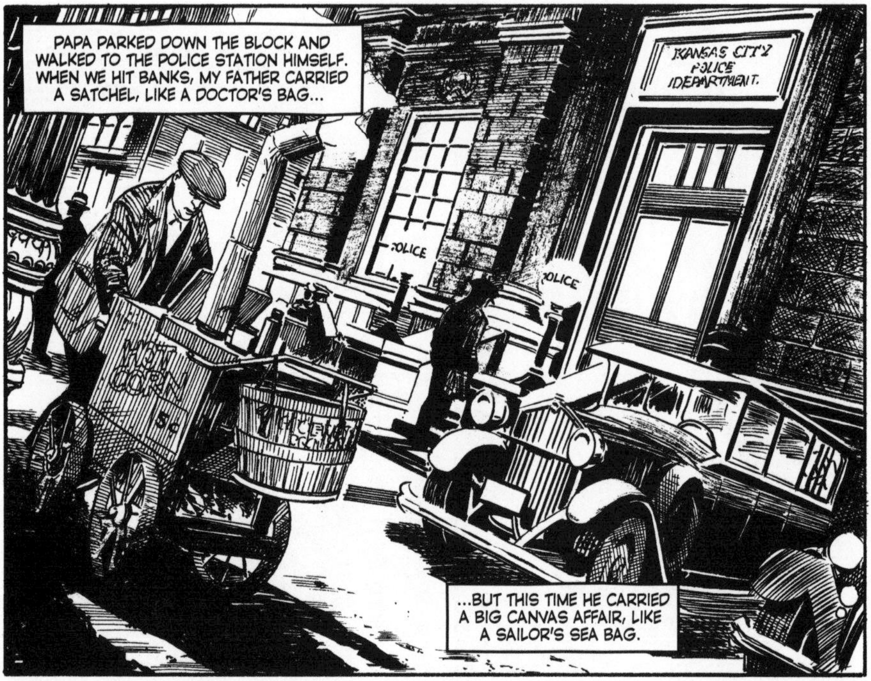
PAPA PARKED DOWN THE BLOCK AND WALKED TO THE POLICE STATION HIMSELF. WHEN WE HIT BANKS, MY FATHER CARRIED A SATCHEL, LIKE A DOCTOR'S BAG...
KANSAS CITY POLICE DEPARTMENT.
POLICE
POLICE
...BUT THIS TIME HE CARRIED A BIG CANVAS AFFAIR, LIKE A SAILOR'S SEA BAG.

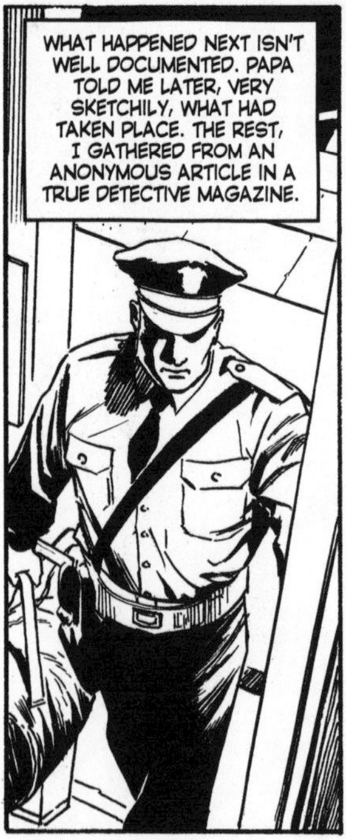
WHAT HAPPENED NEXT ISN'T WELL DOCUMENTED. PAPA TOLD ME LATER, VERY SKETCHILY, WHAT HAD TAKEN PLACE. THE REST, I GATHERED FROM AN ANONYMOUS ARTICLE IN A TRUE DETECTIVE MAGAZINE.

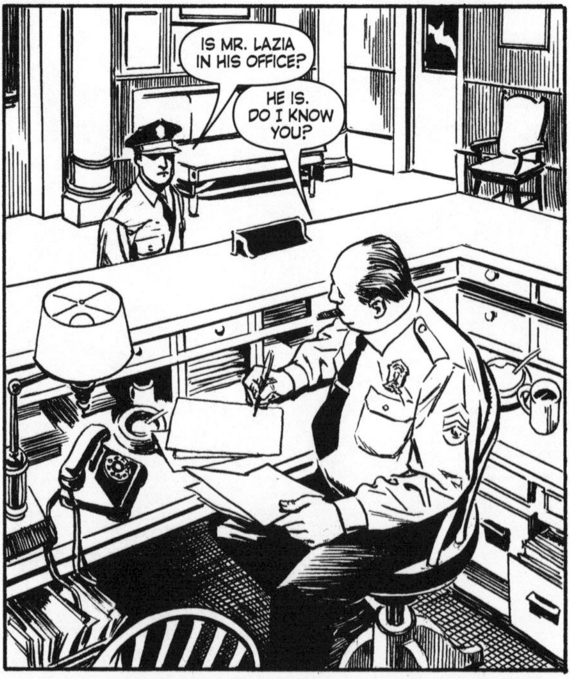
IS MR. LAZIA IN HIS OFFICE?
HE IS. DO I KNOW YOU?

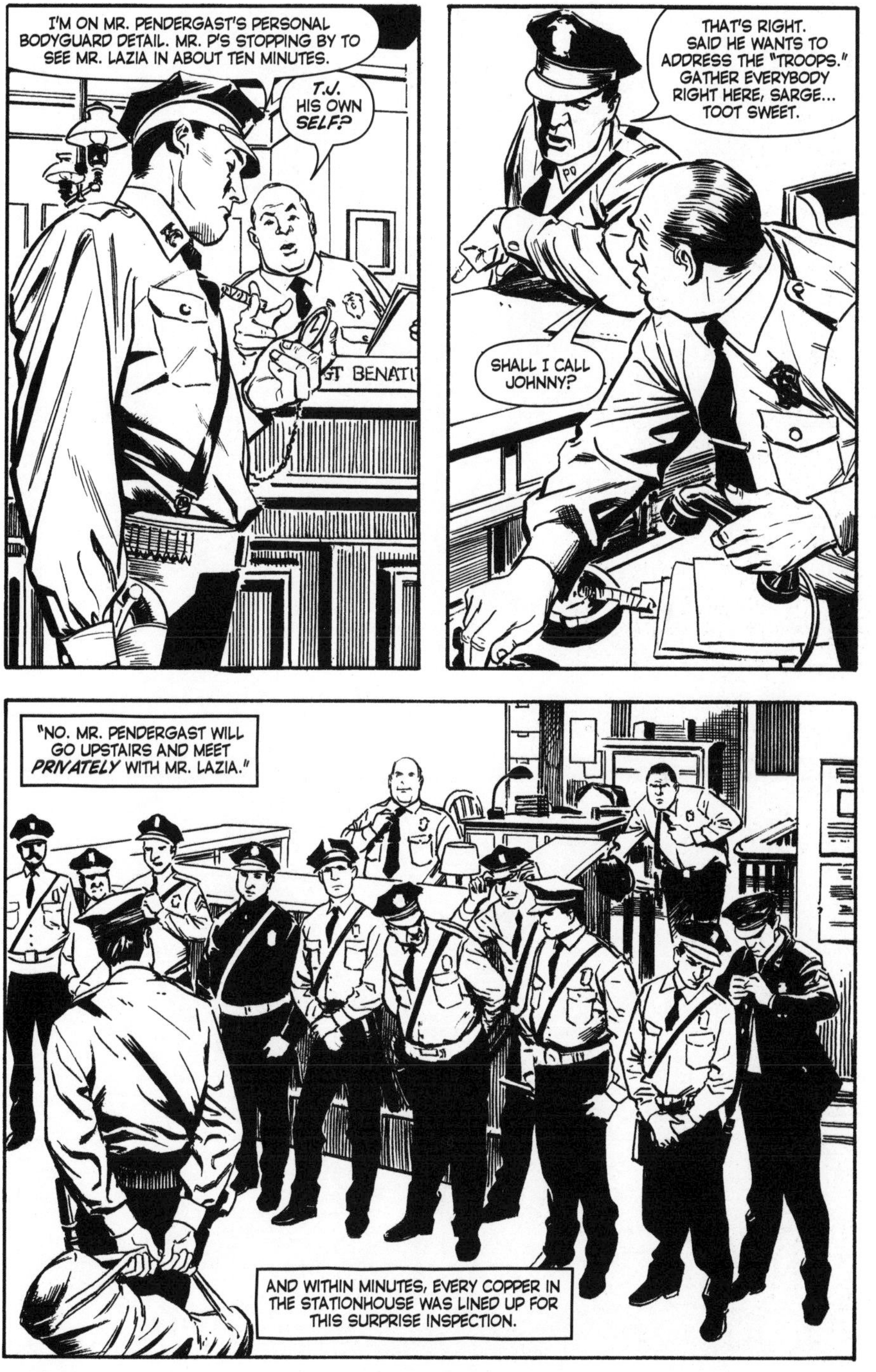
I'M ON MR. PENDERGAST'S PERSONAL BODYGUARD DETAIL. MR. P'S STOPPING BY TO SEE MR. LAZIA IN ABOUT TEN MINUTES.
T.J. HIS OWN *SELF?*
GT BENATI
THAT'S RIGHT. SAID HE WANTS TO ADDRESS THE "TROOPS." GATHER EVERYBODY RIGHT HERE, SARGE... TOOT SWEET.
SHALL I CALL JOHNNY?
"NO. MR. PENDERGAST WILL GO UPSTAIRS AND MEET *PRIVATELY* WITH MR. LAZIA."
AND WITHIN MINUTES, EVERY COPPER IN THE STATIONHOUSE WAS LINED UP FOR THIS SURPRISE INSPECTION.

WHEN CAN WE EXPECT THE BOSS TO STOP BY?
PROBABLY TOMORROW, TO START *FIRING* YOUR ASSES.
TOSS YOUR WEAPONS TO THE FLOOR-- *GENTLE*-LIKE.
AND FEEL FREE TO TRY SOMETHING. I HAVEN'T WRITTEN ANYTHING WITH THIS TYPEWRITER IN MONTHS... AND I *LOVE* TO EXPRESS MYSELF.

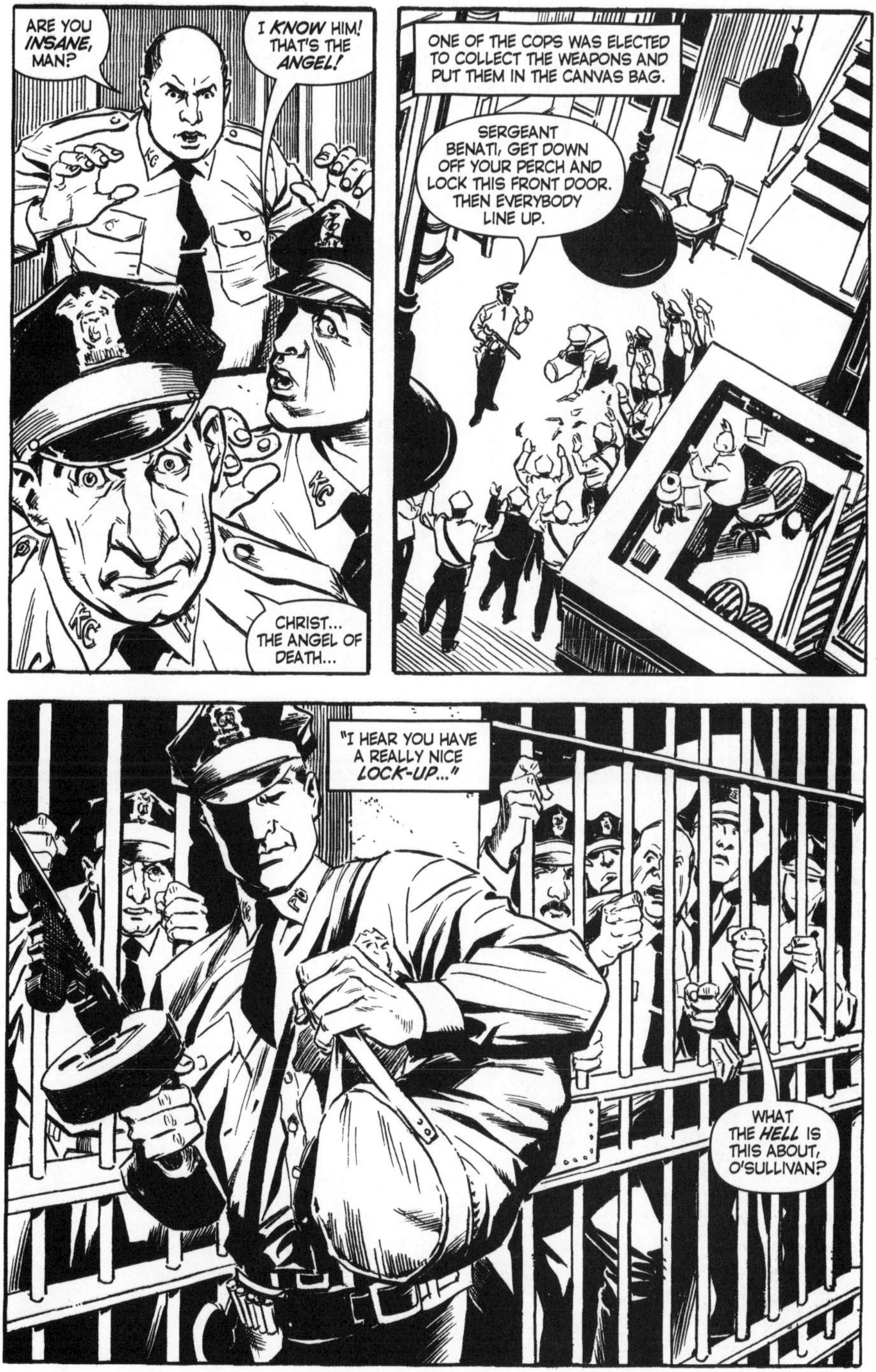
ARE YOU *INSANE,* MAN?
I *KNOW* HIM! THAT'S THE *ANGEL!*
CHRIST... THE ANGEL OF DEATH...
ONE OF THE COPS WAS ELECTED TO COLLECT THE WEAPONS AND PUT THEM IN THE CANVAS BAG.
SERGEANT BENATI, GET DOWN OFF YOUR PERCH AND LOCK THIS FRONT DOOR. THEN EVERYBODY LINE UP.
"I HEAR YOU HAVE A REALLY NICE *LOCK-UP...*"
WHAT THE *HELL* IS THIS ABOUT, O'SULLIVAN?

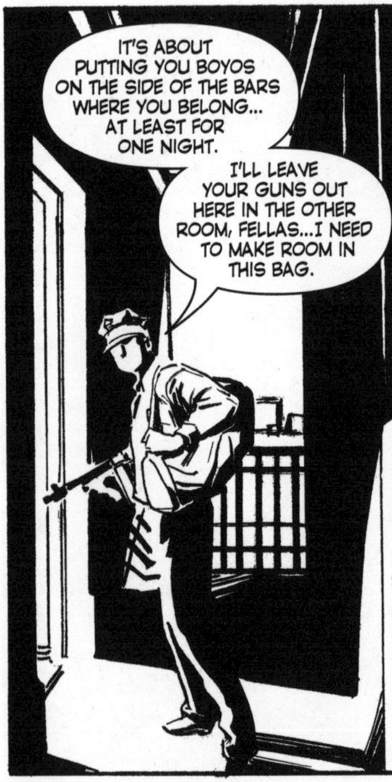
IT'S ABOUT PUTTING YOU BOYOS ON THE SIDE OF THE BARS WHERE YOU BELONG... AT LEAST FOR ONE NIGHT.
I'LL LEAVE YOUR GUNS OUT HERE IN THE OTHER ROOM, FELLAS...I NEED TO MAKE ROOM IN THIS BAG.
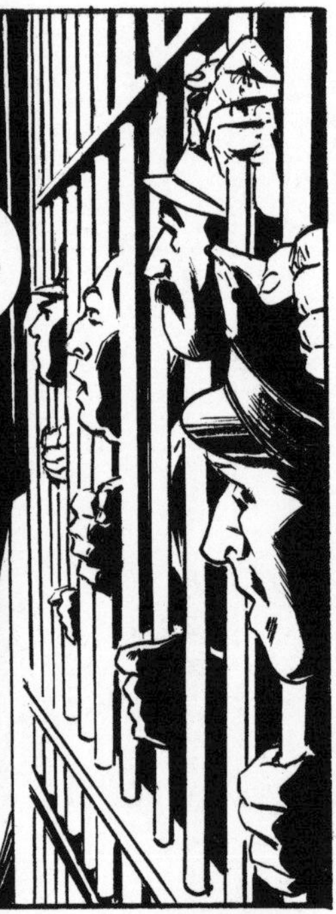
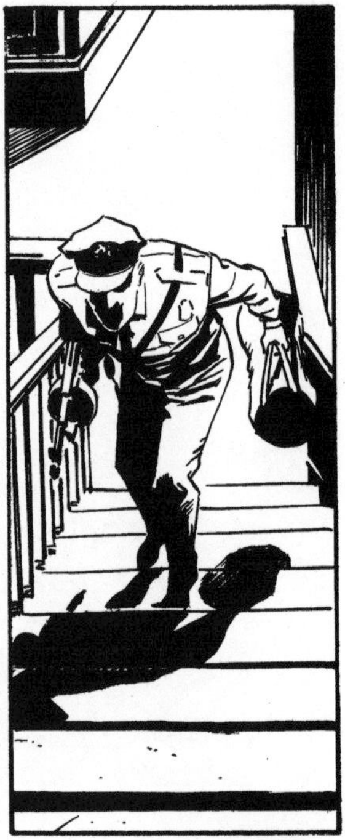
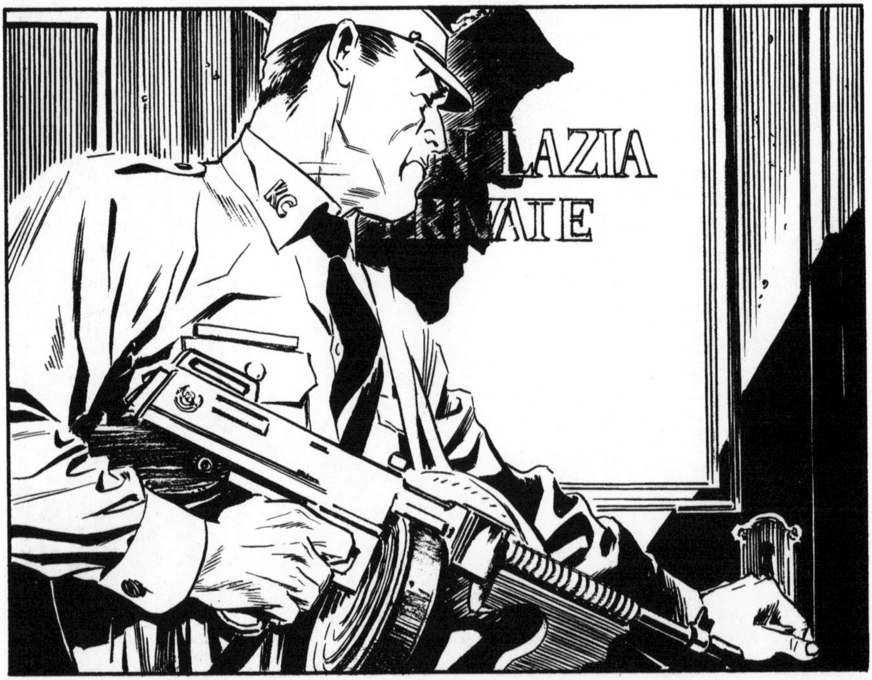
LAZIA
RIVATE

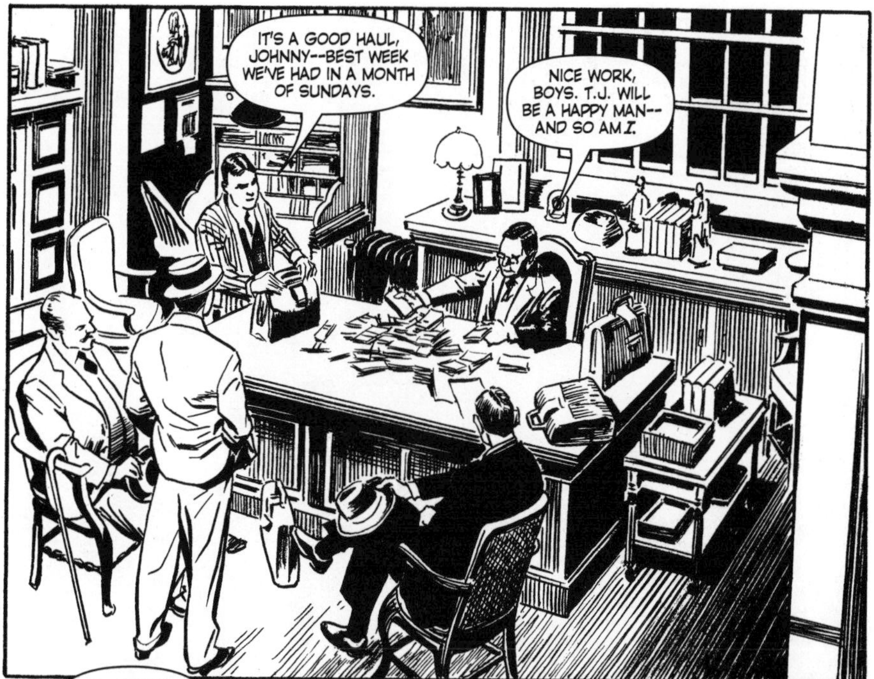
IT'S A GOOD HAUL, JOHNNY--BEST WEEK WE'VE HAD IN A MONTH OF SUNDAYS.
NICE WORK, BOYS. T.J. WILL BE A HAPPY MAN-- AND SO AM *I*.

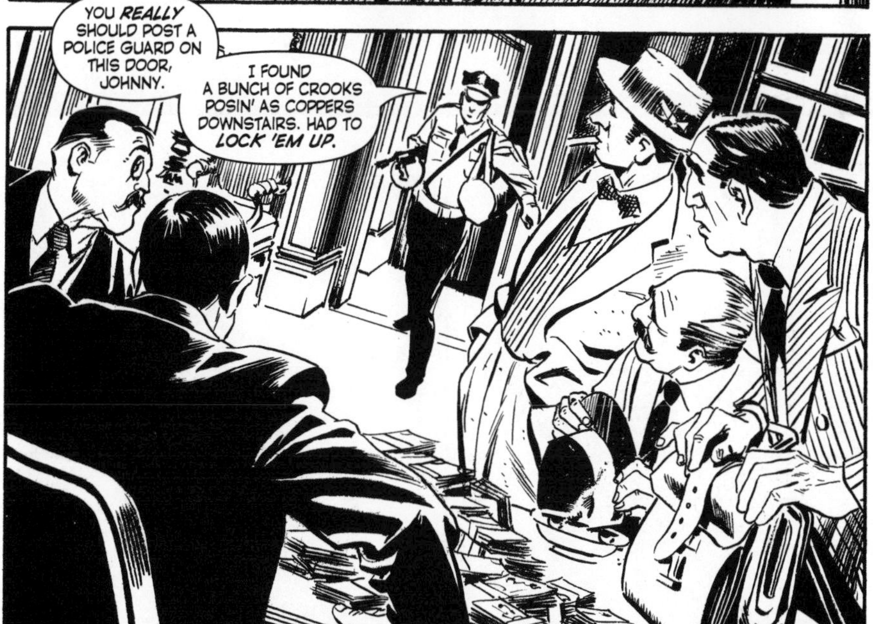
YOU *REALLY* SHOULD POST A POLICE GUARD ON THIS DOOR, JOHNNY.
I FOUND A BUNCH OF CROOKS POSIN' AS COPPERS DOWNSTAIRS. HAD TO *LOCK 'EM UP*.

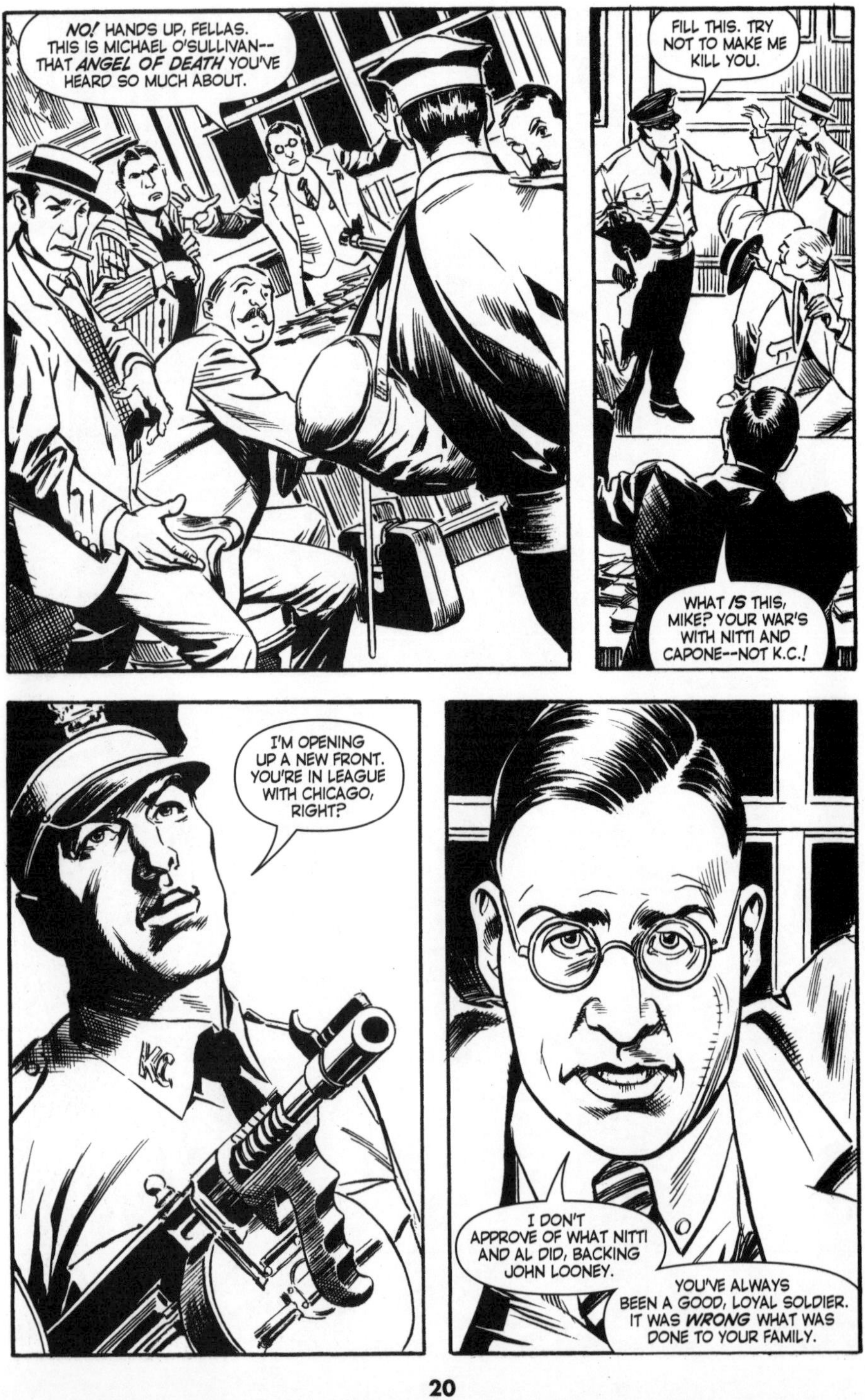
NO! HANDS UP, FELLAS. THIS IS MICHAEL O'SULLIVAN-- THAT ANGEL OF DEATH YOU'VE HEARD SO MUCH ABOUT.
FILL THIS. TRY NOT TO MAKE ME KILL YOU.
WHAT IS THIS, MIKE? YOUR WAR'S WITH NITTI AND CAPONE--NOT K.C.!
I'M OPENING UP A NEW FRONT. YOU'RE IN LEAGUE WITH CHICAGO, RIGHT?
I DON'T APPROVE OF WHAT NITTI AND AL DID, BACKING JOHN LOONEY.
YOU'VE ALWAYS BEEN A GOOD, LOYAL SOLDIER. IT WAS WRONG WHAT WAS DONE TO YOUR FAMILY.

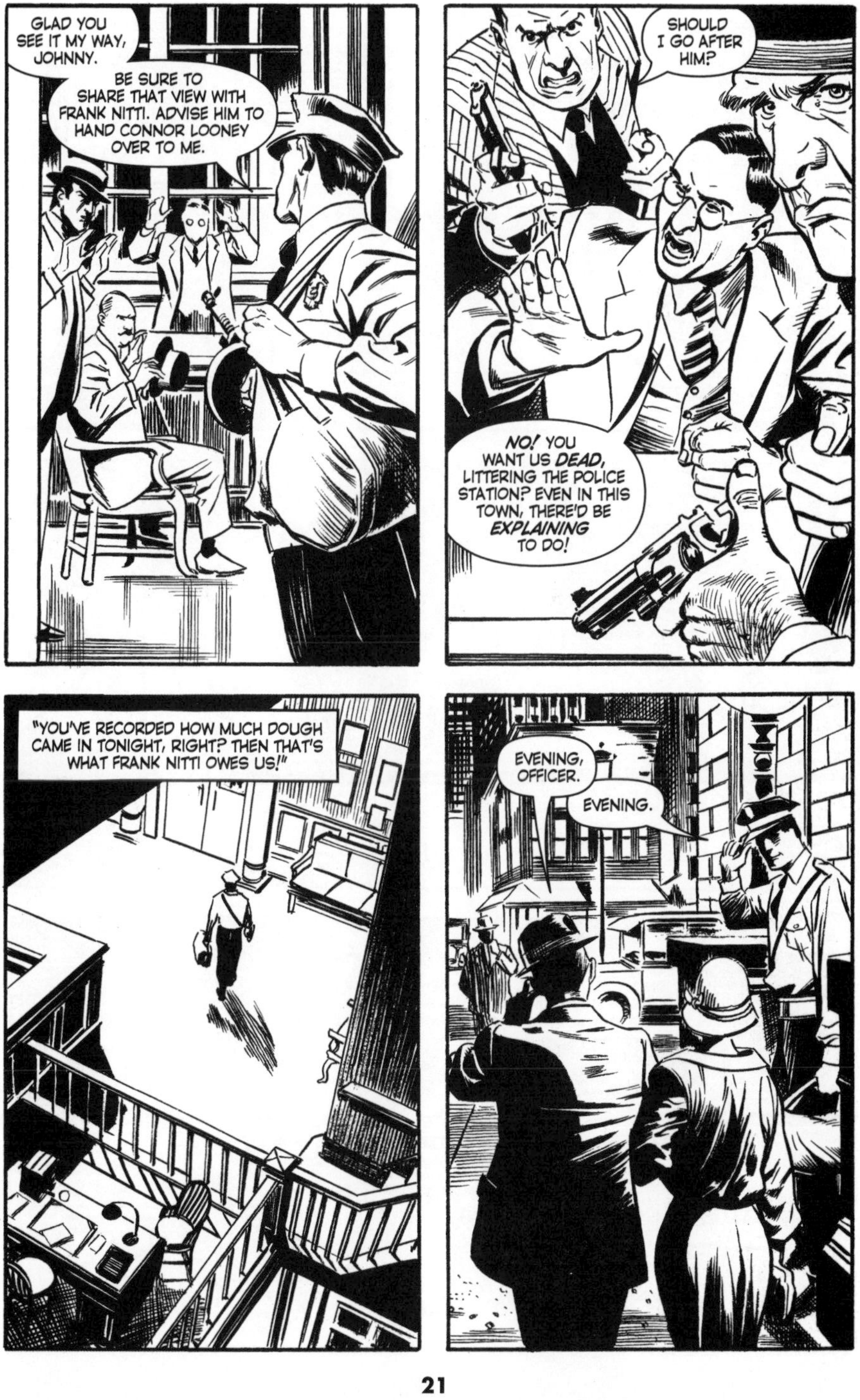
GLAD YOU SEE IT MY WAY, JOHNNY.
BE SURE TO SHARE THAT VIEW WITH FRANK NITTI. ADVISE HIM TO HAND CONNOR LOONEY OVER TO ME.
SHOULD I GO AFTER HIM?
NO! YOU WANT US DEAD, LITTERING THE POLICE STATION? EVEN IN THIS TOWN, THERE'D BE EXPLAINING TO DO!
"YOU'VE RECORDED HOW MUCH DOUGH CAME IN TONIGHT, RIGHT? THEN THAT'S WHAT FRANK NITTI OWES US!"
EVENING, OFFICER.
EVENING.

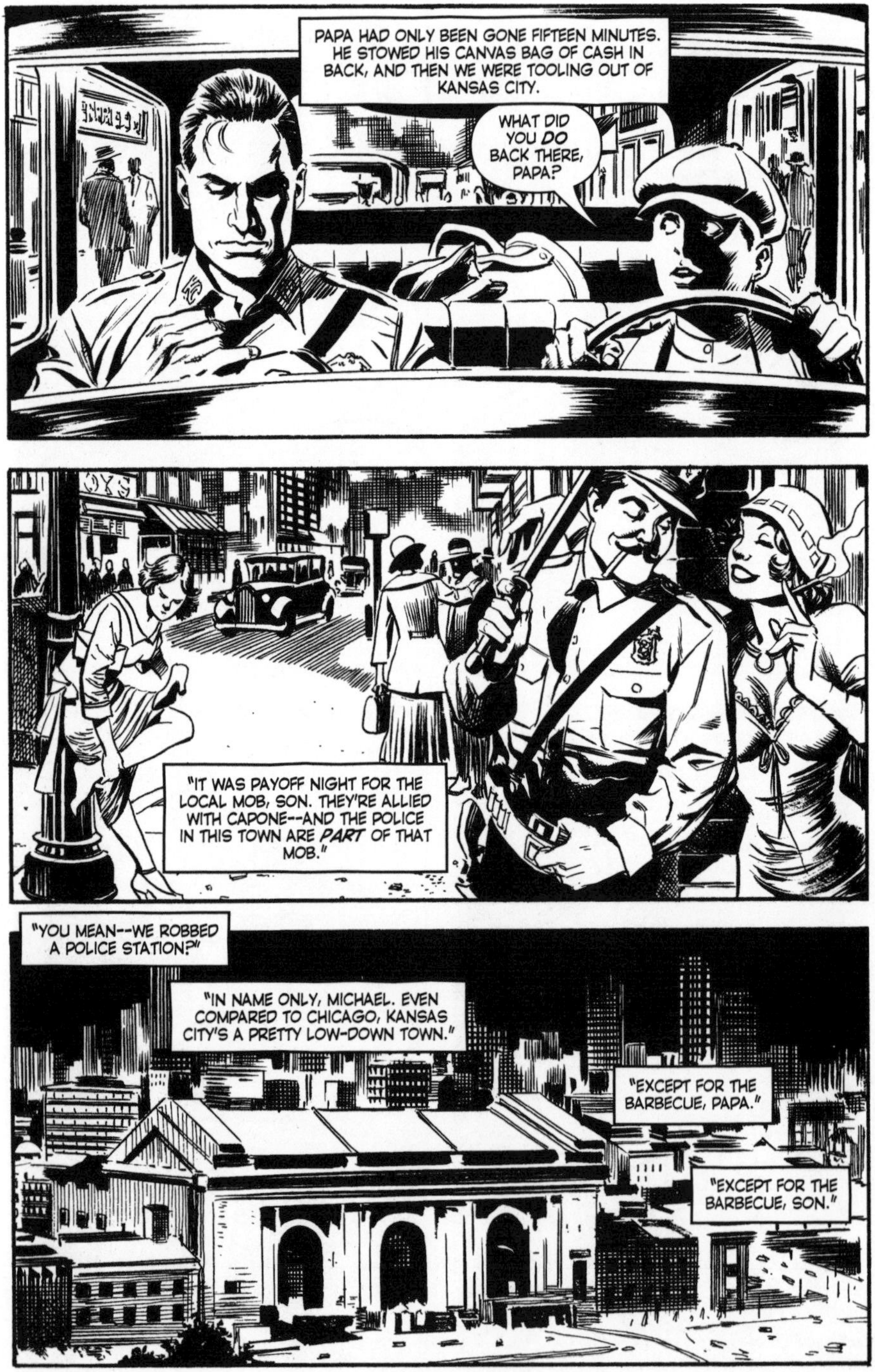
PAPA HAD ONLY BEEN GONE FIFTEEN MINUTES. HE STOWED HIS CANVAS BAG OF CASH IN BACK, AND THEN WE WERE TOOLING OUT OF KANSAS CITY.
WHAT DID YOU DO BACK THERE, PAPA?
"IT WAS PAYOFF NIGHT FOR THE LOCAL MOB, SON. THEY'RE ALLIED WITH CAPONE--AND THE POLICE IN THIS TOWN ARE PART OF THAT MOB."
"YOU MEAN--WE ROBBED A POLICE STATION?"
"IN NAME ONLY, MICHAEL. EVEN COMPARED TO CHICAGO, KANSAS CITY'S A PRETTY LOW-DOWN TOWN."
"EXCEPT FOR THE BARBECUE, PAPA."
"EXCEPT FOR THE BARBECUE, SON."

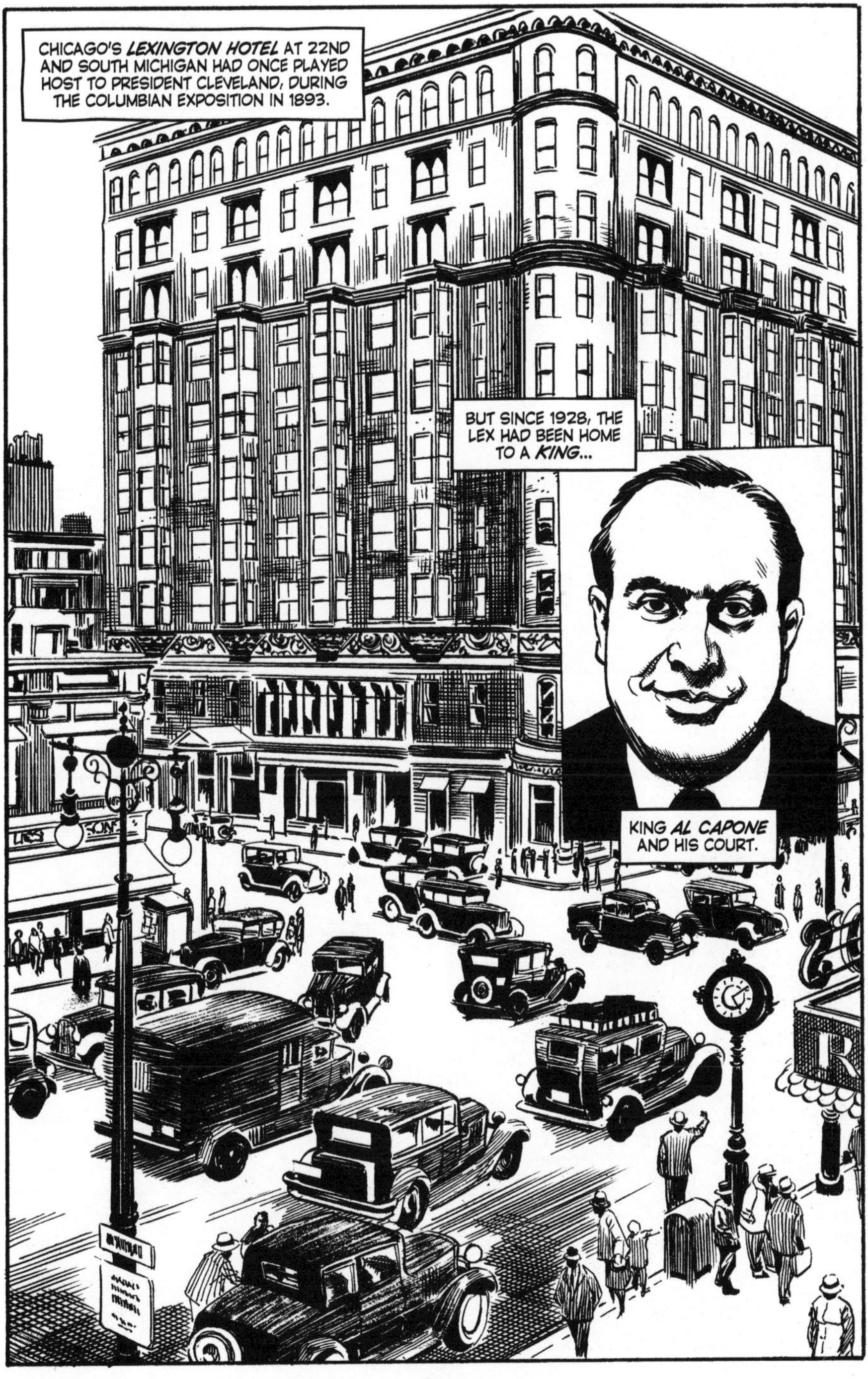
CHICAGO'S *LEXINGTON HOTEL* AT 22ND AND SOUTH MICHIGAN HAD ONCE PLAYED HOST TO PRESIDENT CLEVELAND, DURING THE COLUMBIAN EXPOSITION IN 1893.
BUT SINCE 1928, THE LEX HAD BEEN HOME TO A *KING*...
KING *AL CAPONE* AND HIS COURT.

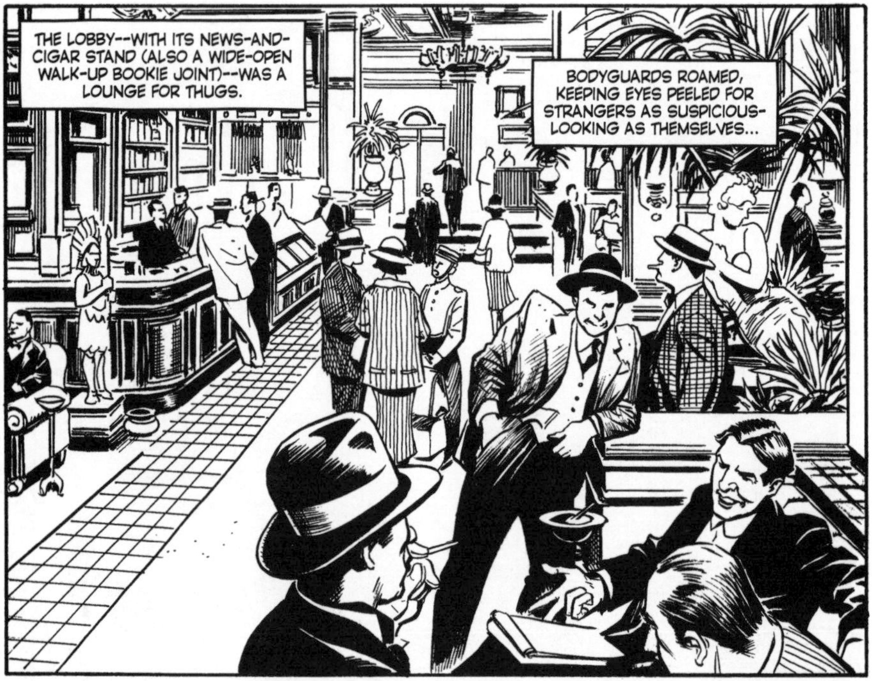
THE LOBBY--WITH ITS NEWS-AND-CIGAR STAND (ALSO A WIDE-OPEN WALK-UP BOOKIE JOINT)--WAS A LOUNGE FOR THUGS.
BODYGUARDS ROAMED, KEEPING EYES PEELED FOR STRANGERS AS SUSPICIOUS-LOOKING AS THEMSELVES...

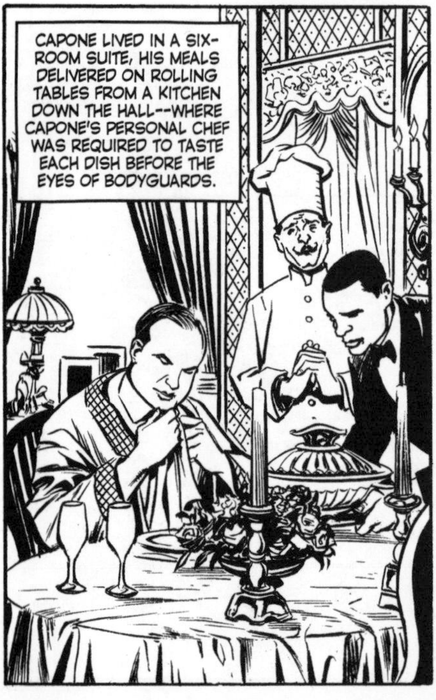
CAPONE LIVED IN A SIX-ROOM SUITE, HIS MEALS DELIVERED ON ROLLING TABLES FROM A KITCHEN DOWN THE HALL--WHERE CAPONE'S PERSONAL CHEF WAS REQUIRED TO TASTE EACH DISH BEFORE THE EYES OF BODYGUARDS.

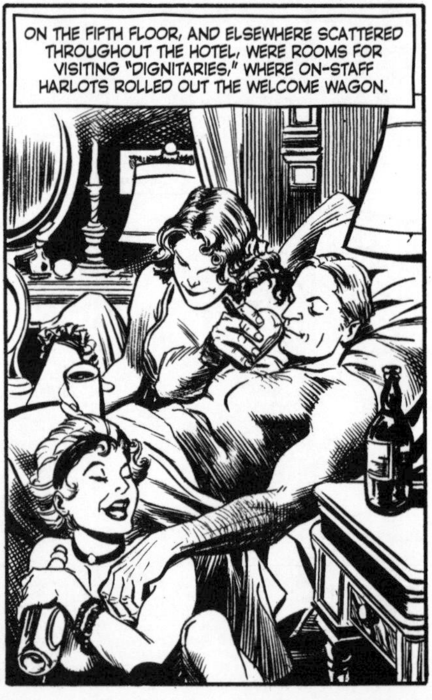
ON THE FIFTH FLOOR, AND ELSEWHERE SCATTERED THROUGHOUT THE HOTEL, WERE ROOMS FOR VISITING "DIGNITARIES," WHERE ON-STAFF HARLOTS ROLLED OUT THE WELCOME WAGON.

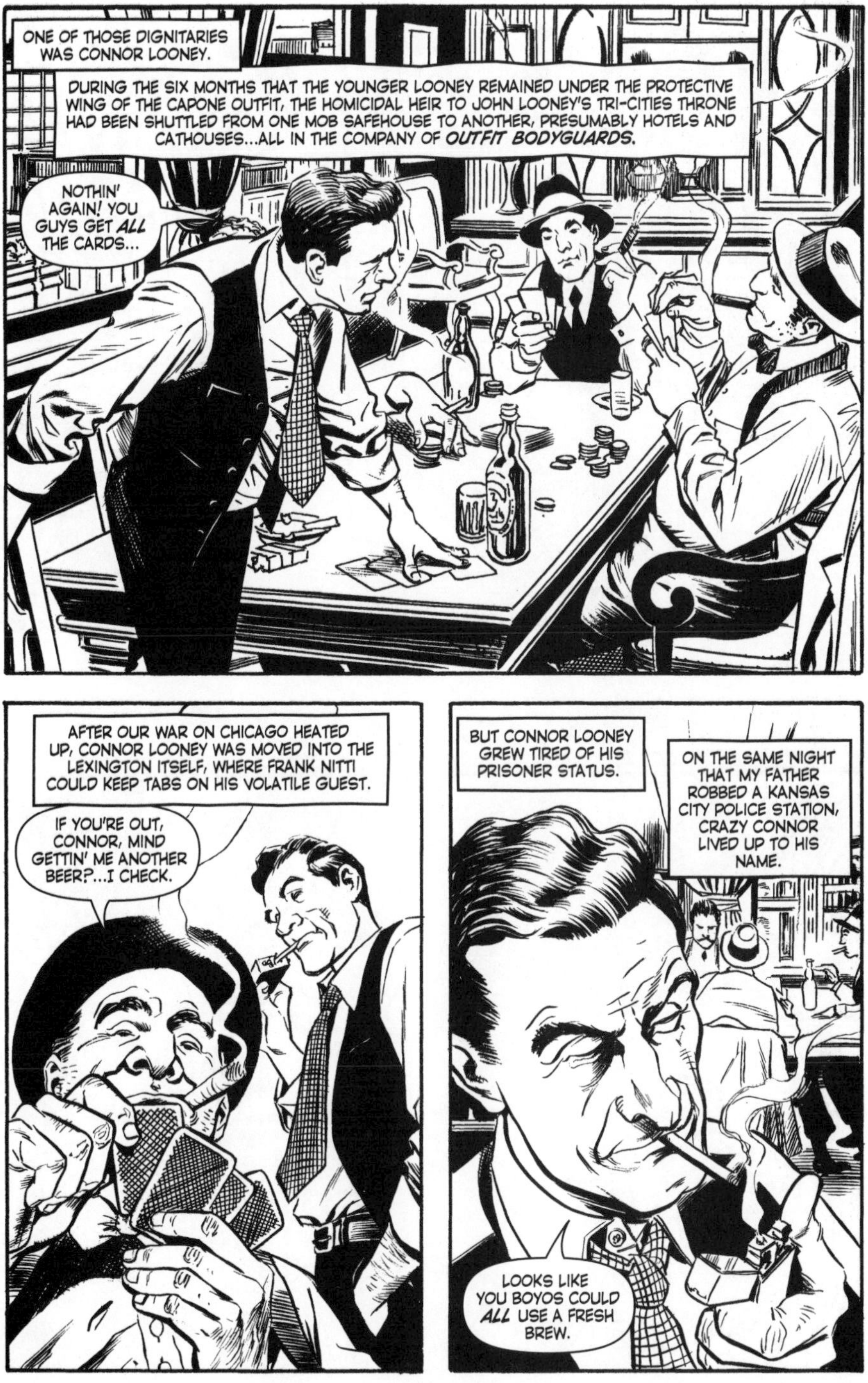
ONE OF THOSE DIGNITARIES WAS CONNOR LOONEY.
DURING THE SIX MONTHS THAT THE YOUNGER LOONEY REMAINED UNDER THE PROTECTIVE WING OF THE CAPONE OUTFIT, THE HOMICIDAL HEIR TO JOHN LOONEY'S TRI-CITIES THRONE HAD BEEN SHUTTLED FROM ONE MOB SAFEHOUSE TO ANOTHER, PRESUMABLY HOTELS AND CATHOUSES...ALL IN THE COMPANY OF *OUTFIT BODYGUARDS*.
NOTHIN' AGAIN! YOU GUYS GET *ALL* THE CARDS...
AFTER OUR WAR ON CHICAGO HEATED UP, CONNOR LOONEY WAS MOVED INTO THE LEXINGTON ITSELF, WHERE FRANK NITTI COULD KEEP TABS ON HIS VOLATILE GUEST.
IF YOU'RE OUT, CONNOR, MIND GETTIN' ME ANOTHER BEER?...I CHECK.
BUT CONNOR LOONEY GREW TIRED OF HIS PRISONER STATUS.
ON THE SAME NIGHT THAT MY FATHER ROBBED A KANSAS CITY POLICE STATION, CRAZY CONNOR LIVED UP TO HIS NAME.
LOOKS LIKE YOU BOYOS COULD *ALL* USE A FRESH BREW.

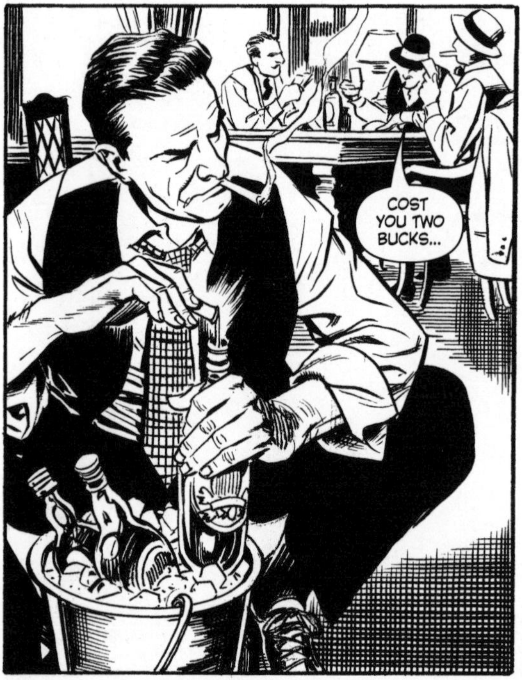
COST YOU TWO BUCKS...

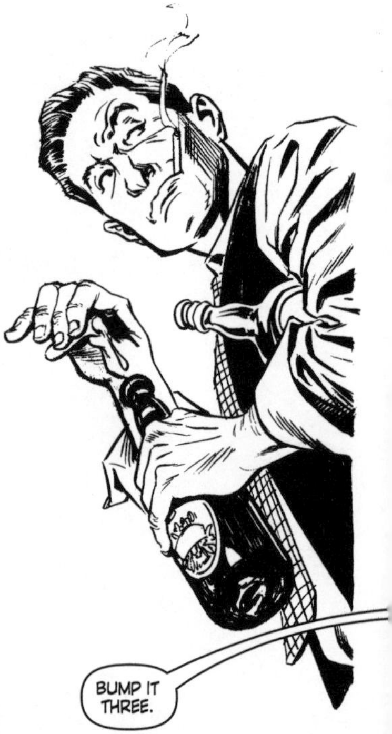
BUMP IT THREE.

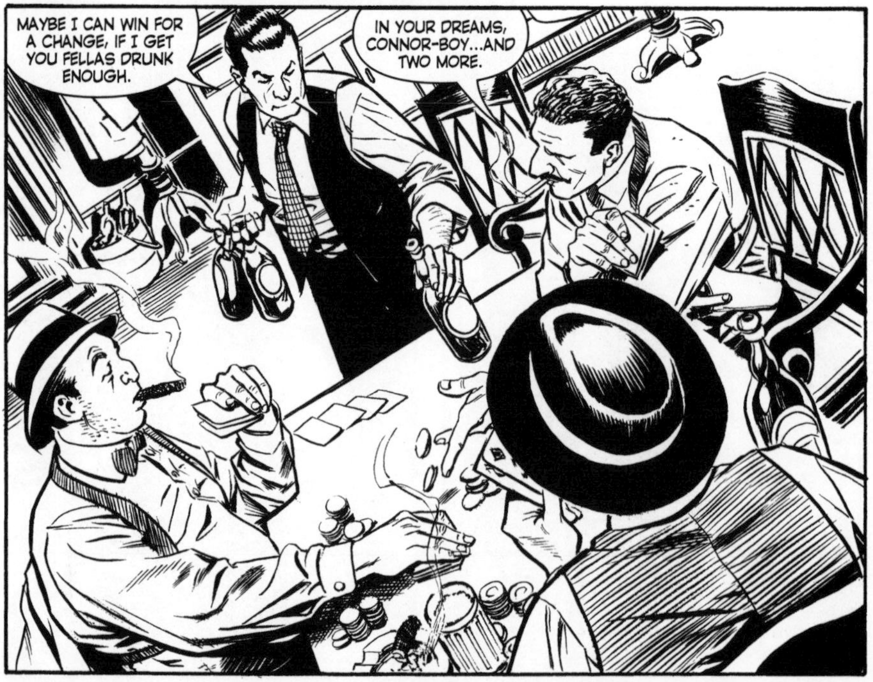
MAYBE I CAN WIN FOR A CHANGE, IF I GET YOU FELLAS DRUNK ENOUGH.
IN YOUR DREAMS, CONNOR-BOY...AND TWO MORE.

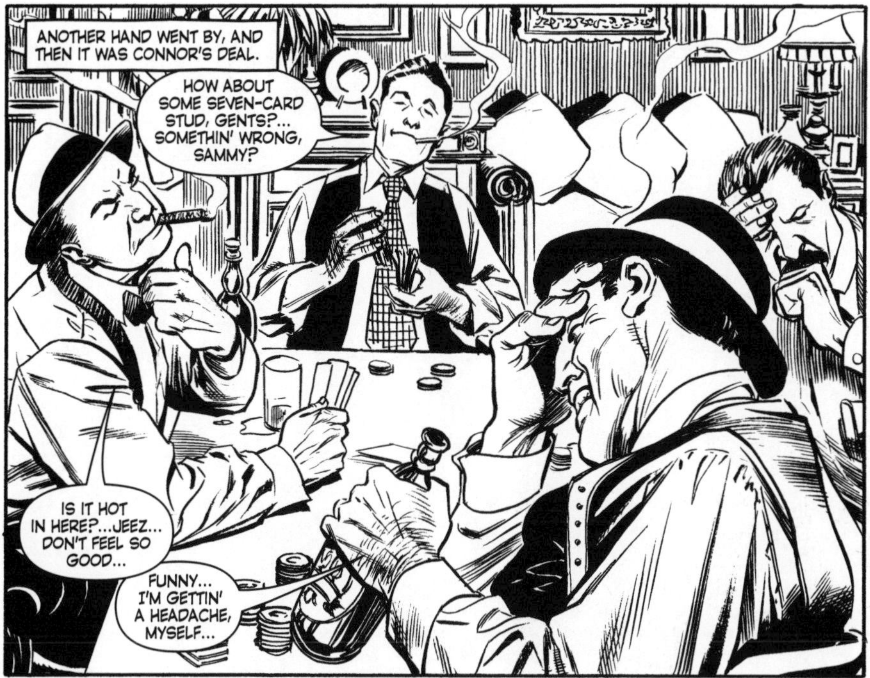
ANOTHER HAND WENT BY, AND THEN IT WAS CONNOR'S DEAL.
HOW ABOUT SOME SEVEN-CARD STUD, GENTS?... SOMETHIN' WRONG, SAMMY?
IS IT HOT IN HERE?...JEEZ... DON'T FEEL SO GOOD...
FUNNY... I'M GETTIN' A HEADACHE, MYSELF...

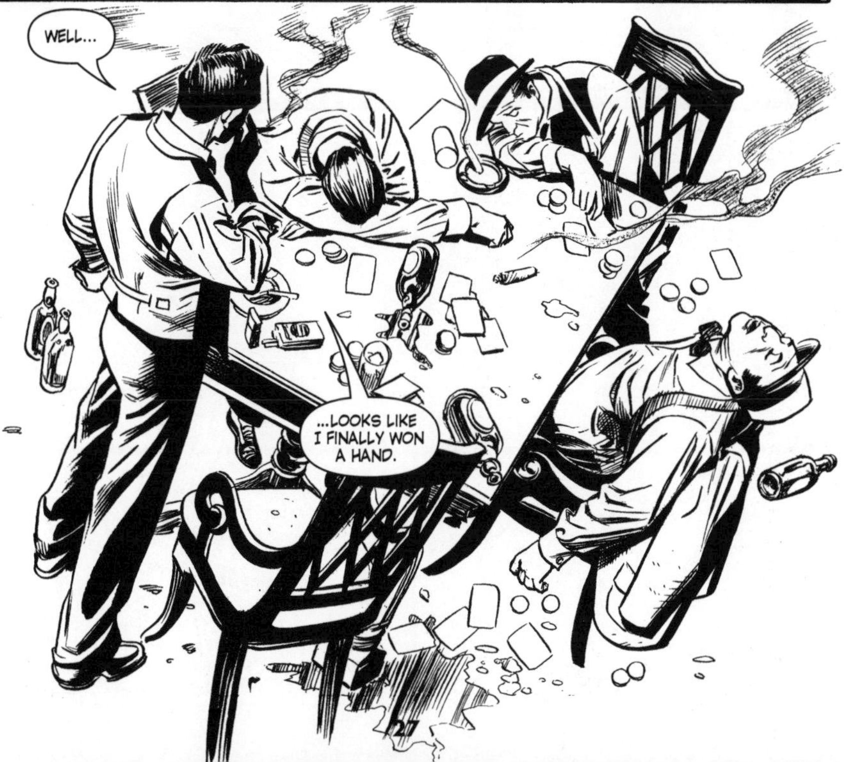
WELL...
...LOOKS LIKE I FINALLY WON A HAND.

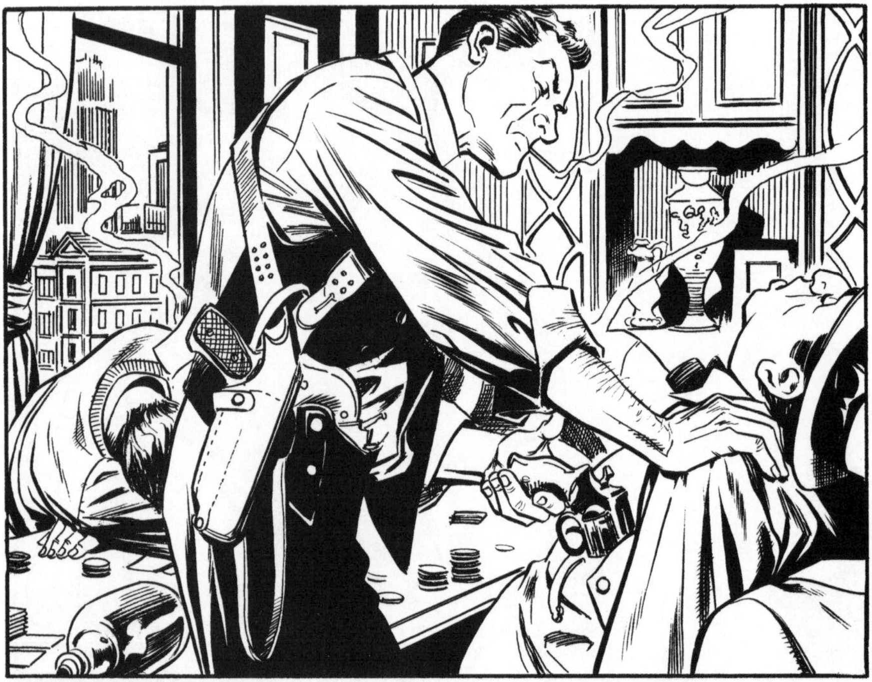

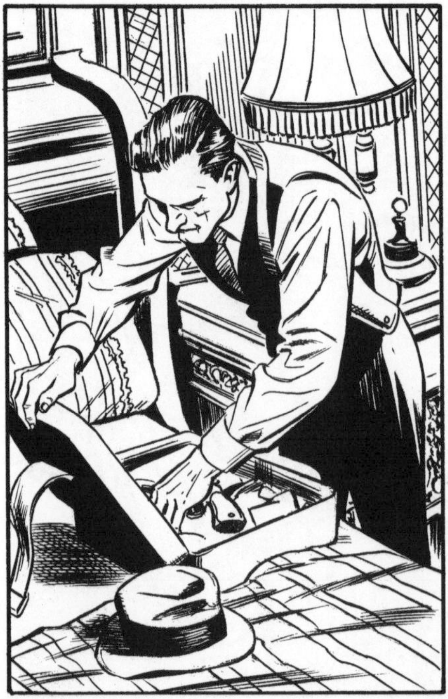

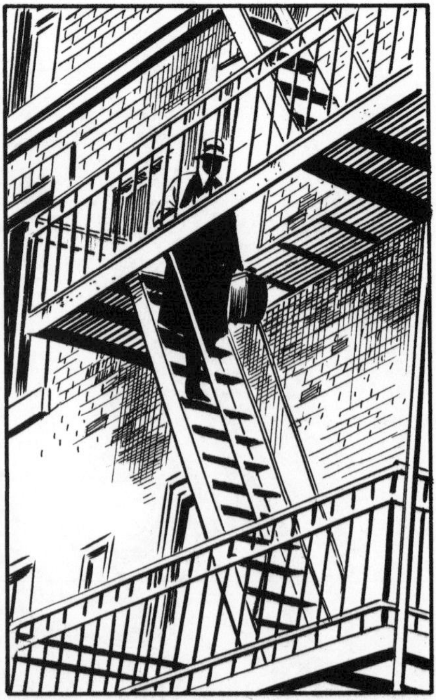

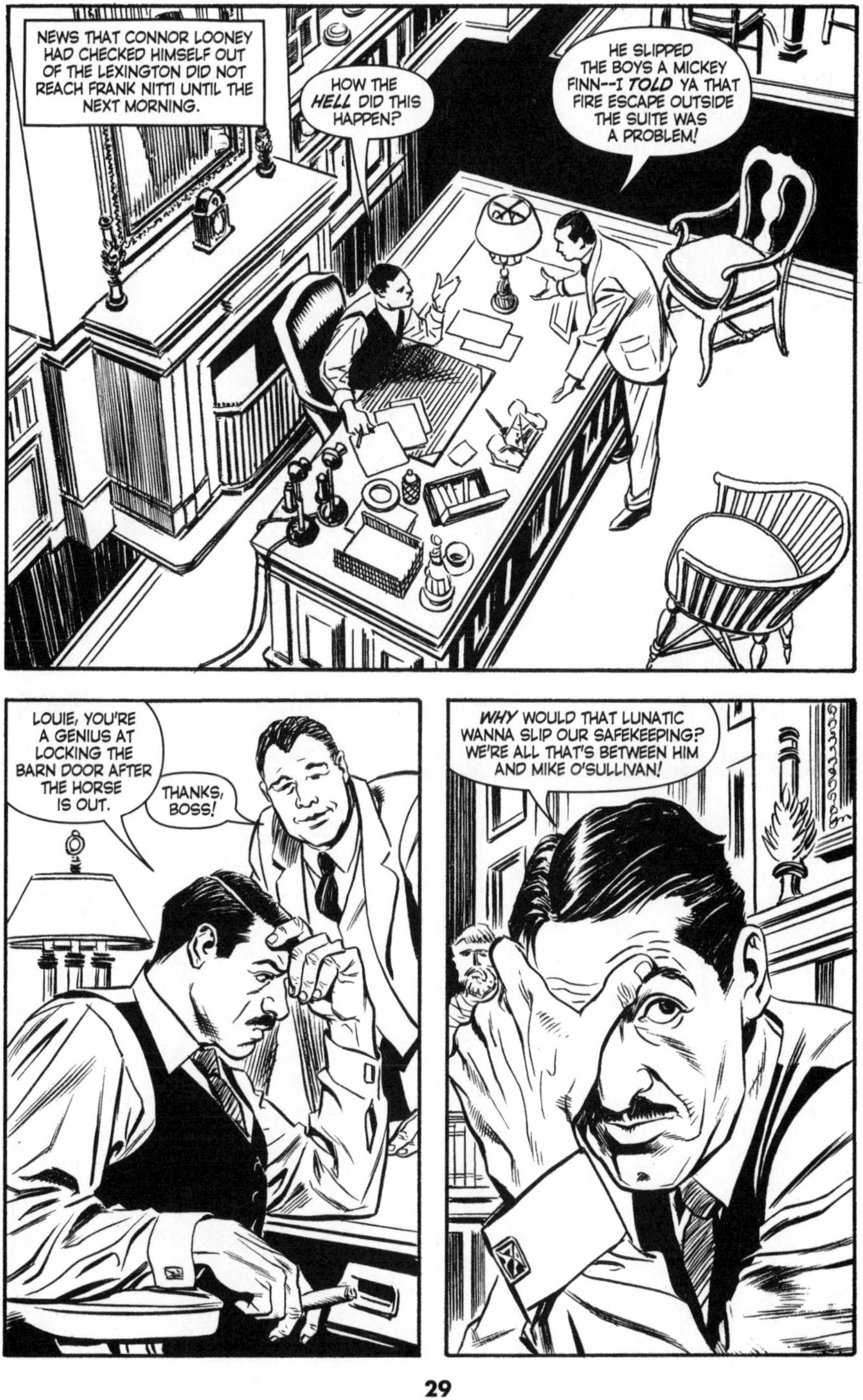
NEWS THAT CONNOR LOONEY HAD CHECKED HIMSELF OUT OF THE LEXINGTON DID NOT REACH FRANK NITTI UNTIL THE NEXT MORNING.
HOW THE HELL DID THIS HAPPEN?
HE SLIPPED THE BOYS A MICKEY FINN--I TOLD YA THAT FIRE ESCAPE OUTSIDE THE SUITE WAS A PROBLEM!
LOUIE, YOU'RE A GENIUS AT LOCKING THE BARN DOOR AFTER THE HORSE IS OUT.
THANKS, BOSS!
WHY WOULD THAT LUNATIC WANNA SLIP OUR SAFEKEEPING? WE'RE ALL THAT'S BETWEEN HIM AND MIKE O'SULLIVAN!

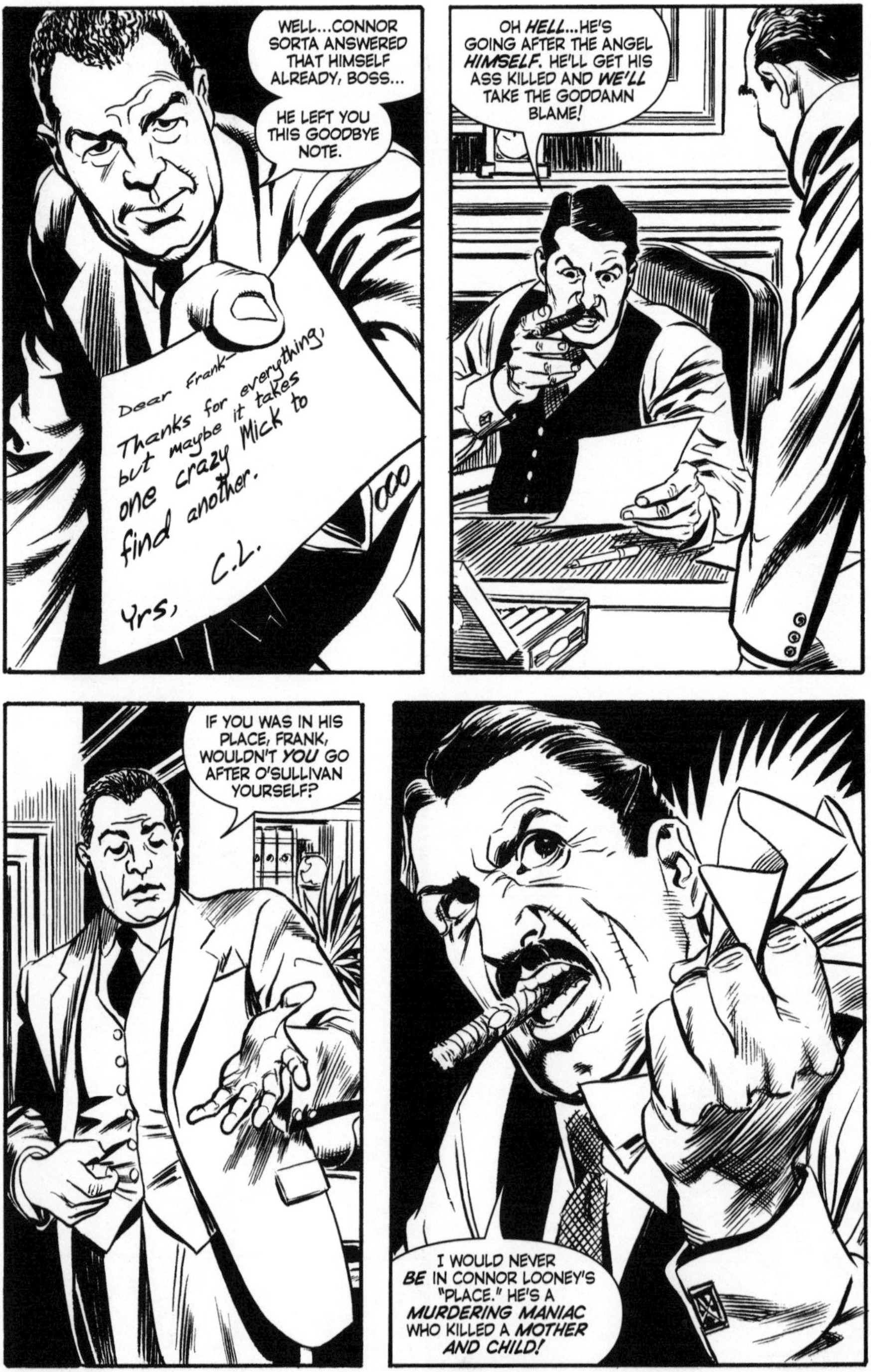
WELL...CONNOR SORTA ANSWERED THAT HIMSELF ALREADY, BOSS...
HE LEFT YOU THIS GOODBYE NOTE.
Dear Frank— Thanks for everything, but maybe it takes one crazy Mick to find another. Yrs, C.L.
OH HELL...HE'S GOING AFTER THE ANGEL HIMSELF. HE'LL GET HIS ASS KILLED AND WE'LL TAKE THE GODDAMN BLAME!
IF YOU WAS IN HIS PLACE, FRANK, WOULDN'T YOU GO AFTER O'SULLIVAN YOURSELF?
I WOULD NEVER BE IN CONNOR LOONEY'S "PLACE." HE'S A MURDERING MANIAC WHO KILLED A MOTHER AND CHILD!

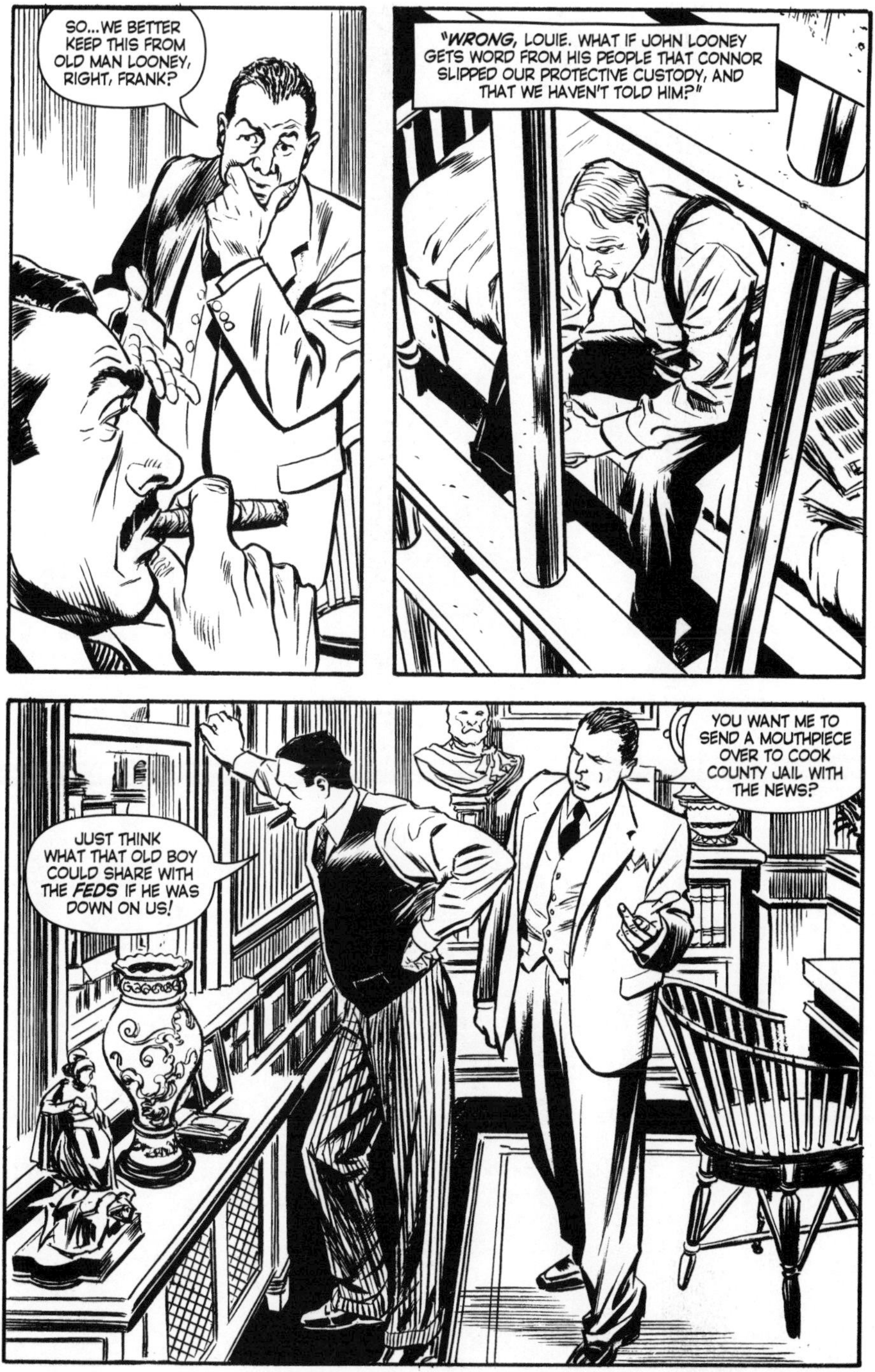
SO...WE BETTER KEEP THIS FROM OLD MAN LOONEY, RIGHT, FRANK?
"WRONG, LOUIE. WHAT IF JOHN LOONEY GETS WORD FROM HIS PEOPLE THAT CONNOR SLIPPED OUR PROTECTIVE CUSTODY, AND THAT WE HAVEN'T TOLD HIM?"
YOU WANT ME TO SEND A MOUTHPIECE OVER TO COOK COUNTY JAIL WITH THE NEWS?
JUST THINK WHAT THAT OLD BOY COULD SHARE WITH THE FEDS IF HE WAS DOWN ON US!

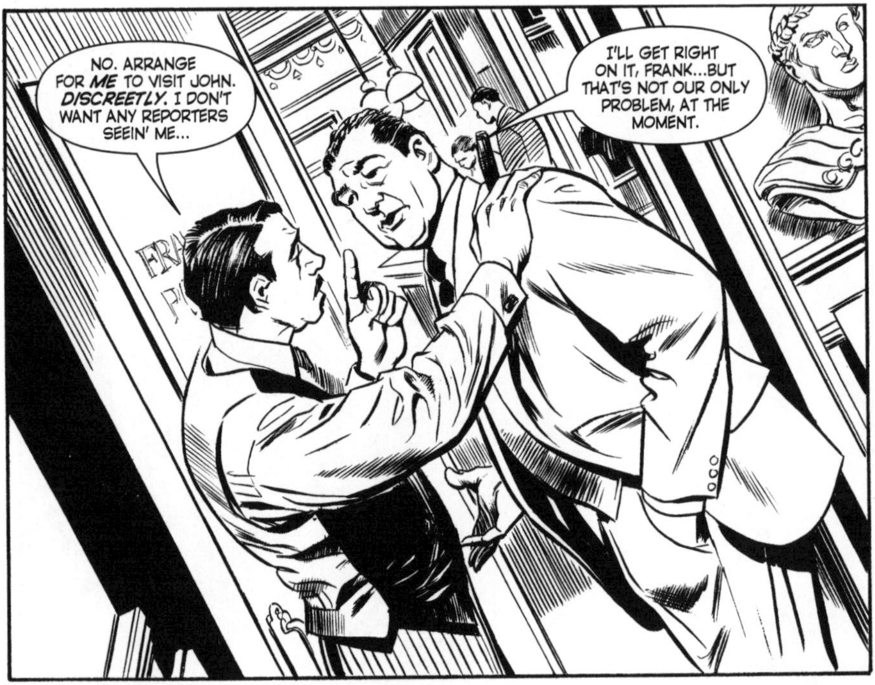
NO. ARRANGE FOR *ME* TO VISIT JOHN. *DISCREETLY.* I DON'T WANT ANY REPORTERS SEEIN' ME...
I'LL GET RIGHT ON IT, FRANK...BUT THAT'S NOT OUR ONLY PROBLEM, AT THE MOMENT.

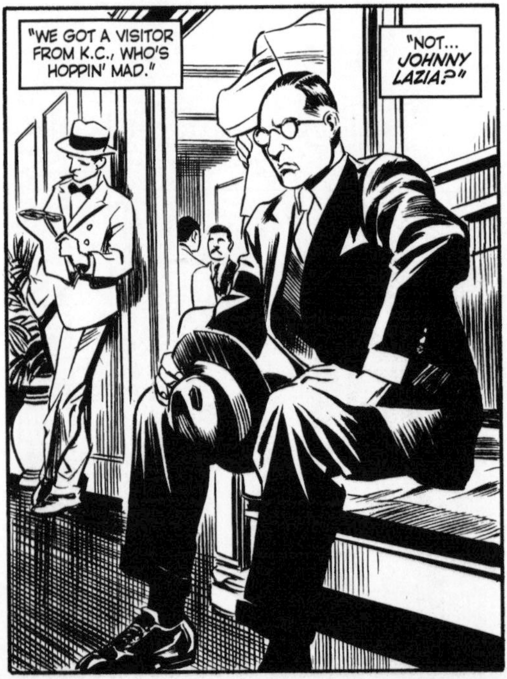
"WE GOT A VISITOR FROM K.C., WHO'S HOPPIN' MAD."
"NOT... *JOHNNY LAZIA?*"

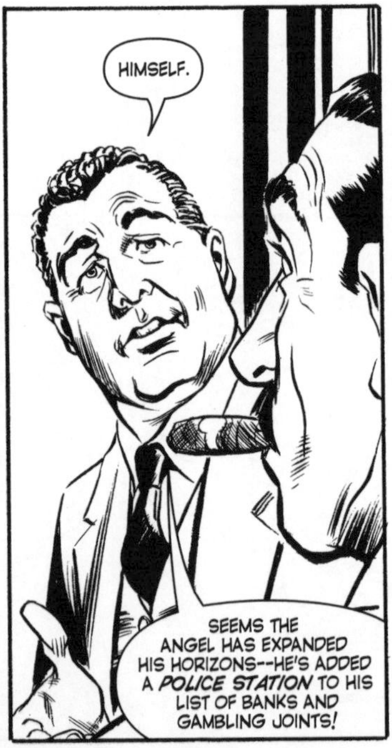
HIMSELF.
SEEMS THE ANGEL HAS EXPANDED HIS HORIZONS--HE'S ADDED A *POLICE STATION* TO HIS LIST OF BANKS AND GAMBLING JOINTS!

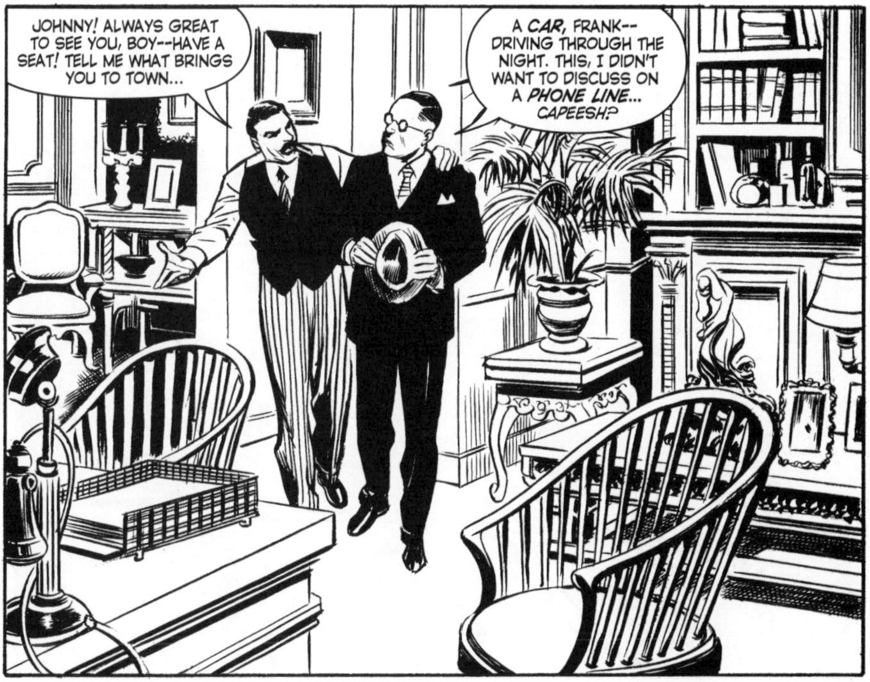
JOHNNY! ALWAYS GREAT TO SEE YOU, BOY--HAVE A SEAT! TELL ME WHAT BRINGS YOU TO TOWN...
A CAR, FRANK-- DRIVING THROUGH THE NIGHT. THIS, I DIDN'T WANT TO DISCUSS ON A PHONE LINE... CAPEESH?

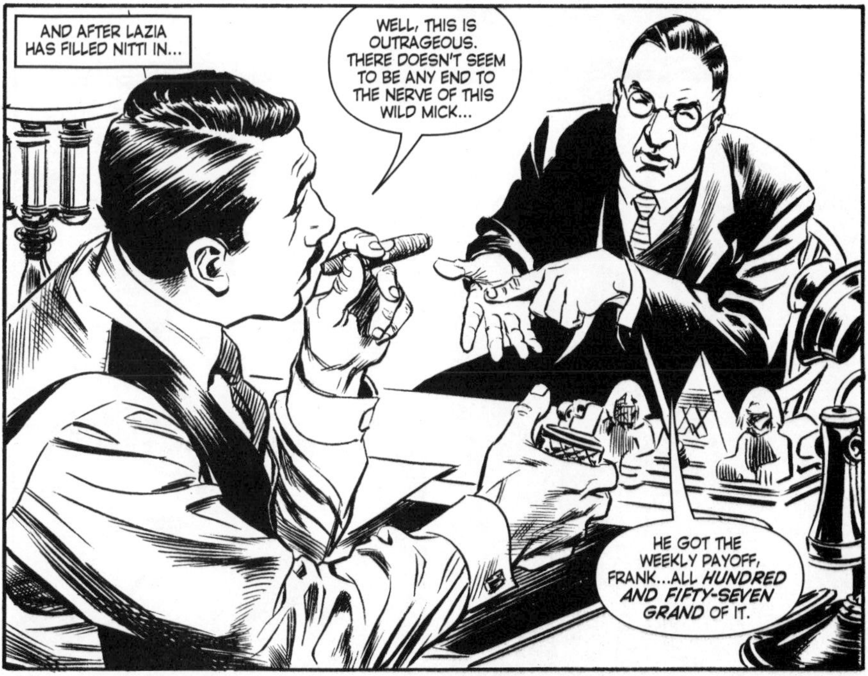
AND AFTER LAZIA HAS FILLED NITTI IN...
WELL, THIS IS OUTRAGEOUS. THERE DOESN'T SEEM TO BE ANY END TO THE NERVE OF THIS WILD MICK...
HE GOT THE WEEKLY PAYOFF, FRANK...ALL HUNDRED AND FIFTY-SEVEN GRAND OF IT.

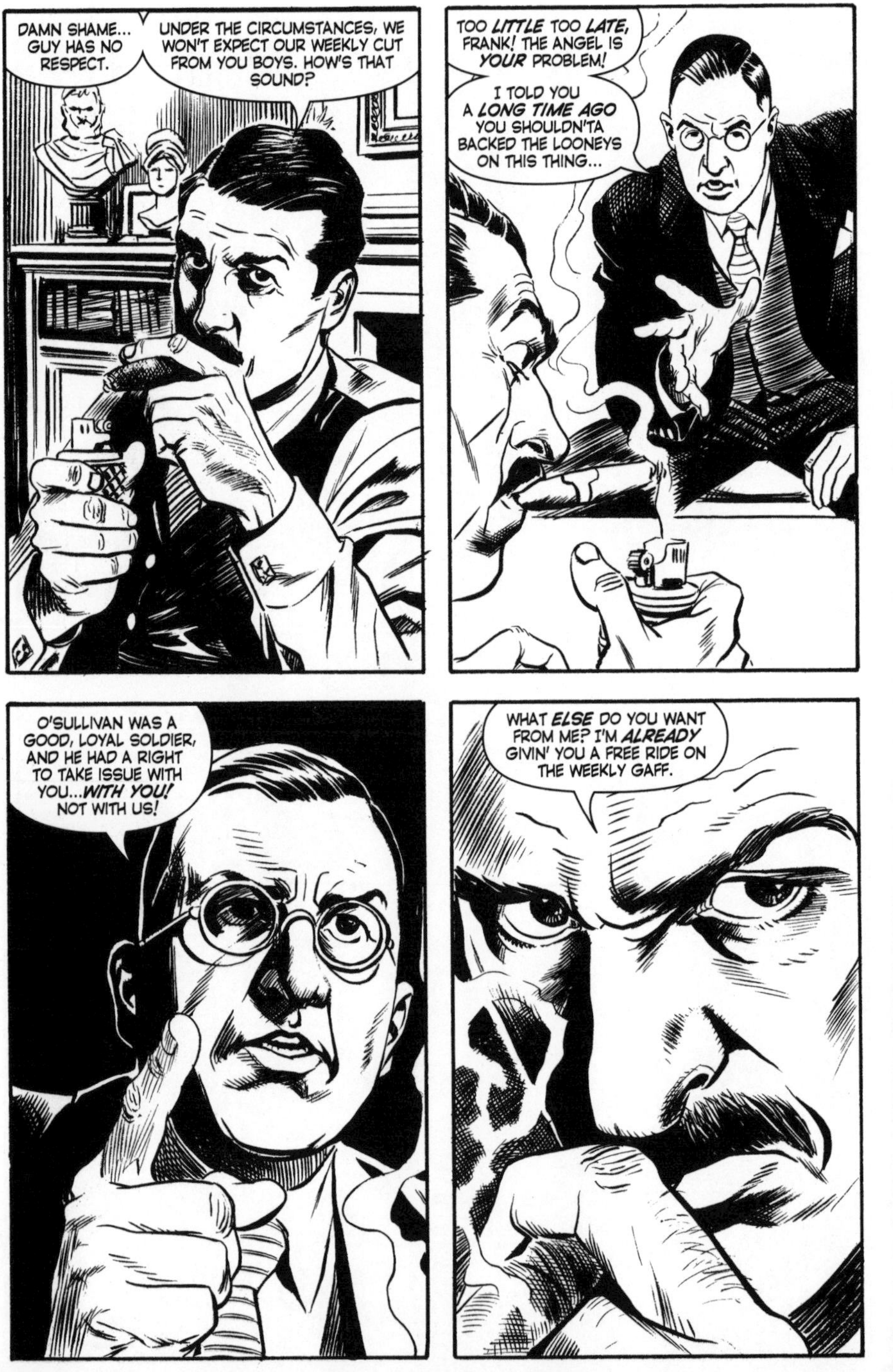
DAMN SHAME... GUY HAS NO RESPECT.
UNDER THE CIRCUMSTANCES, WE WON'T EXPECT OUR WEEKLY CUT FROM YOU BOYS. HOW'S THAT SOUND?
TOO LITTLE TOO LATE, FRANK! THE ANGEL IS YOUR PROBLEM!
I TOLD YOU A LONG TIME AGO YOU SHOULDN'TA BACKED THE LOONEYS ON THIS THING...
O'SULLIVAN WAS A GOOD, LOYAL SOLDIER, AND HE HAD A RIGHT TO TAKE ISSUE WITH YOU...WITH YOU! NOT WITH US!
WHAT ELSE DO YOU WANT FROM ME? I'M ALREADY GIVIN' YOU A FREE RIDE ON THE WEEKLY GAFF.

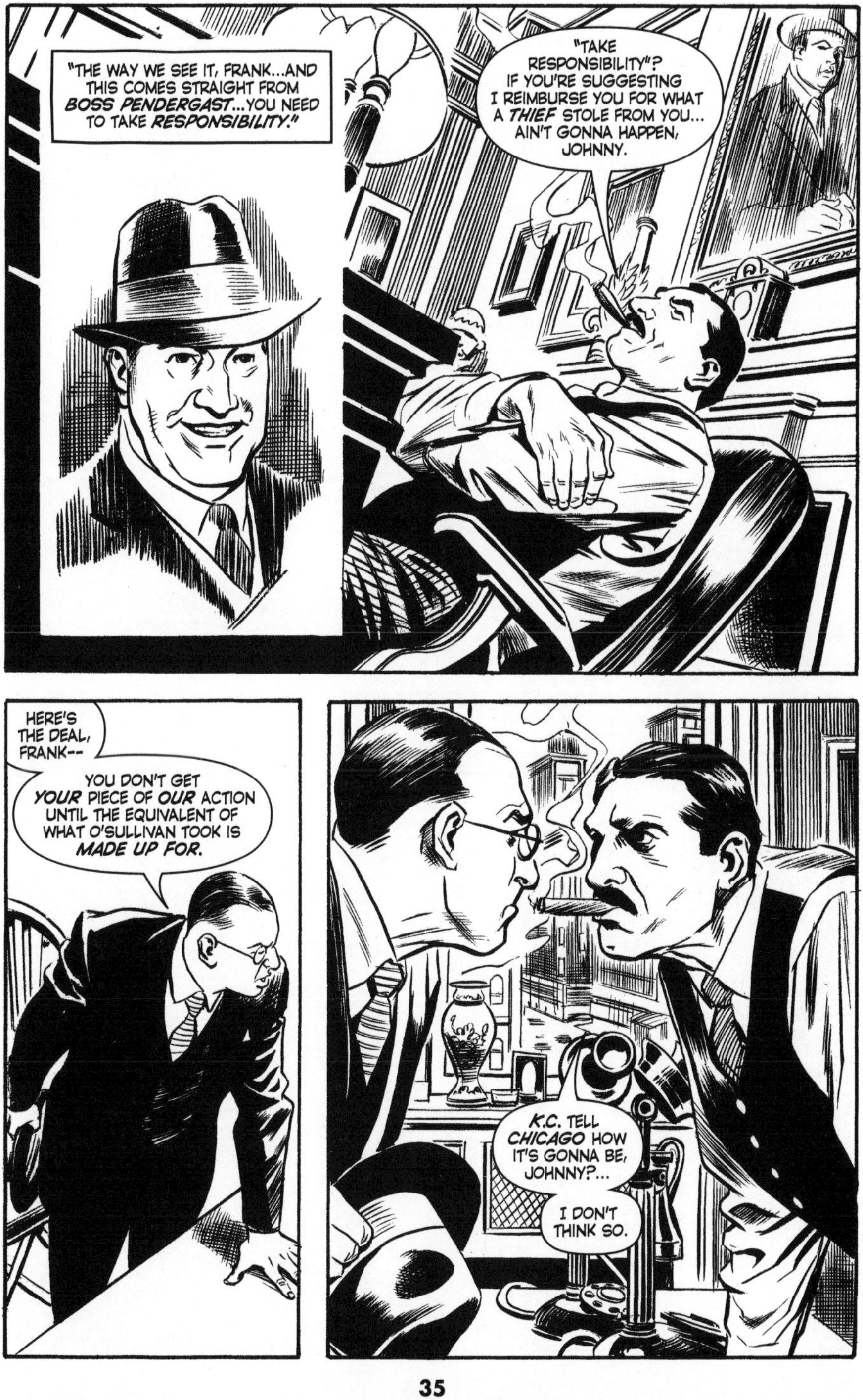
"THE WAY WE SEE IT, FRANK...AND THIS COMES STRAIGHT FROM BOSS PENDERGAST...YOU NEED TO TAKE RESPONSIBILITY."
"TAKE RESPONSIBILITY"? IF YOU'RE SUGGESTING I REIMBURSE YOU FOR WHAT A THIEF STOLE FROM YOU... AIN'T GONNA HAPPEN, JOHNNY.
HERE'S THE DEAL, FRANK--
YOU DON'T GET YOUR PIECE OF OUR ACTION UNTIL THE EQUIVALENT OF WHAT O'SULLIVAN TOOK IS MADE UP FOR.
K.C. TELL CHICAGO HOW IT'S GONNA BE, JOHNNY?...
I DON'T THINK SO.

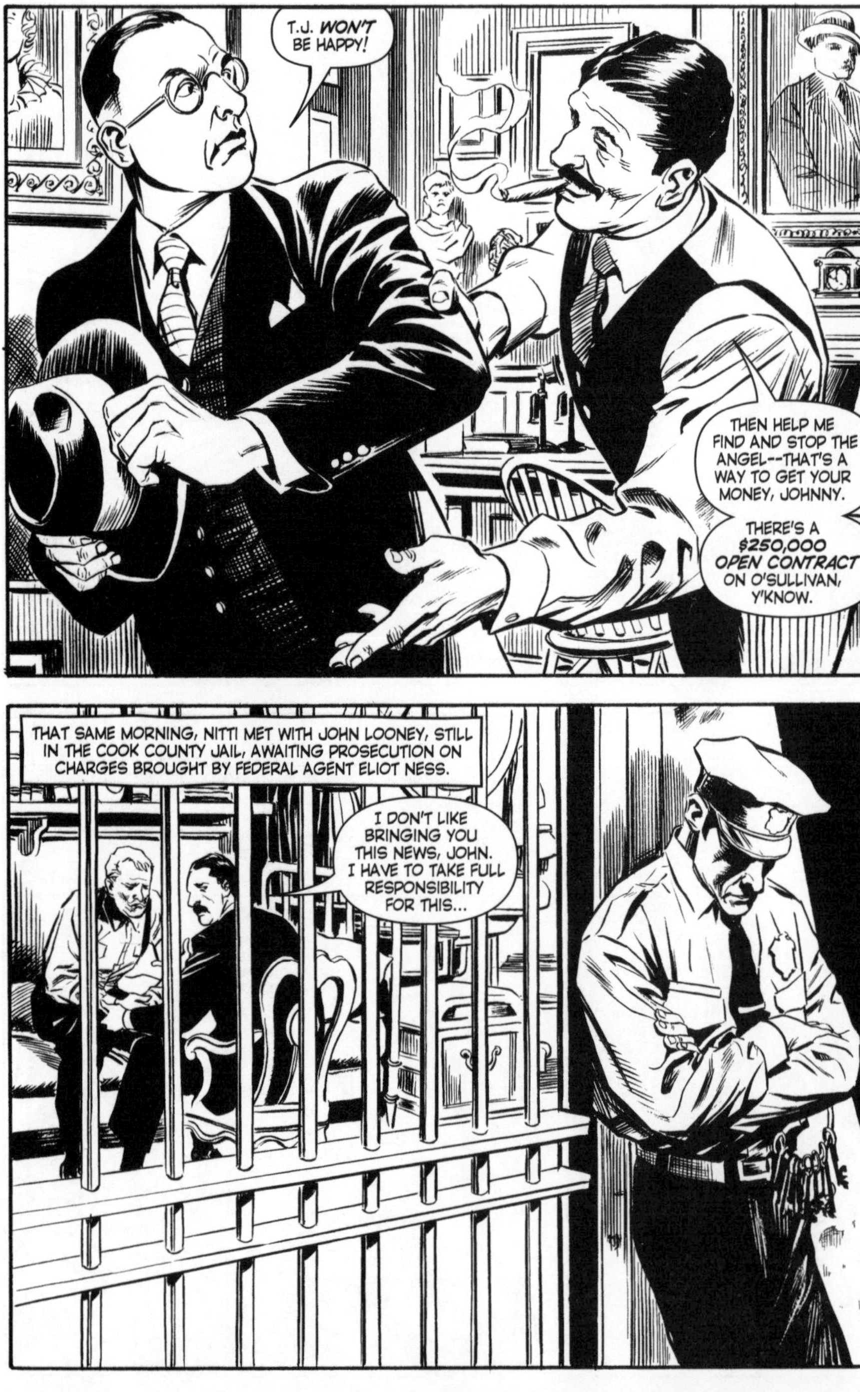
T.J. *WON'T* BE HAPPY!
THEN HELP ME FIND AND STOP THE ANGEL--THAT'S A WAY TO GET YOUR MONEY, JOHNNY.
THERE'S A *$250,000 OPEN CONTRACT* ON O'SULLIVAN, Y'KNOW.
THAT SAME MORNING, NITTI MET WITH JOHN LOONEY, STILL IN THE COOK COUNTY JAIL, AWAITING PROSECUTION ON CHARGES BROUGHT BY FEDERAL AGENT ELIOT NESS.
I DON'T LIKE BRINGING YOU THIS NEWS, JOHN. I HAVE TO TAKE FULL RESPONSIBILITY FOR THIS...

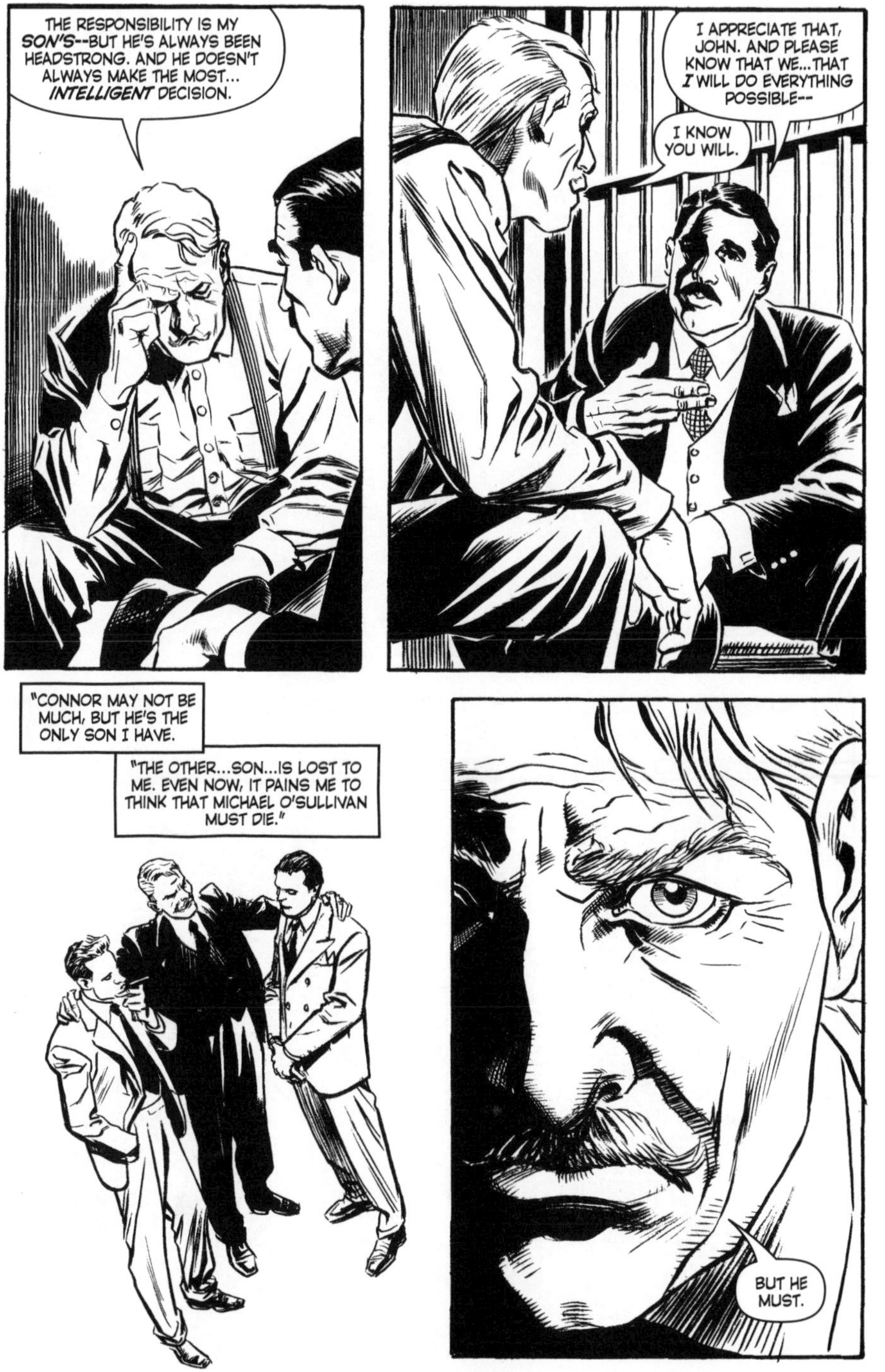
THE RESPONSIBILITY IS MY *SON'S*--BUT HE'S ALWAYS BEEN HEADSTRONG. AND HE DOESN'T ALWAYS MAKE THE MOST... *INTELLIGENT* DECISION.
I APPRECIATE THAT, JOHN. AND PLEASE KNOW THAT WE...THAT *I* WILL DO EVERYTHING POSSIBLE--
I KNOW YOU WILL.
"CONNOR MAY NOT BE MUCH, BUT HE'S THE ONLY SON I HAVE.
"THE OTHER...SON...IS LOST TO ME. EVEN NOW, IT PAINS ME TO THINK THAT MICHAEL O'SULLIVAN MUST DIE."
BUT HE MUST.

MY RELATIONSHIP WITH YOU AND AL GOES WAY BACK, FRANK. AND I'M CALLING ON THAT ASSOCIATION, THAT FRIENDSHIP, NOW. YOU *MUST* RETRIEVE CONNOR, BACK INTO YOUR SAFE HAVEN.

I WILL NOT ABIDE THE DEATH OF MY SON AT O'SULLIVAN'S HANDS. DO I MAKE MYSELF *CLEAR*, FRANK?

YOU DO, JOHN.

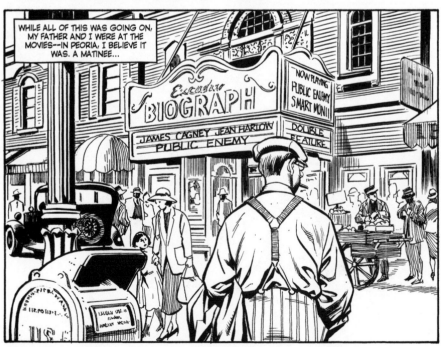

WHILE ALL OF THIS WAS GOING ON, MY FATHER AND I WERE AT THE MOVIES--IN PEORIA, I BELIEVE IT WAS. A MATINEE...

Excelsior BIOGRAPH

NOW PLAYING PUBLIC ENEMY SMART MONEY

JAMES CAGNEY JEAN HARLOW PUBLIC ENEMY

DOUBLE FEATURE

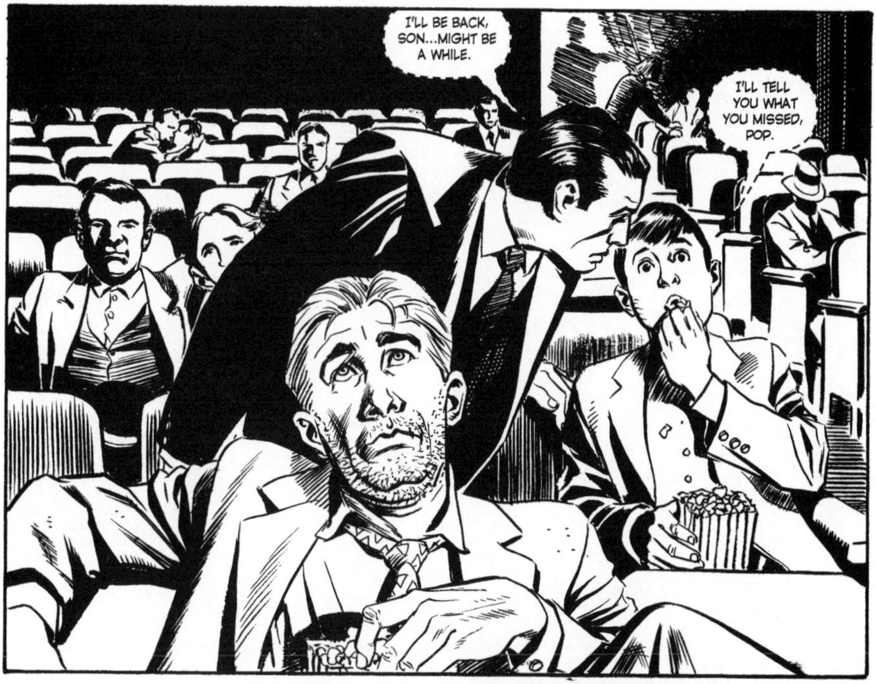
I'LL BE BACK, SON...MIGHT BE A WHILE.
I'LL TELL YOU WHAT YOU MISSED, POP.

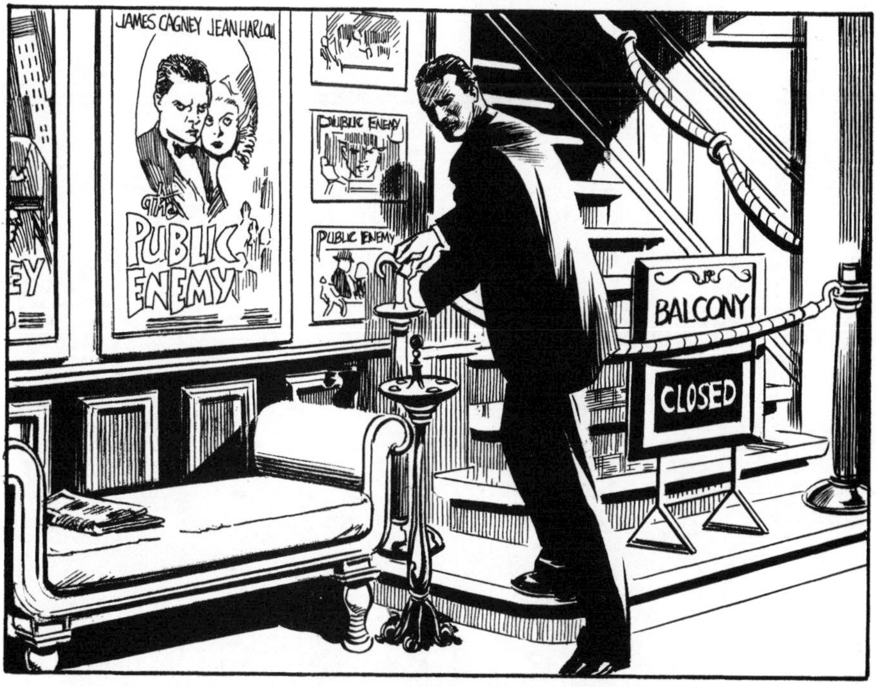
JAMES CAGNEY JEAN HARLOW
PUBLIC ENEMY
PUBLIC ENEMY
PUBLIC ENEMY
BALCONY
CLOSED

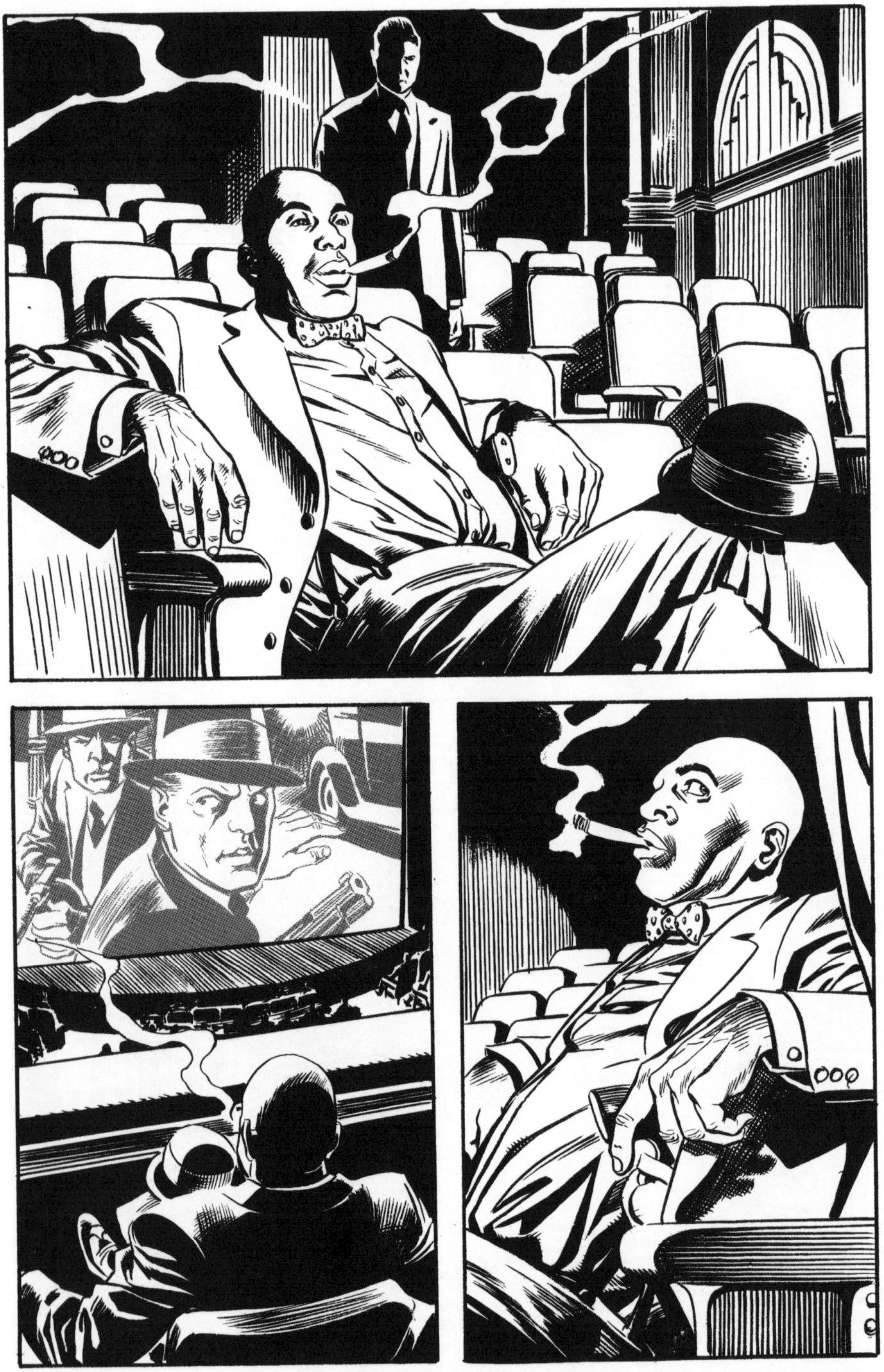

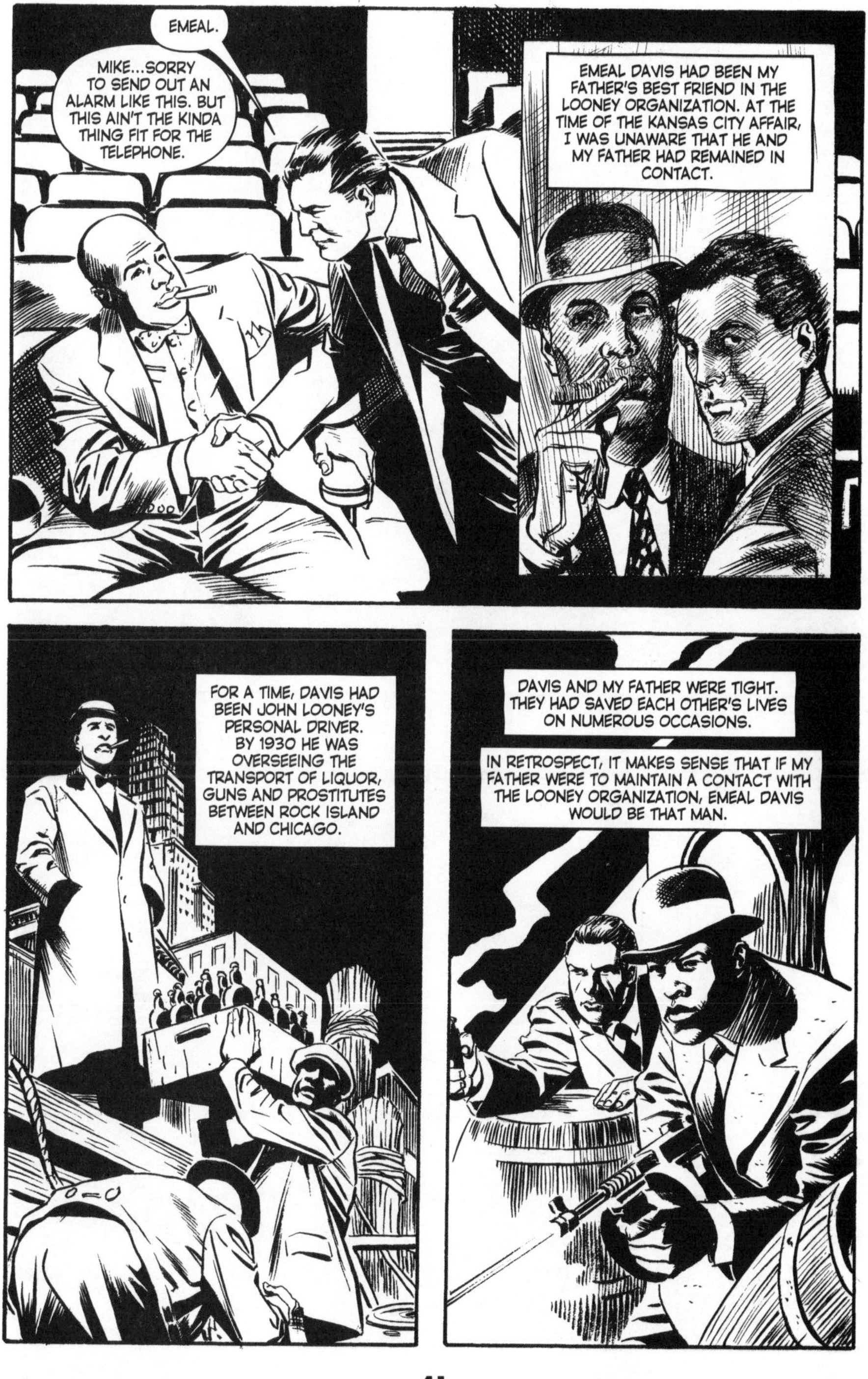
EMEAL.
MIKE...SORRY TO SEND OUT AN ALARM LIKE THIS. BUT THIS AIN'T THE KINDA THING FIT FOR THE TELEPHONE.
EMEAL DAVIS HAD BEEN MY FATHER'S BEST FRIEND IN THE LOONEY ORGANIZATION. AT THE TIME OF THE KANSAS CITY AFFAIR, I WAS UNAWARE THAT HE AND MY FATHER HAD REMAINED IN CONTACT.
FOR A TIME, DAVIS HAD BEEN JOHN LOONEY'S PERSONAL DRIVER. BY 1930 HE WAS OVERSEEING THE TRANSPORT OF LIQUOR, GUNS AND PROSTITUTES BETWEEN ROCK ISLAND AND CHICAGO.
DAVIS AND MY FATHER WERE TIGHT. THEY HAD SAVED EACH OTHER'S LIVES ON NUMEROUS OCCASIONS.
IN RETROSPECT, IT MAKES SENSE THAT IF MY FATHER WERE TO MAINTAIN A CONTACT WITH THE LOONEY ORGANIZATION, EMEAL DAVIS WOULD BE THAT MAN.

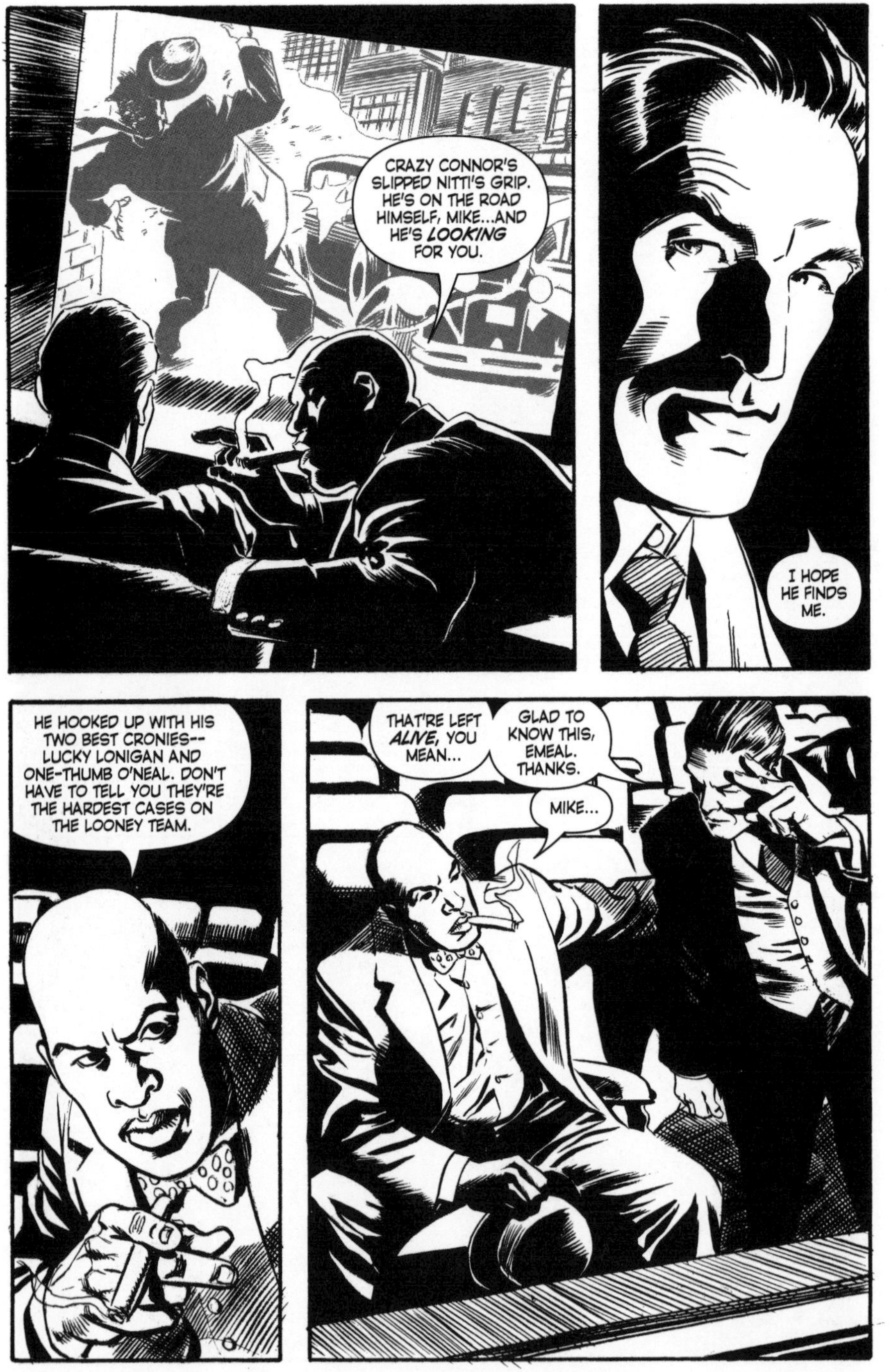
CRAZY CONNOR'S SLIPPED NITTI'S GRIP. HE'S ON THE ROAD HIMSELF, MIKE...AND HE'S *LOOKING* FOR YOU.
I HOPE HE FINDS ME.
HE HOOKED UP WITH HIS TWO BEST CRONIES-- LUCKY LONIGAN AND ONE-THUMB O'NEAL. DON'T HAVE TO TELL YOU THEY'RE THE HARDEST CASES ON THE LOONEY TEAM.
THAT'RE LEFT *ALIVE,* YOU MEAN...
GLAD TO KNOW THIS, EMEAL. THANKS.
MIKE...

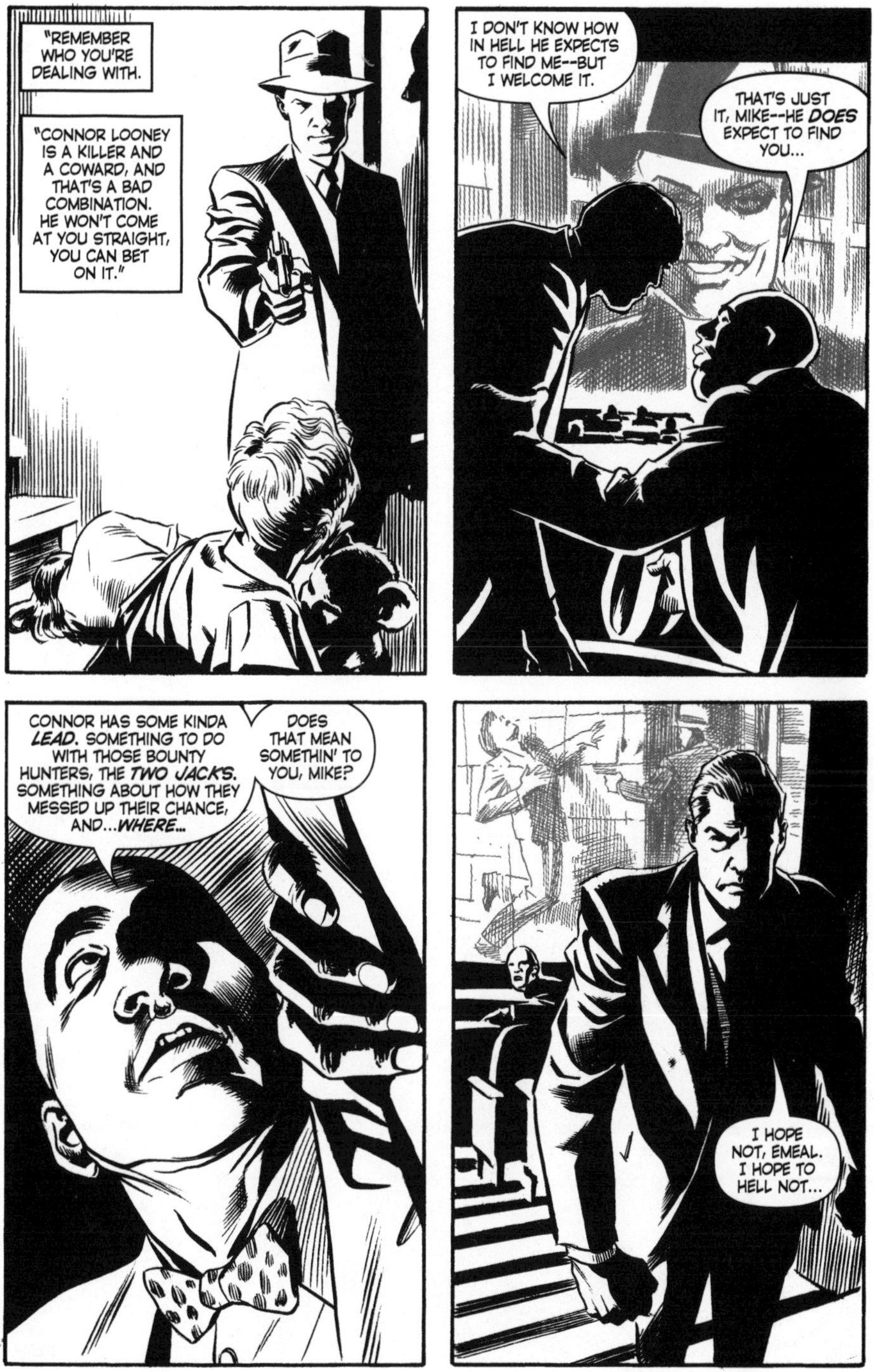
"REMEMBER WHO YOU'RE DEALING WITH.
"CONNOR LOONEY IS A KILLER AND A COWARD, AND THAT'S A BAD COMBINATION. HE WON'T COME AT YOU STRAIGHT, YOU CAN BET ON IT."
I DON'T KNOW HOW IN HELL HE EXPECTS TO FIND ME--BUT I WELCOME IT.
THAT'S JUST IT, MIKE--HE *DOES* EXPECT TO FIND YOU...
CONNOR HAS SOME KINDA *LEAD*. SOMETHING TO DO WITH THOSE BOUNTY HUNTERS, THE *TWO JACKS*. SOMETHING ABOUT HOW THEY MESSED UP THEIR CHANCE, AND...*WHERE*...
DOES THAT MEAN SOMETHIN' TO YOU, MIKE?
I HOPE NOT, EMEAL. I HOPE TO HELL NOT...

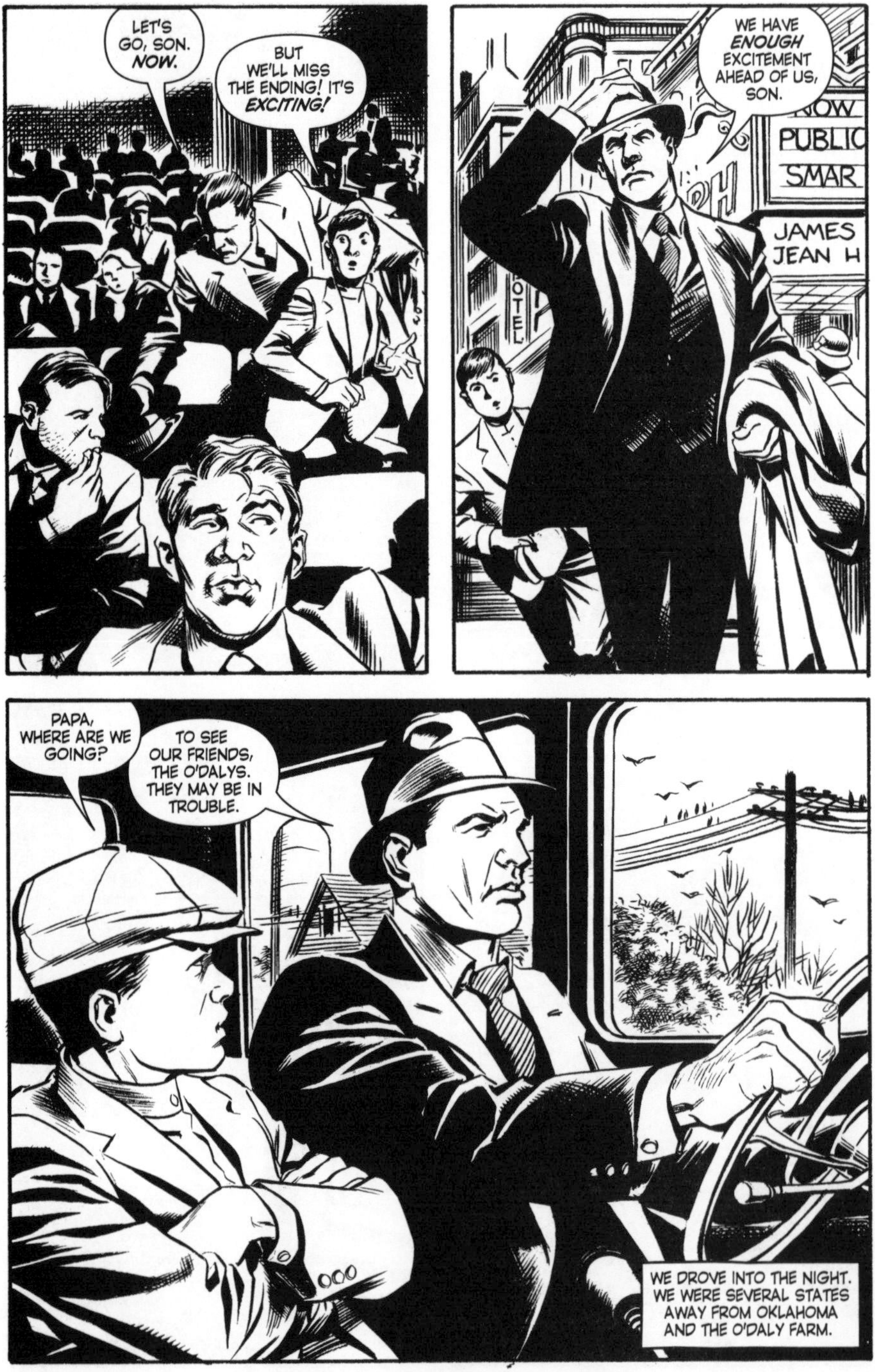
LET'S GO, SON. *NOW.*
BUT WE'LL MISS THE ENDING! IT'S *EXCITING!*
WE HAVE *ENOUGH* EXCITEMENT AHEAD OF US, SON.
NOW
PUBLIC
SMAR
JAMES
JEAN H
PAPA, WHERE ARE WE GOING?
TO SEE OUR FRIENDS, THE O'DALYS. THEY MAY BE IN TROUBLE.
WE DROVE INTO THE NIGHT. WE WERE SEVERAL STATES AWAY FROM OKLAHOMA AND THE O'DALY FARM.

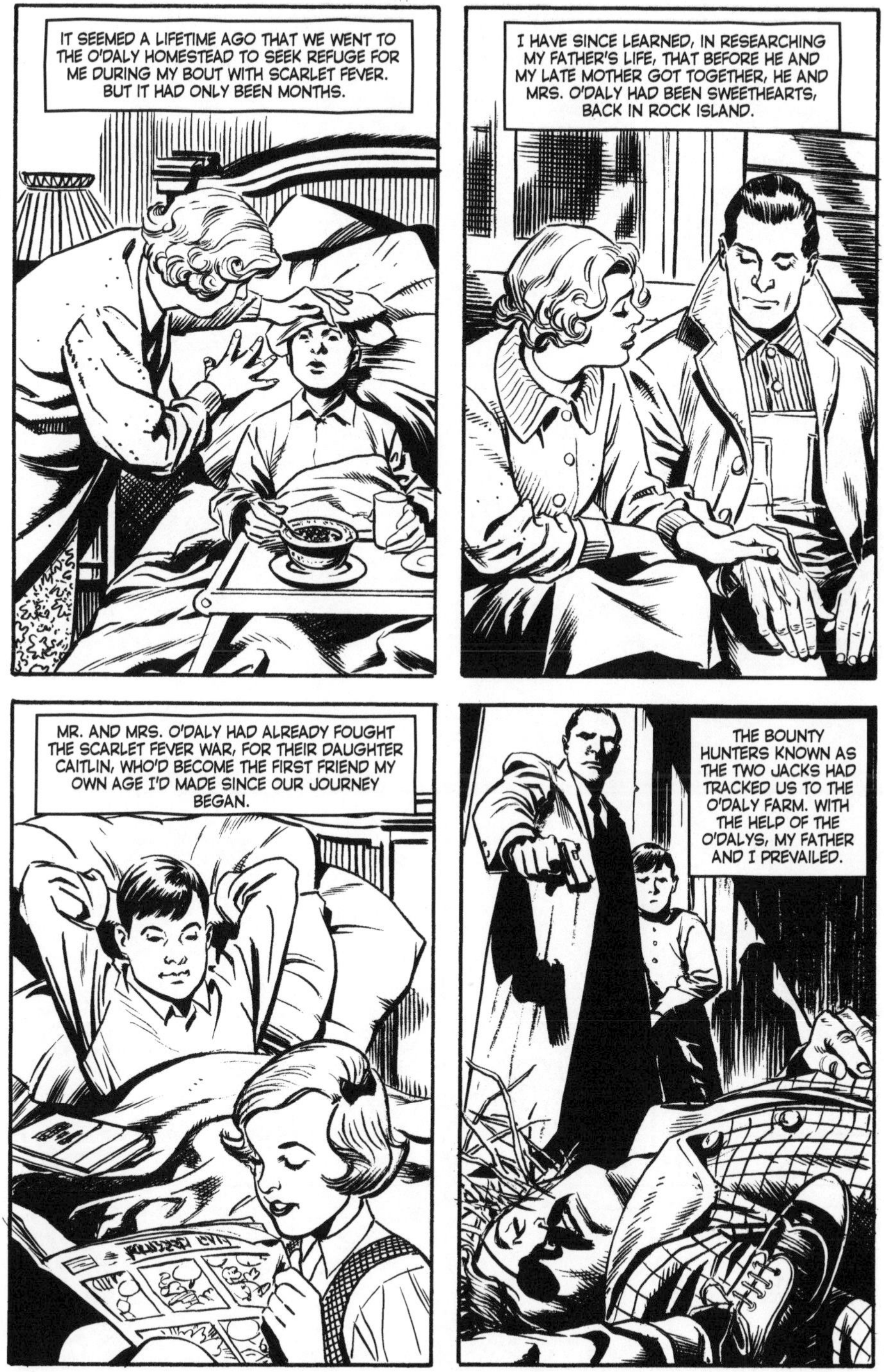
IT SEEMED A LIFETIME AGO THAT WE WENT TO THE O'DALY HOMESTEAD TO SEEK REFUGE FOR ME DURING MY BOUT WITH SCARLET FEVER. BUT IT HAD ONLY BEEN MONTHS.
I HAVE SINCE LEARNED, IN RESEARCHING MY FATHER'S LIFE, THAT BEFORE HE AND MY LATE MOTHER GOT TOGETHER, HE AND MRS. O'DALY HAD BEEN SWEETHEARTS, BACK IN ROCK ISLAND.
MR. AND MRS. O'DALY HAD ALREADY FOUGHT THE SCARLET FEVER WAR, FOR THEIR DAUGHTER CAITLIN, WHO'D BECOME THE FIRST FRIEND MY OWN AGE I'D MADE SINCE OUR JOURNEY BEGAN.
THE BOUNTY HUNTERS KNOWN AS THE TWO JACKS HAD TRACKED US TO THE O'DALY FARM. WITH THE HELP OF THE O'DALYS, MY FATHER AND I PREVAILED.

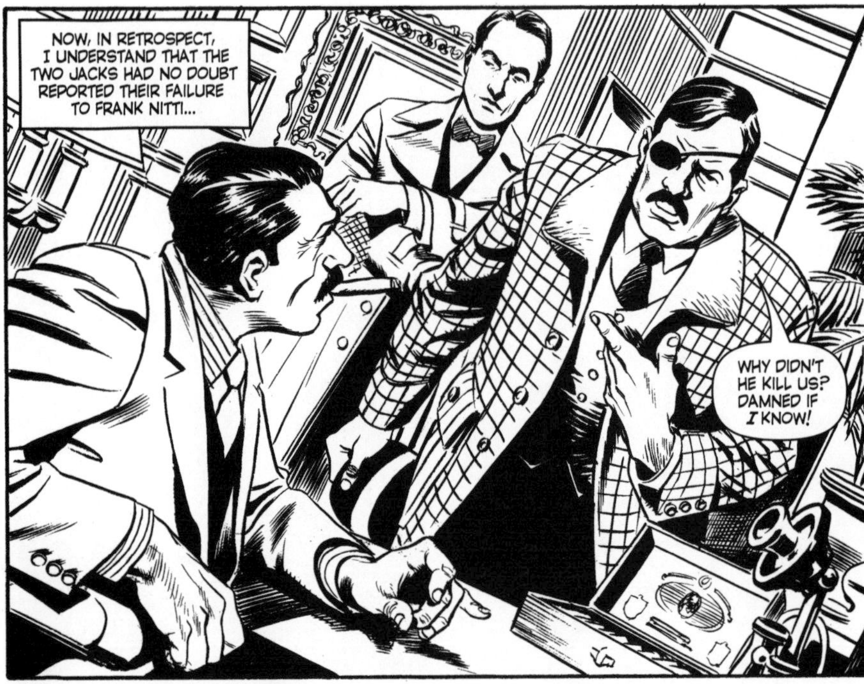
NOW, IN RETROSPECT, I UNDERSTAND THAT THE TWO JACKS HAD NO DOUBT REPORTED THEIR FAILURE TO FRANK NITTI...
WHY DIDN'T HE KILL US? DAMNED IF *I* KNOW!

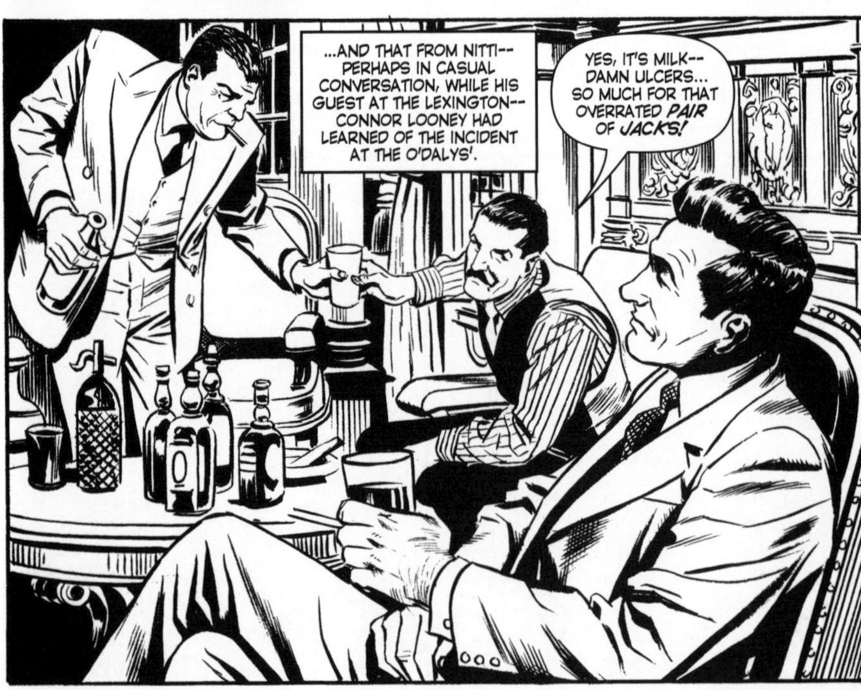
...AND THAT FROM NITTI-- PERHAPS IN CASUAL CONVERSATION, WHILE HIS GUEST AT THE LEXINGTON-- CONNOR LOONEY HAD LEARNED OF THE INCIDENT AT THE O'DALYS'.
YES, IT'S MILK-- DAMN ULCERS... SO MUCH FOR THAT OVERRATED *PAIR OF JACKS!*

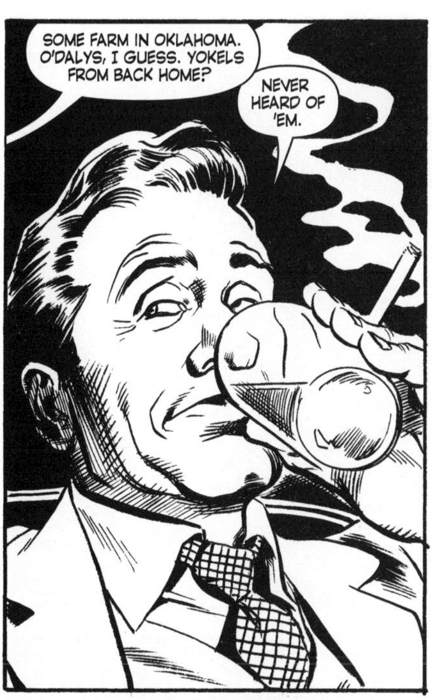
SOME FARM IN OKLAHOMA. O'DALYS, I GUESS. YOKELS FROM BACK HOME?
NEVER HEARD OF 'EM.

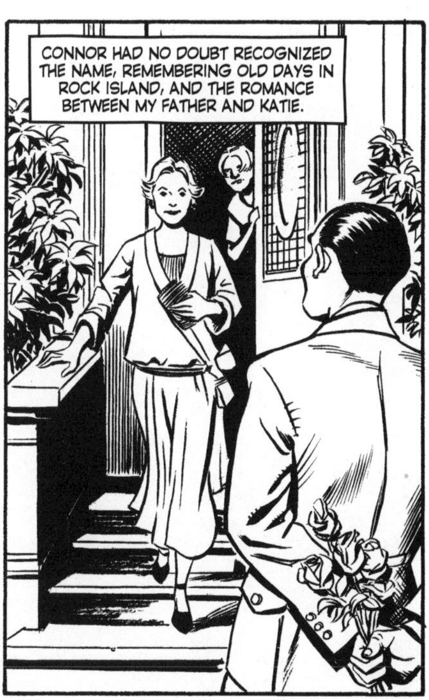
CONNOR HAD NO DOUBT RECOGNIZED THE NAME, REMEMBERING OLD DAYS IN ROCK ISLAND, AND THE ROMANCE BETWEEN MY FATHER AND KATIE.

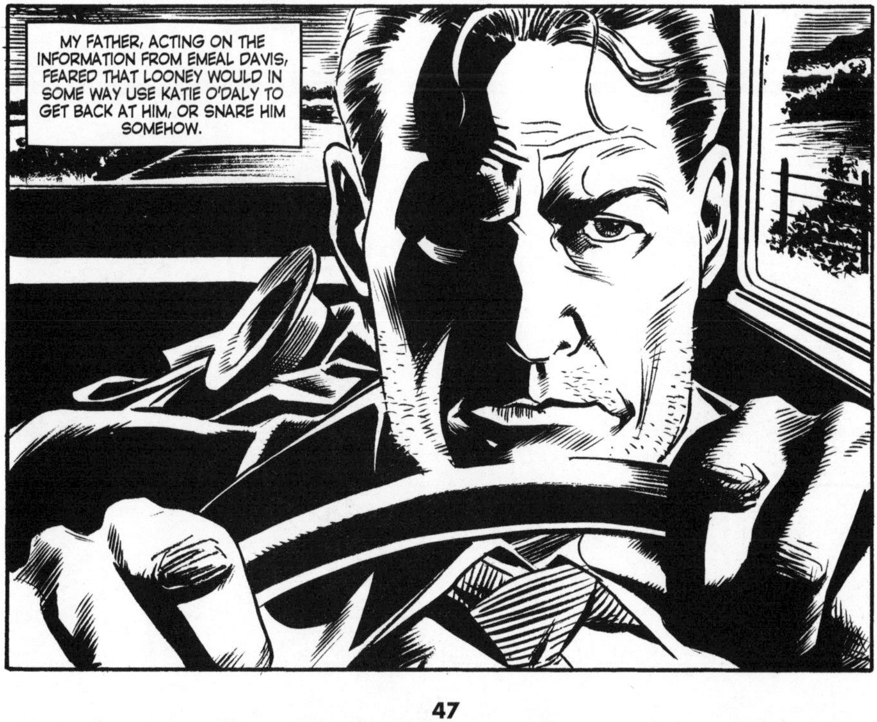
MY FATHER, ACTING ON THE INFORMATION FROM EMEAL DAVIS, FEARED THAT LOONEY WOULD IN SOME WAY USE KATIE O'DALY TO GET BACK AT HIM, OR SNARE HIM SOMEHOW.

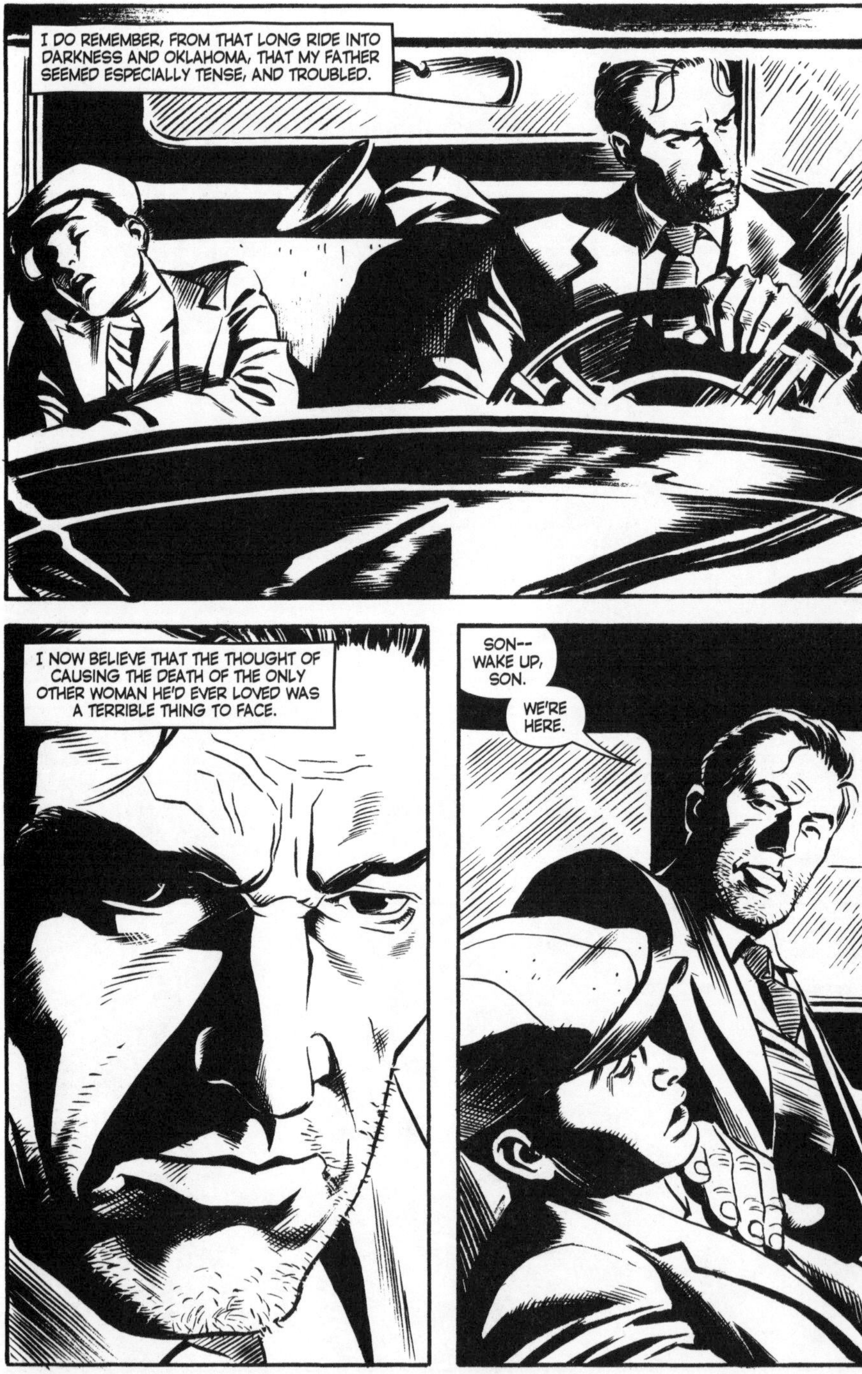
I DO REMEMBER, FROM THAT LONG RIDE INTO DARKNESS AND OKLAHOMA, THAT MY FATHER SEEMED ESPECIALLY TENSE, AND TROUBLED.
I NOW BELIEVE THAT THE THOUGHT OF CAUSING THE DEATH OF THE ONLY OTHER WOMAN HE'D EVER LOVED WAS A TERRIBLE THING TO FACE.
SON-- WAKE UP, SON.
WE'RE HERE.

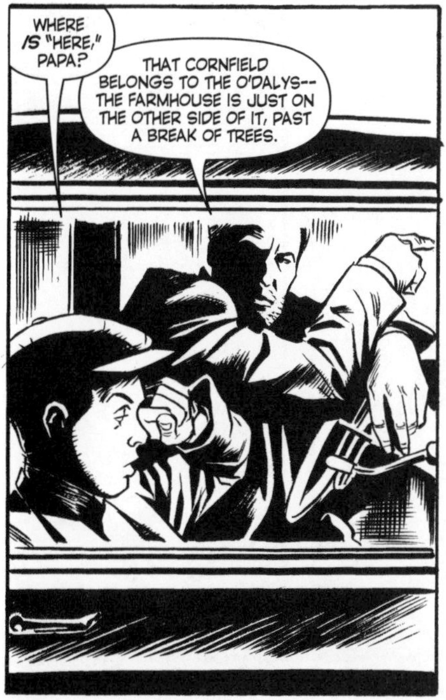
WHERE *IS* "HERE," PAPA?
THAT CORNFIELD BELONGS TO THE O'DALYS-- THE FARMHOUSE IS JUST ON THE OTHER SIDE OF IT, PAST A BREAK OF TREES.

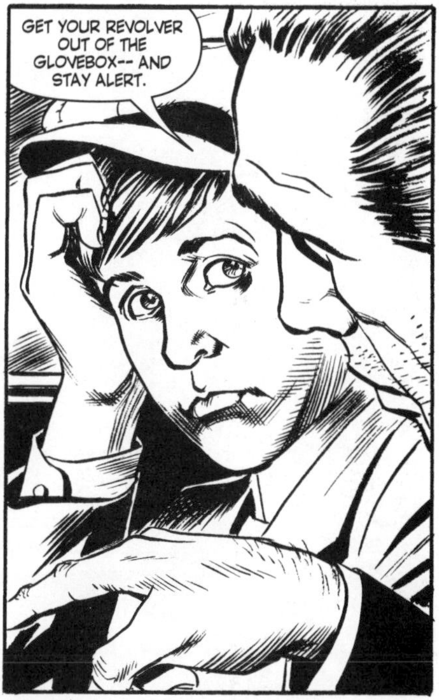
GET YOUR REVOLVER OUT OF THE GLOVEBOX-- AND STAY ALERT.

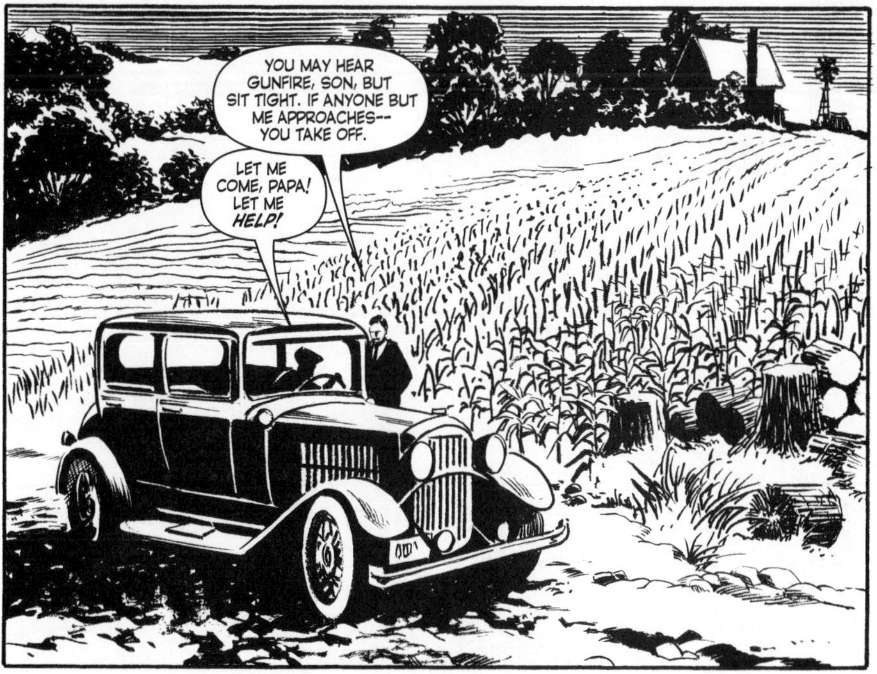
YOU MAY HEAR GUNFIRE, SON, BUT SIT TIGHT. IF ANYONE BUT ME APPROACHES-- YOU TAKE OFF.
LET ME COME, PAPA! LET ME ***HELP!***

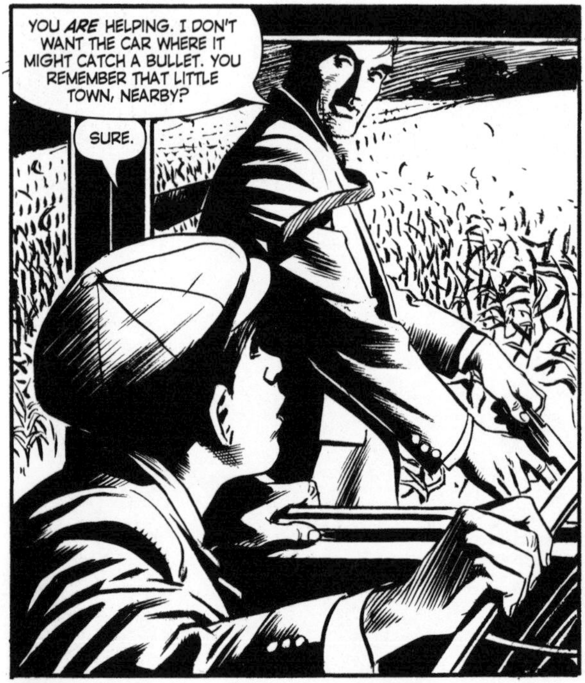
YOU ***ARE*** HELPING. I DON'T WANT THE CAR WHERE IT MIGHT CATCH A BULLET. YOU REMEMBER THAT LITTLE TOWN, NEARBY?
SURE.

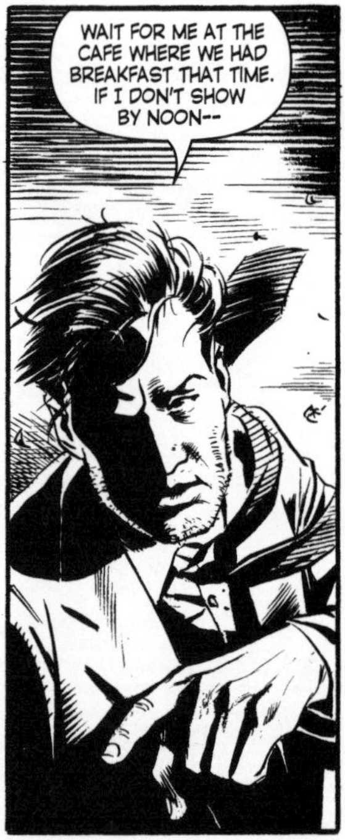
WAIT FOR ME AT THE CAFE WHERE WE HAD BREAKFAST THAT TIME. IF I DON'T SHOW BY NOON--

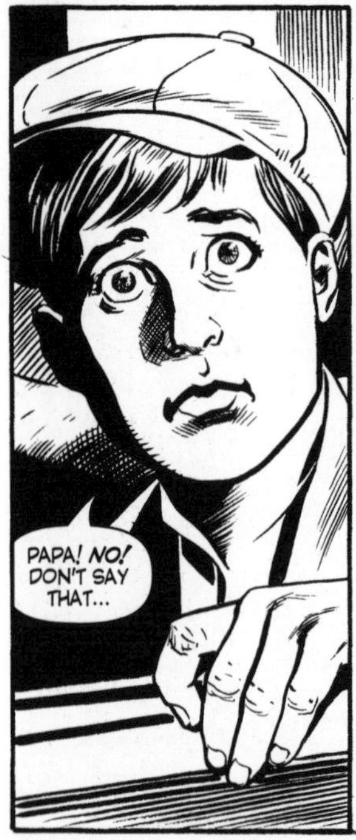
PAPA! ***NO!*** DON'T SAY THAT...

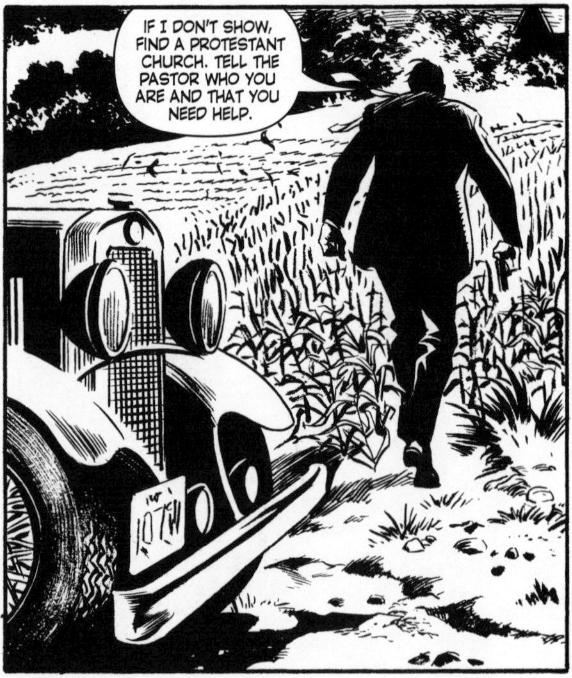
IF I DON'T SHOW, FIND A PROTESTANT CHURCH. TELL THE PASTOR WHO YOU ARE AND THAT YOU NEED HELP.

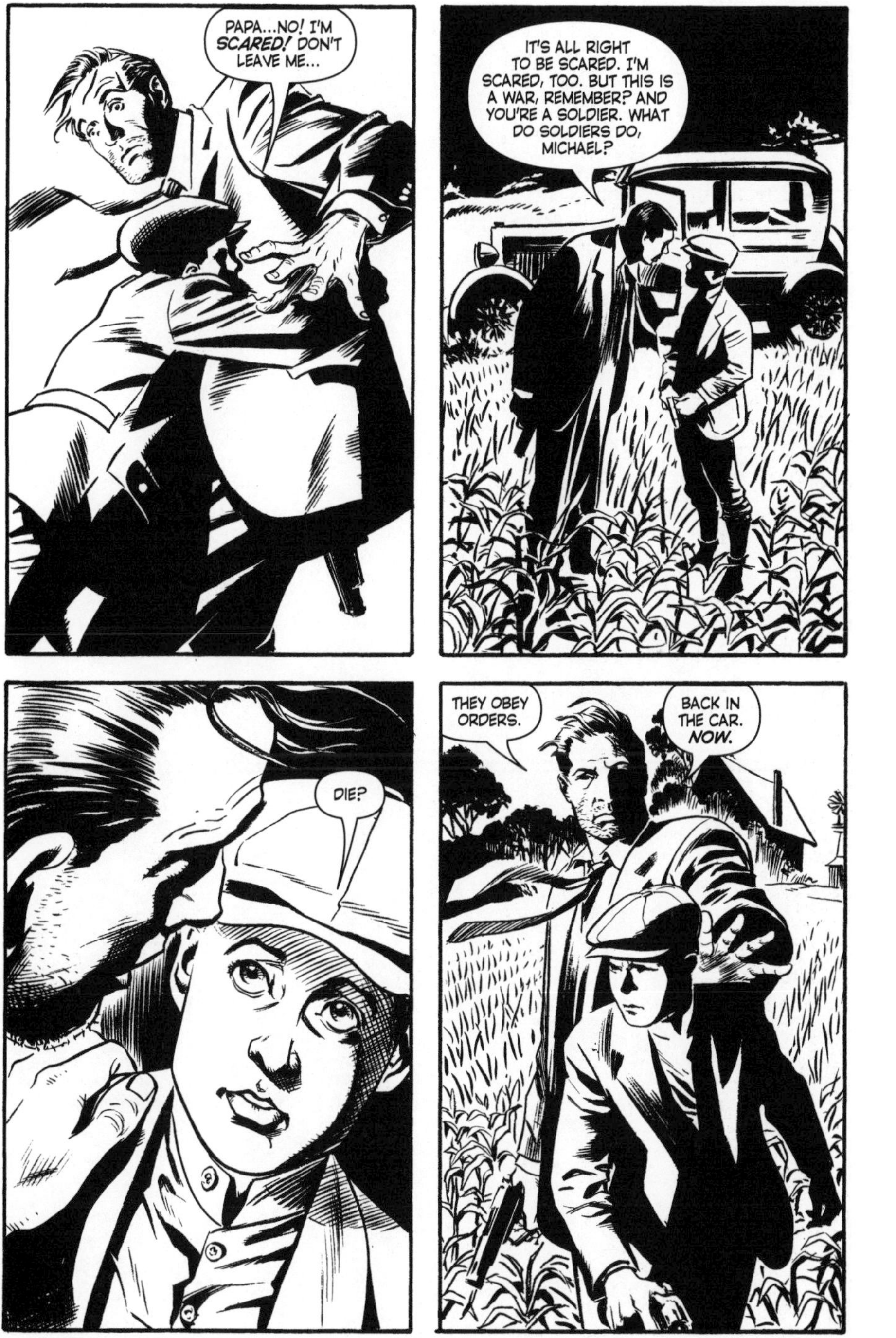
PAPA...NO! I'M *SCARED!* DON'T LEAVE ME...
IT'S ALL RIGHT TO BE SCARED. I'M SCARED, TOO. BUT THIS IS A WAR, REMEMBER? AND YOU'RE A SOLDIER. WHAT DO SOLDIERS DO, MICHAEL?
DIE?
THEY OBEY ORDERS.
BACK IN THE CAR. ***NOW.***

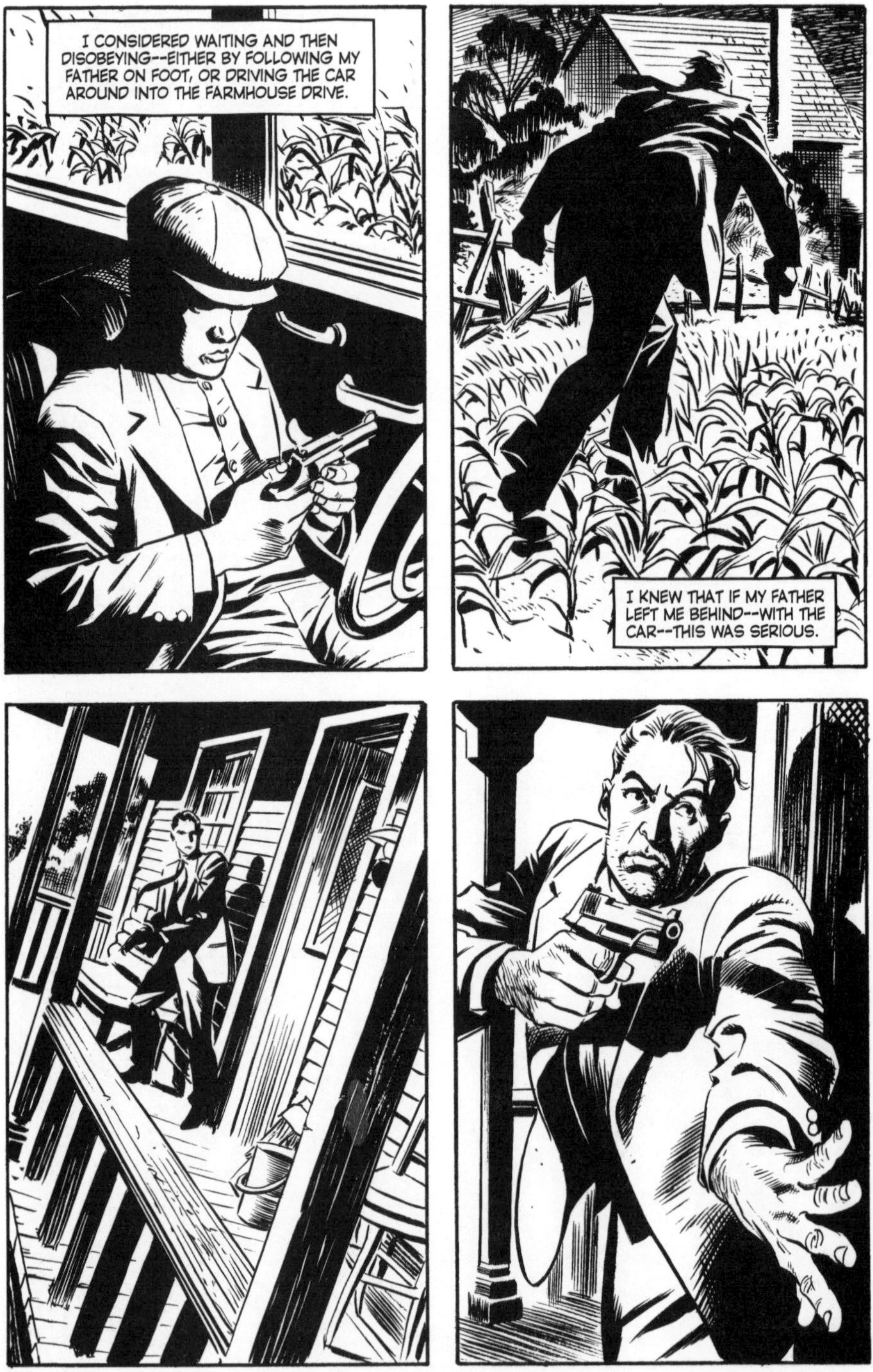
I CONSIDERED WAITING AND THEN DISOBEYING--EITHER BY FOLLOWING MY FATHER ON FOOT, OR DRIVING THE CAR AROUND INTO THE FARMHOUSE DRIVE.
I KNEW THAT IF MY FATHER LEFT ME BEHIND--WITH THE CAR--THIS WAS SERIOUS.

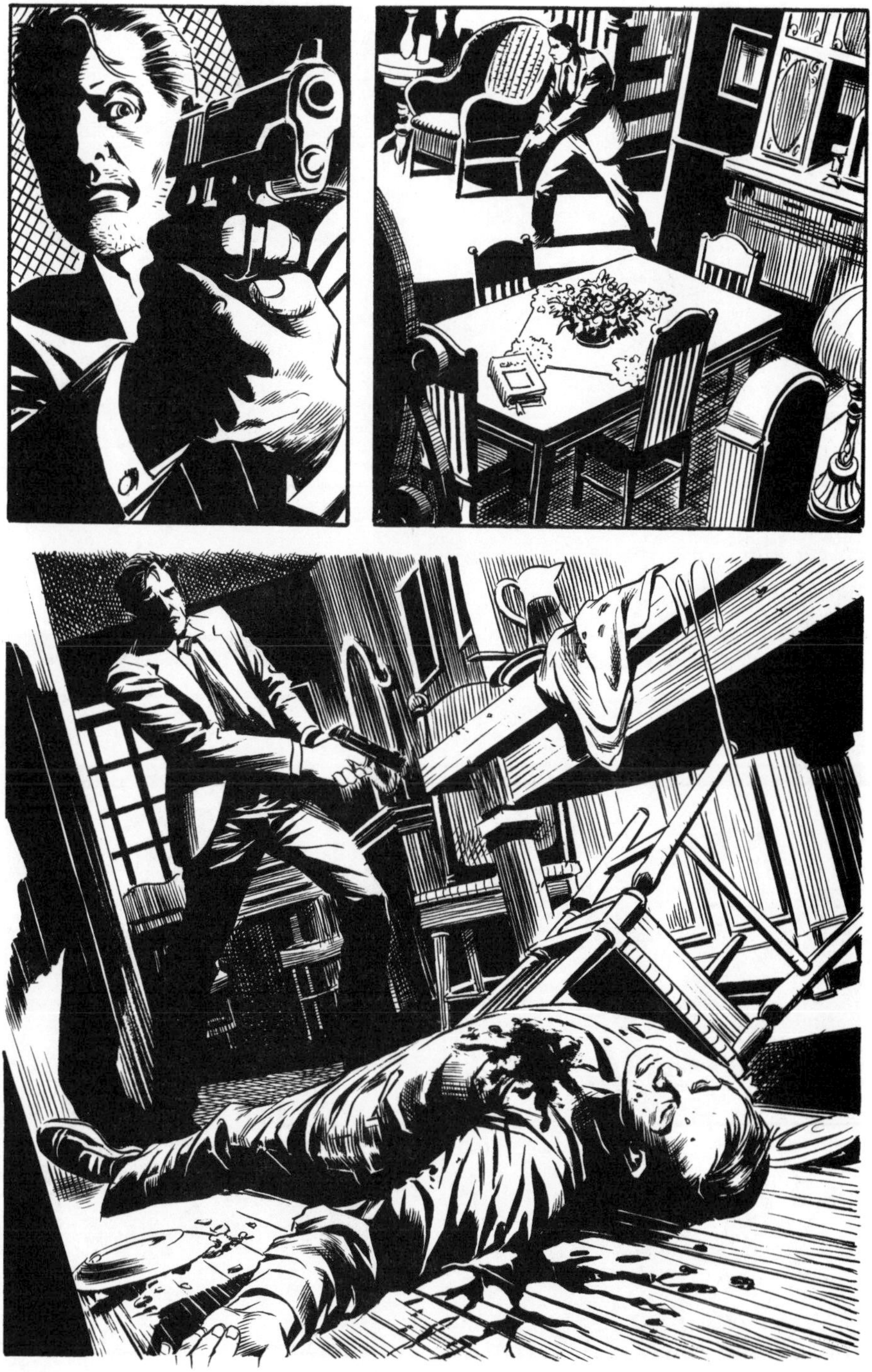

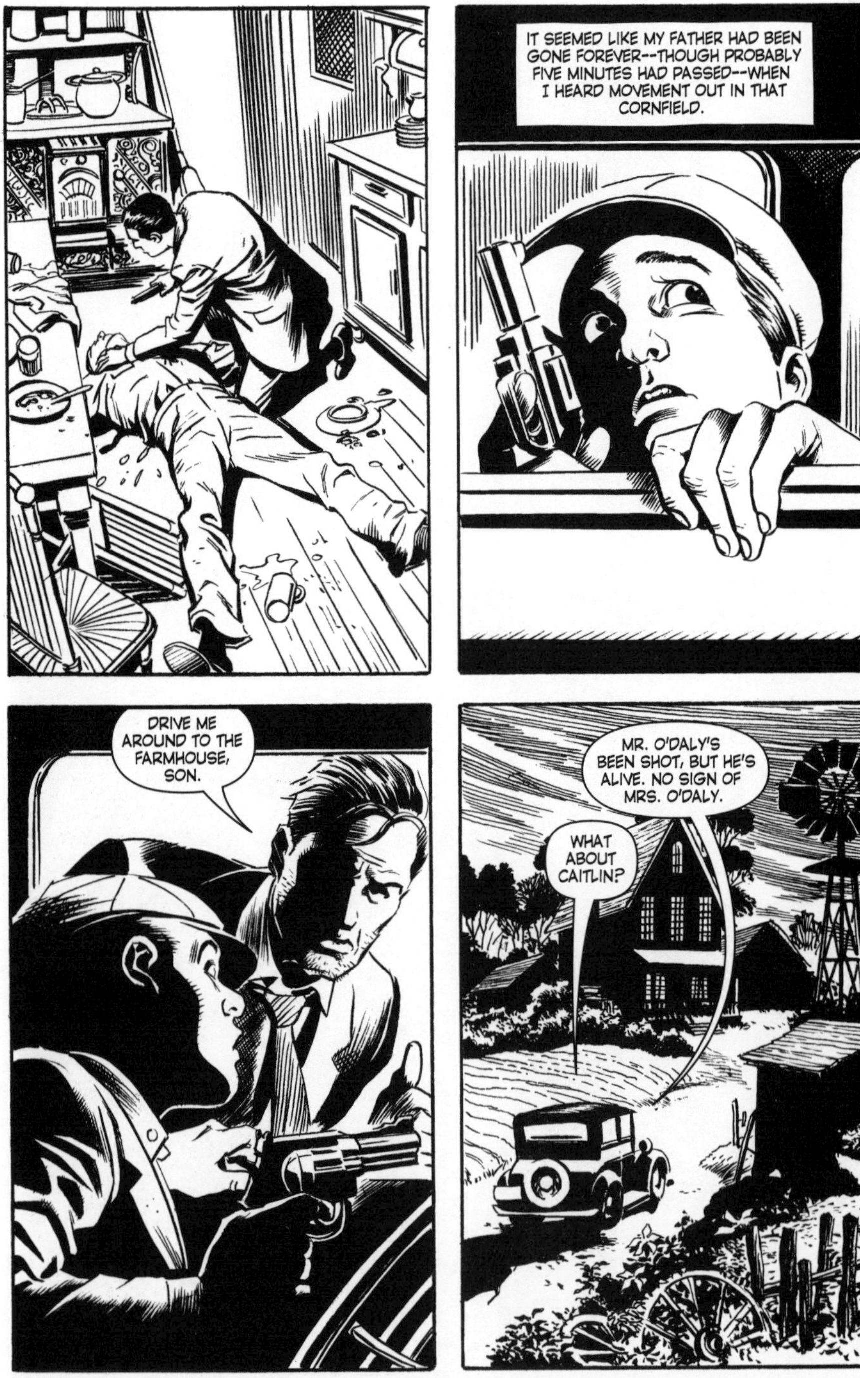
IT SEEMED LIKE MY FATHER HAD BEEN GONE FOREVER--THOUGH PROBABLY FIVE MINUTES HAD PASSED--WHEN I HEARD MOVEMENT OUT IN THAT CORNFIELD.
DRIVE ME AROUND TO THE FARMHOUSE, SON.
MR. O'DALY'S BEEN SHOT, BUT HE'S ALIVE. NO SIGN OF MRS. O'DALY.
WHAT ABOUT CAITLIN?

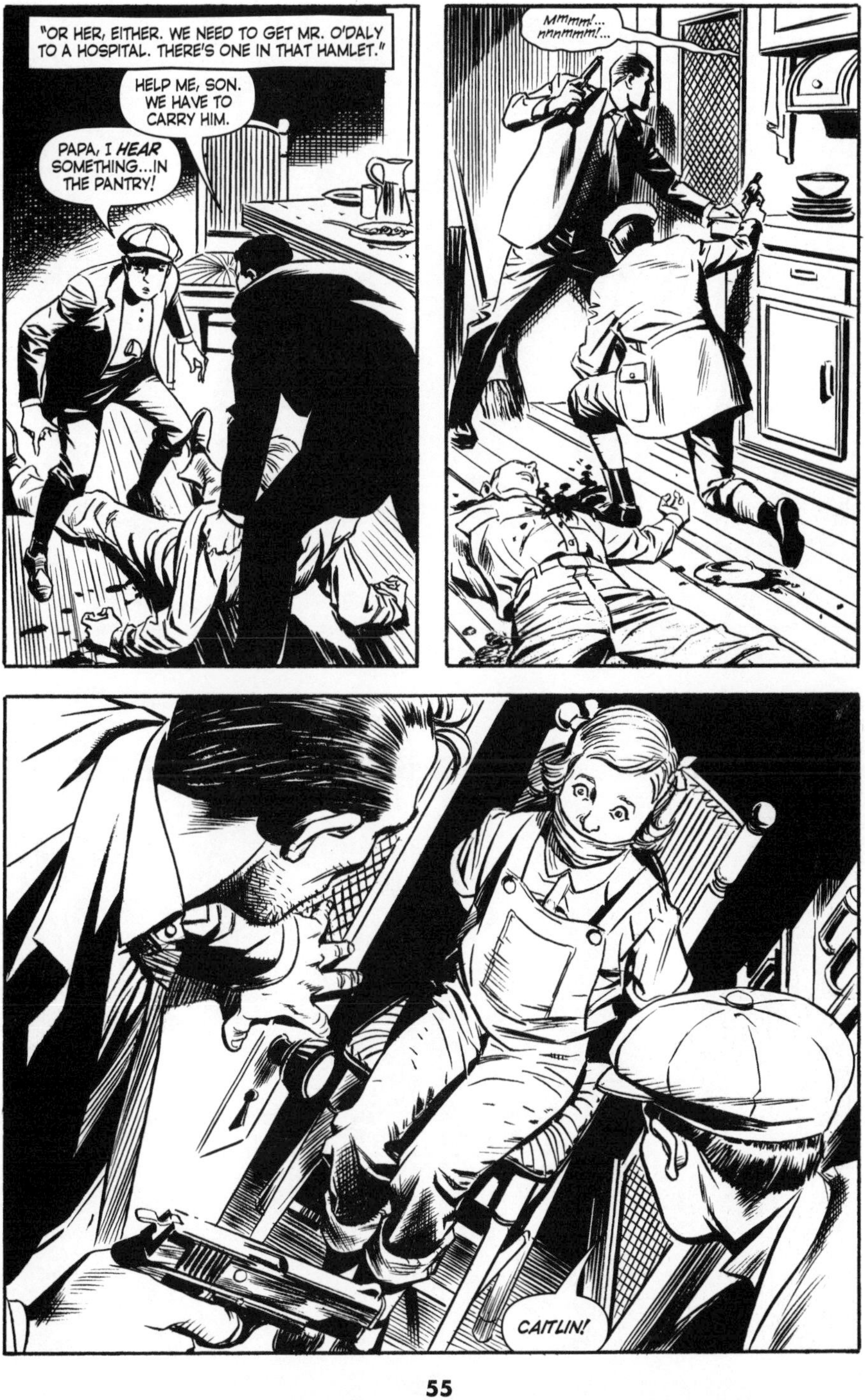
"OR HER, EITHER. WE NEED TO GET MR. O'DALY TO A HOSPITAL. THERE'S ONE IN THAT HAMLET."
HELP ME, SON. WE HAVE TO CARRY HIM.
PAPA, I HEAR SOMETHING...IN THE PANTRY!
Mmmm!... nnnmmm!...
CAITLIN!

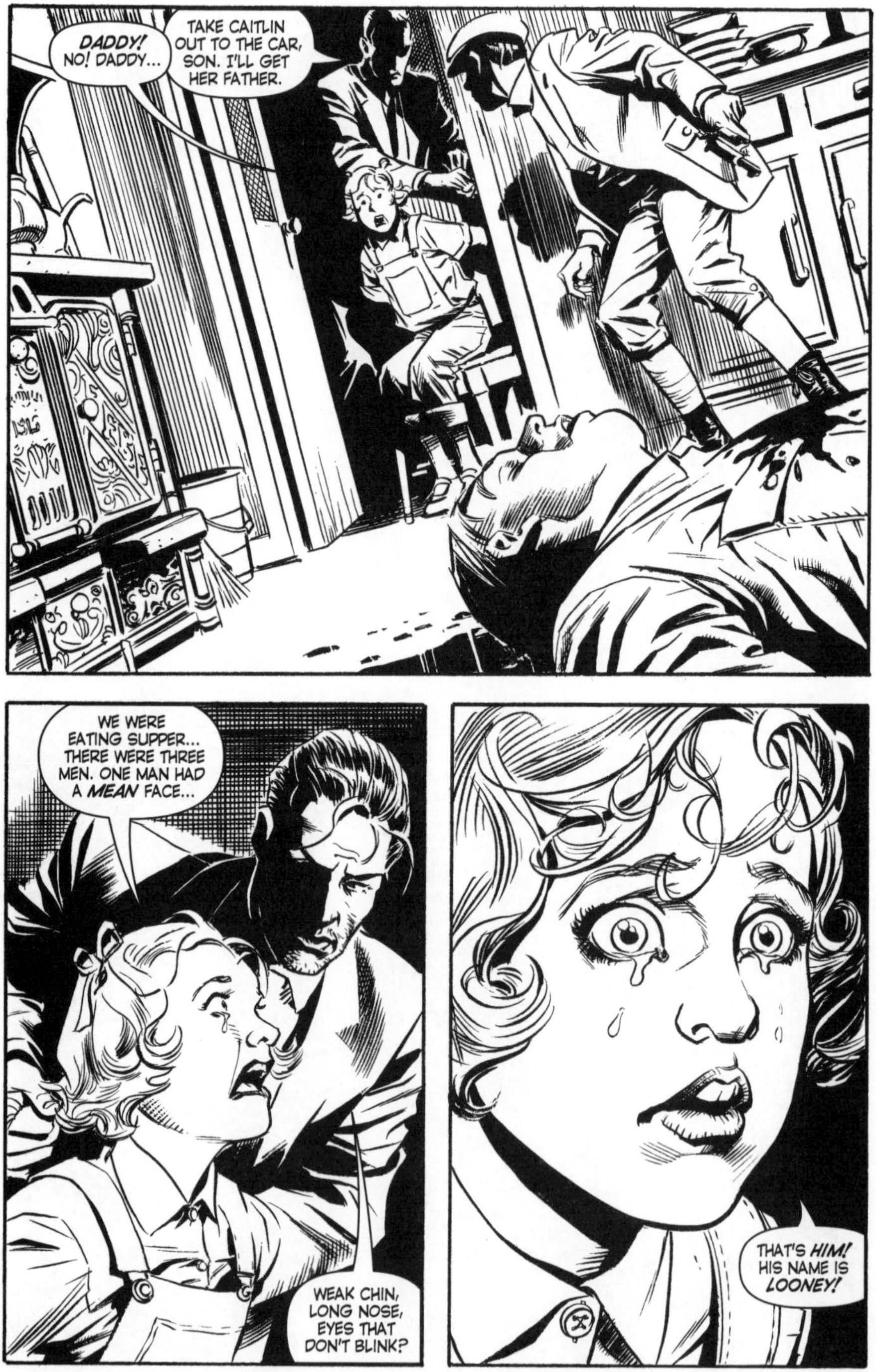
DADDY! NO! DADDY...
TAKE CAITLIN OUT TO THE CAR, SON. I'LL GET HER FATHER.
WE WERE EATING SUPPER... THERE WERE THREE MEN. ONE MAN HAD A MEAN FACE...
WEAK CHIN, LONG NOSE, EYES THAT DON'T BLINK?
THAT'S HIM! HIS NAME IS LOONEY!

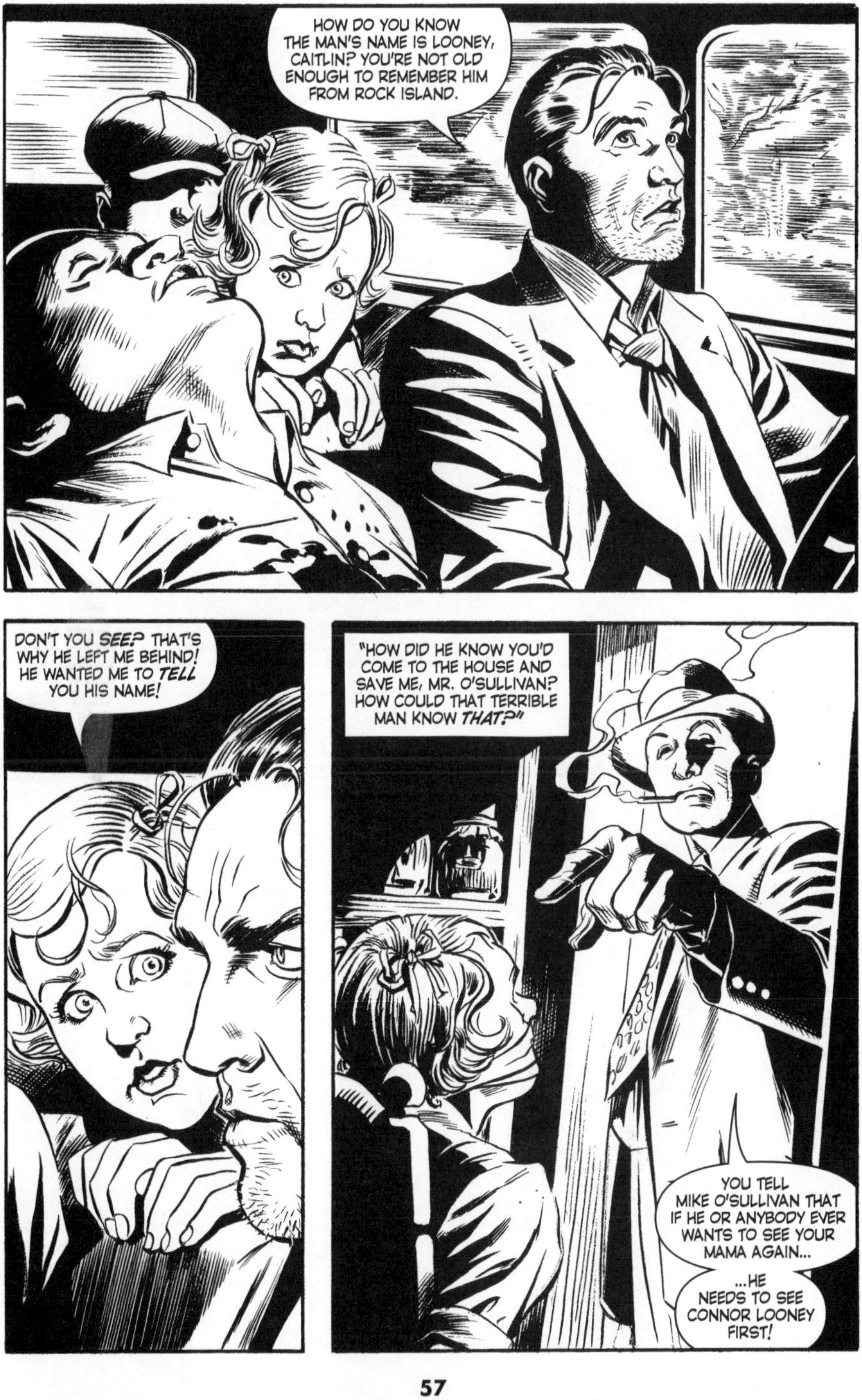
HOW DO YOU KNOW THE MAN'S NAME IS LOONEY, CAITLIN? YOU'RE NOT OLD ENOUGH TO REMEMBER HIM FROM ROCK ISLAND.
DON'T YOU SEE? THAT'S WHY HE LEFT ME BEHIND! HE WANTED ME TO TELL YOU HIS NAME!
"HOW DID HE KNOW YOU'D COME TO THE HOUSE AND SAVE ME, MR. O'SULLIVAN? HOW COULD THAT TERRIBLE MAN KNOW THAT?"
YOU TELL MIKE O'SULLIVAN THAT IF HE OR ANYBODY EVER WANTS TO SEE YOUR MAMA AGAIN...
...HE NEEDS TO SEE CONNOR LOONEY FIRST!

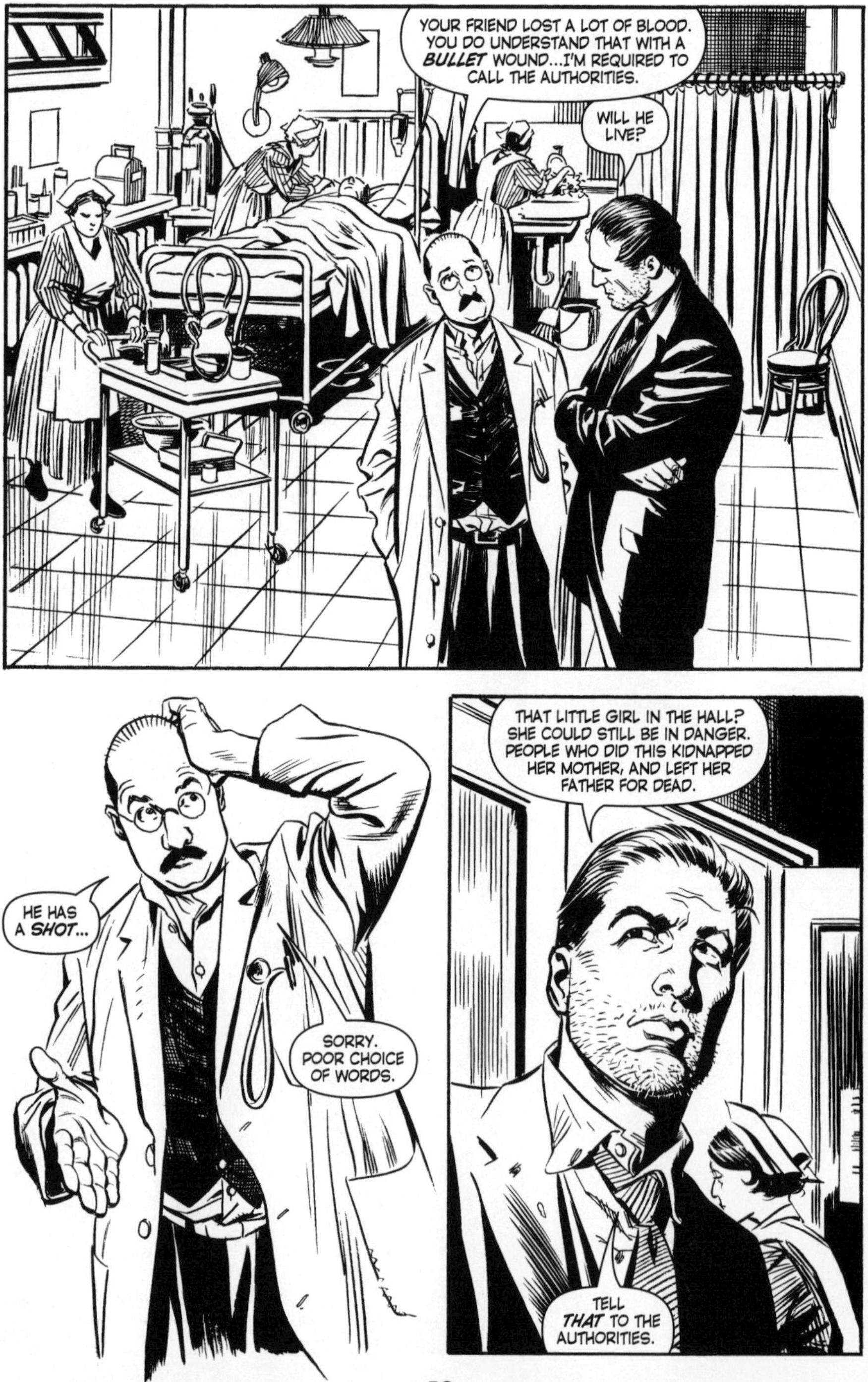
YOUR FRIEND LOST A LOT OF BLOOD. YOU DO UNDERSTAND THAT WITH A *BULLET* WOUND...I'M REQUIRED TO CALL THE AUTHORITIES.
WILL HE LIVE?
HE HAS A *SHOT*...
SORRY. POOR CHOICE OF WORDS.
THAT LITTLE GIRL IN THE HALL? SHE COULD STILL BE IN DANGER. PEOPLE WHO DID THIS KIDNAPPED HER MOTHER, AND LEFT HER FATHER FOR DEAD.
TELL *THAT* TO THE AUTHORITIES.

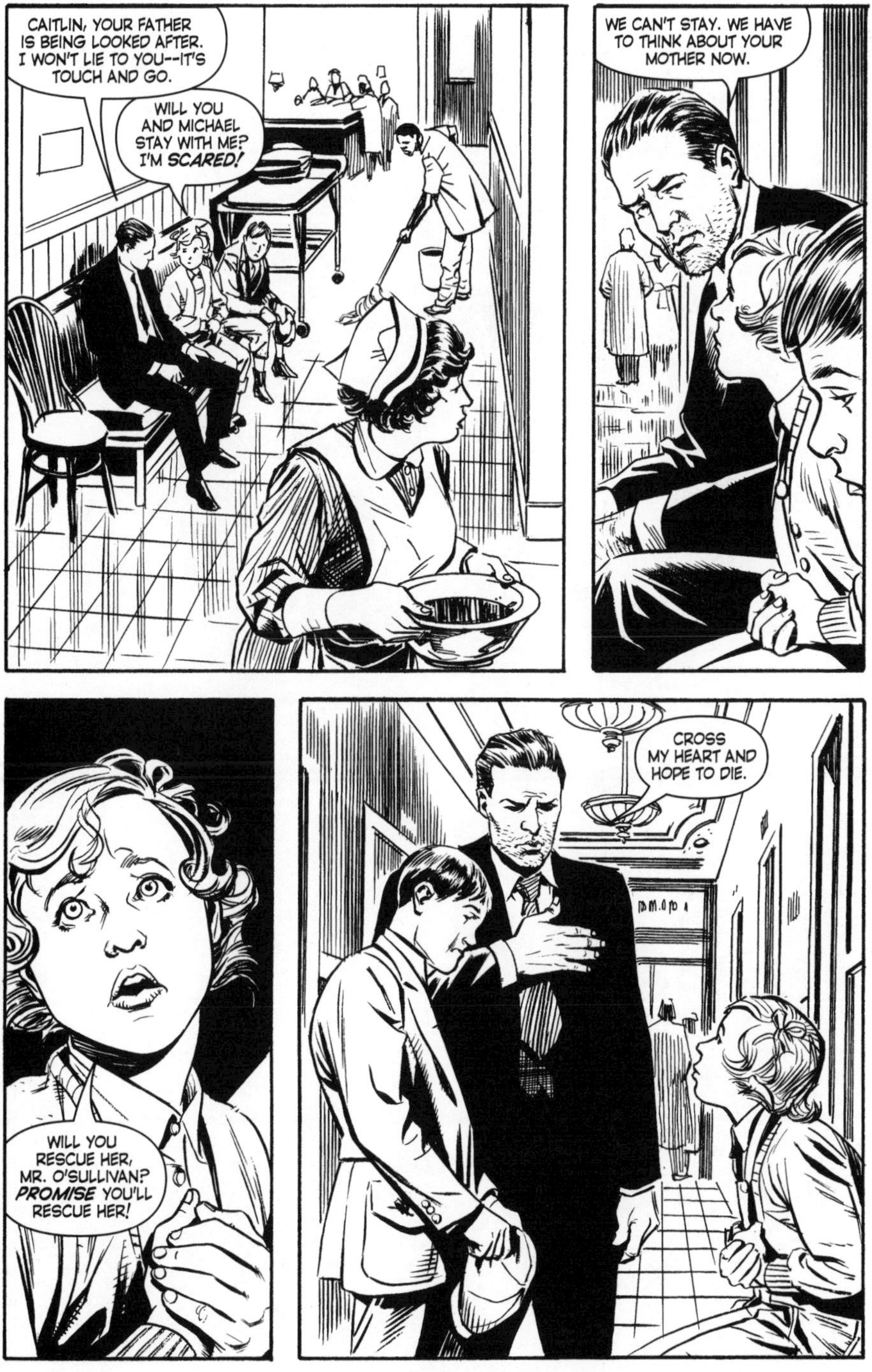
CAITLIN, YOUR FATHER IS BEING LOOKED AFTER. I WON'T LIE TO YOU--IT'S TOUCH AND GO.
WILL YOU AND MICHAEL STAY WITH ME? I'M *SCARED!*
WE CAN'T STAY. WE HAVE TO THINK ABOUT YOUR MOTHER NOW.
WILL YOU RESCUE HER, MR. O'SULLIVAN? ***PROMISE*** YOU'LL RESCUE HER!
CROSS MY HEART AND HOPE TO DIE.

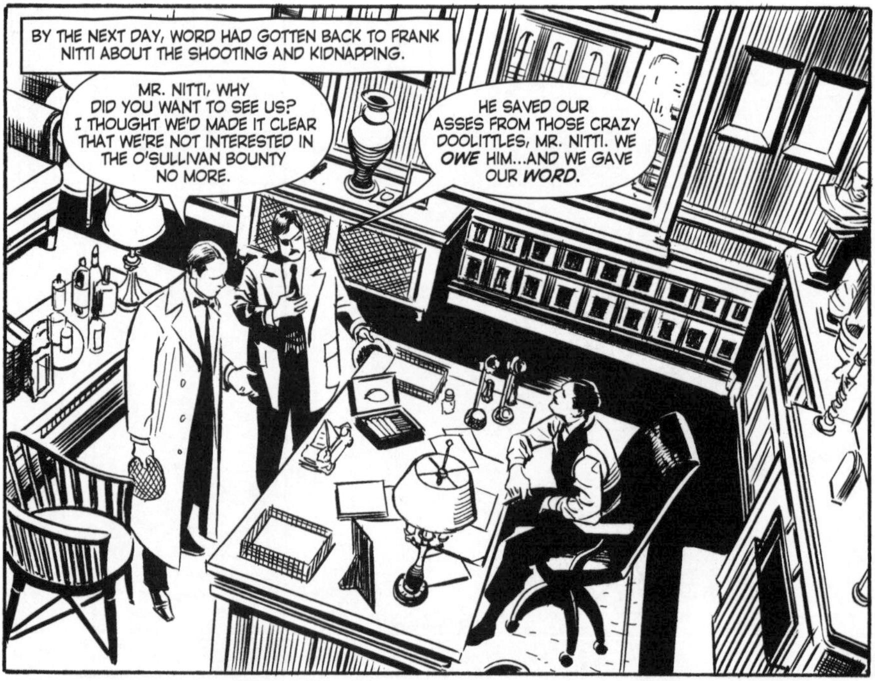
BY THE NEXT DAY, WORD HAD GOTTEN BACK TO FRANK NITTI ABOUT THE SHOOTING AND KIDNAPPING.
MR. NITTI, WHY DID YOU WANT TO SEE US? I THOUGHT WE'D MADE IT CLEAR THAT WE'RE NOT INTERESTED IN THE O'SULLIVAN BOUNTY NO MORE.
HE SAVED OUR ASSES FROM THOSE CRAZY DOOLITTLES, MR. NITTI. WE *OWE* HIM...AND WE GAVE OUR *WORD*.

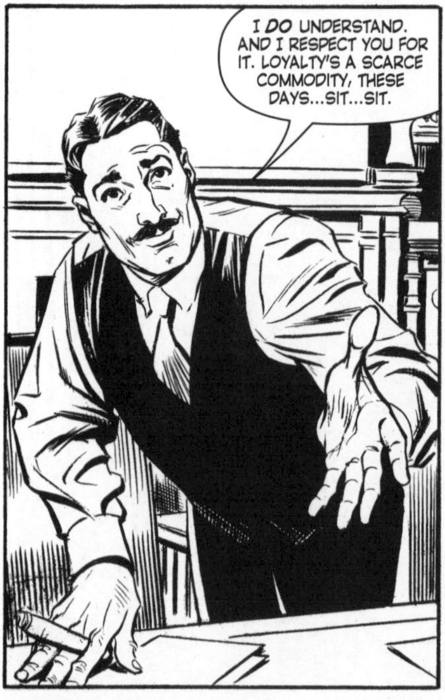
I *DO* UNDERSTAND. AND I RESPECT YOU FOR IT. LOYALTY'S A SCARCE COMMODITY, THESE DAYS...SIT...SIT.

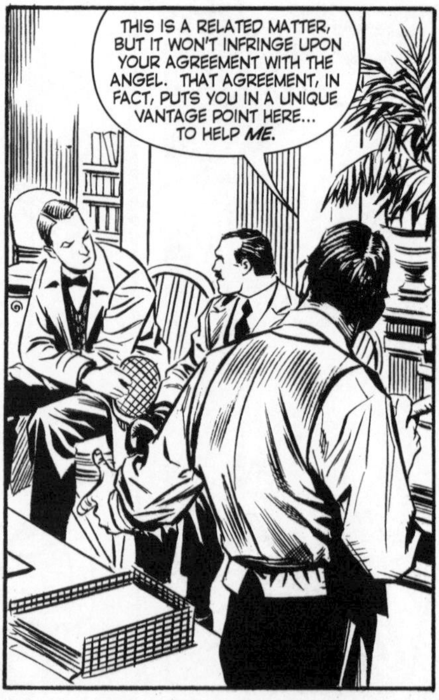
THIS IS A RELATED MATTER, BUT IT WON'T INFRINGE UPON YOUR AGREEMENT WITH THE ANGEL. THAT AGREEMENT, IN FACT, PUTS YOU IN A UNIQUE VANTAGE POINT HERE... TO HELP *ME*.

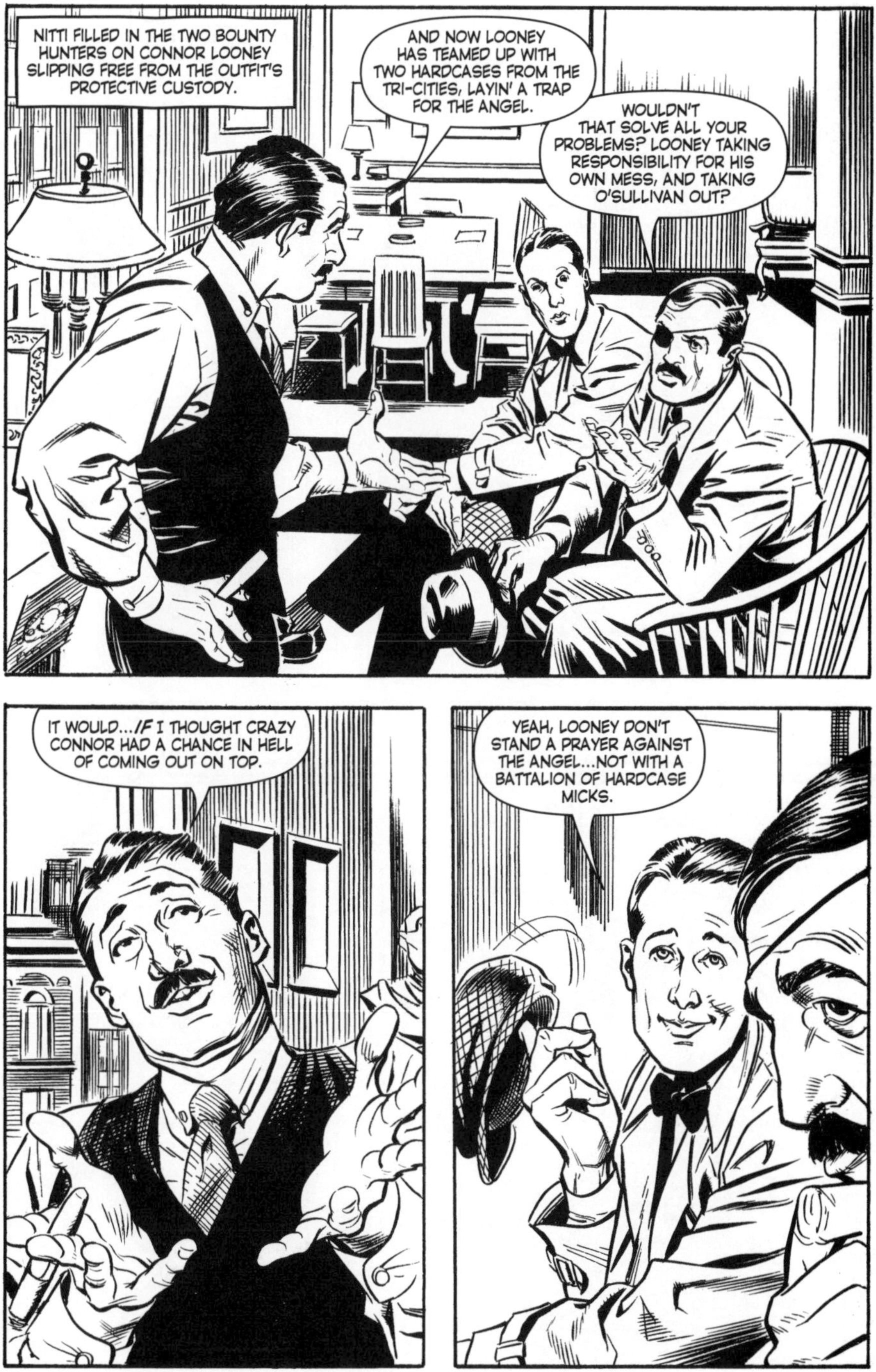
NITTI FILLED IN THE TWO BOUNTY HUNTERS ON CONNOR LOONEY SLIPPING FREE FROM THE OUTFIT'S PROTECTIVE CUSTODY.
AND NOW LOONEY HAS TEAMED UP WITH TWO HARDCASES FROM THE TRI-CITIES, LAYIN' A TRAP FOR THE ANGEL.
WOULDN'T THAT SOLVE ALL YOUR PROBLEMS? LOONEY TAKING RESPONSIBILITY FOR HIS OWN MESS, AND TAKING O'SULLIVAN OUT?
IT WOULD.../F I THOUGHT CRAZY CONNOR HAD A CHANCE IN HELL OF COMING OUT ON TOP.
YEAH, LOONEY DON'T STAND A PRAYER AGAINST THE ANGEL...NOT WITH A BATTALION OF HARDCASE MICKS.

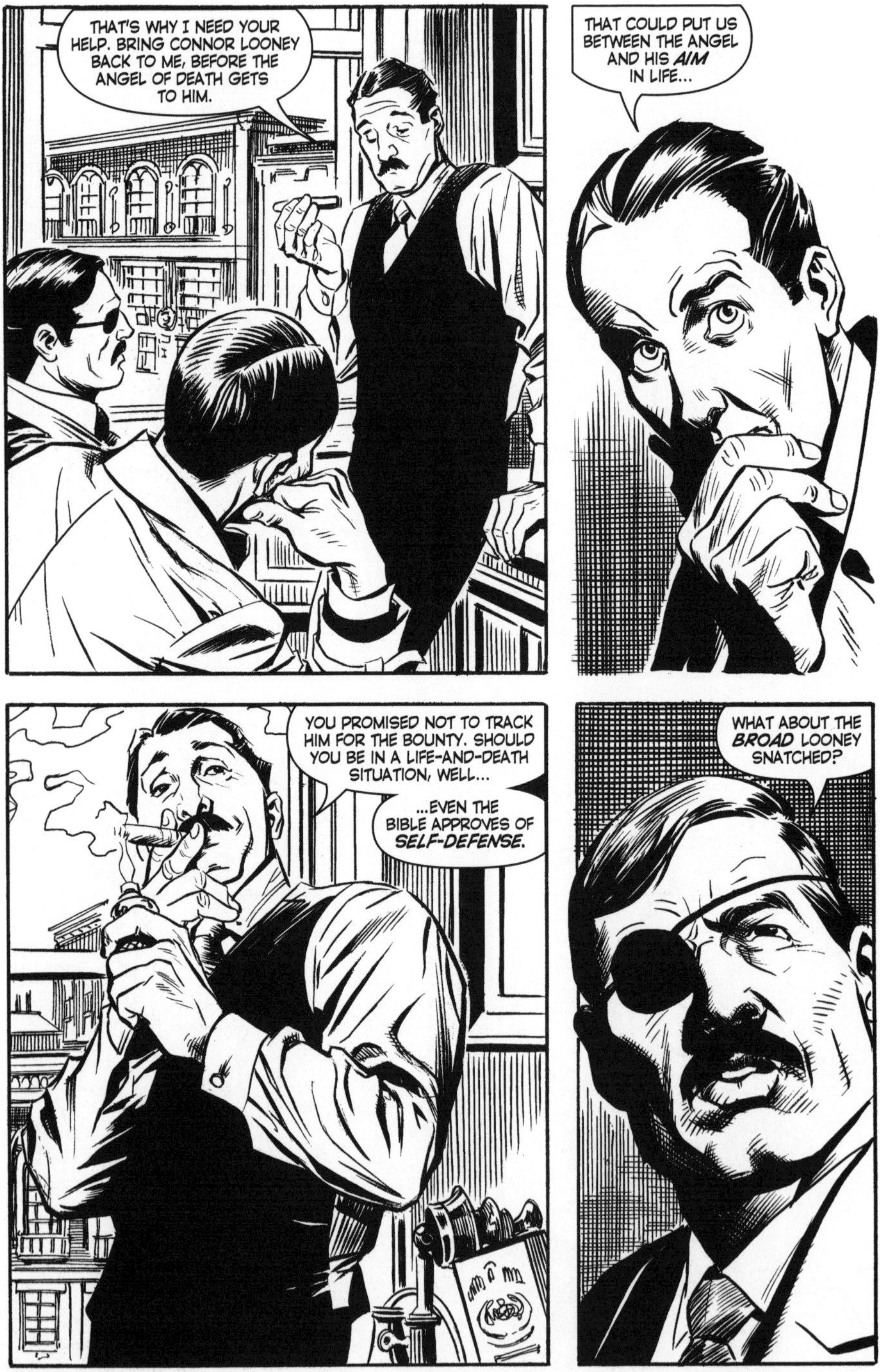
THAT'S WHY I NEED YOUR HELP. BRING CONNOR LOONEY BACK TO ME, BEFORE THE ANGEL OF DEATH GETS TO HIM.
THAT COULD PUT US BETWEEN THE ANGEL AND HIS *AIM* IN LIFE...
YOU PROMISED NOT TO TRACK HIM FOR THE BOUNTY. SHOULD YOU BE IN A LIFE-AND-DEATH SITUATION, WELL...
...EVEN THE BIBLE APPROVES OF *SELF-DEFENSE*.
WHAT ABOUT THE *BROAD* LOONEY SNATCHED?

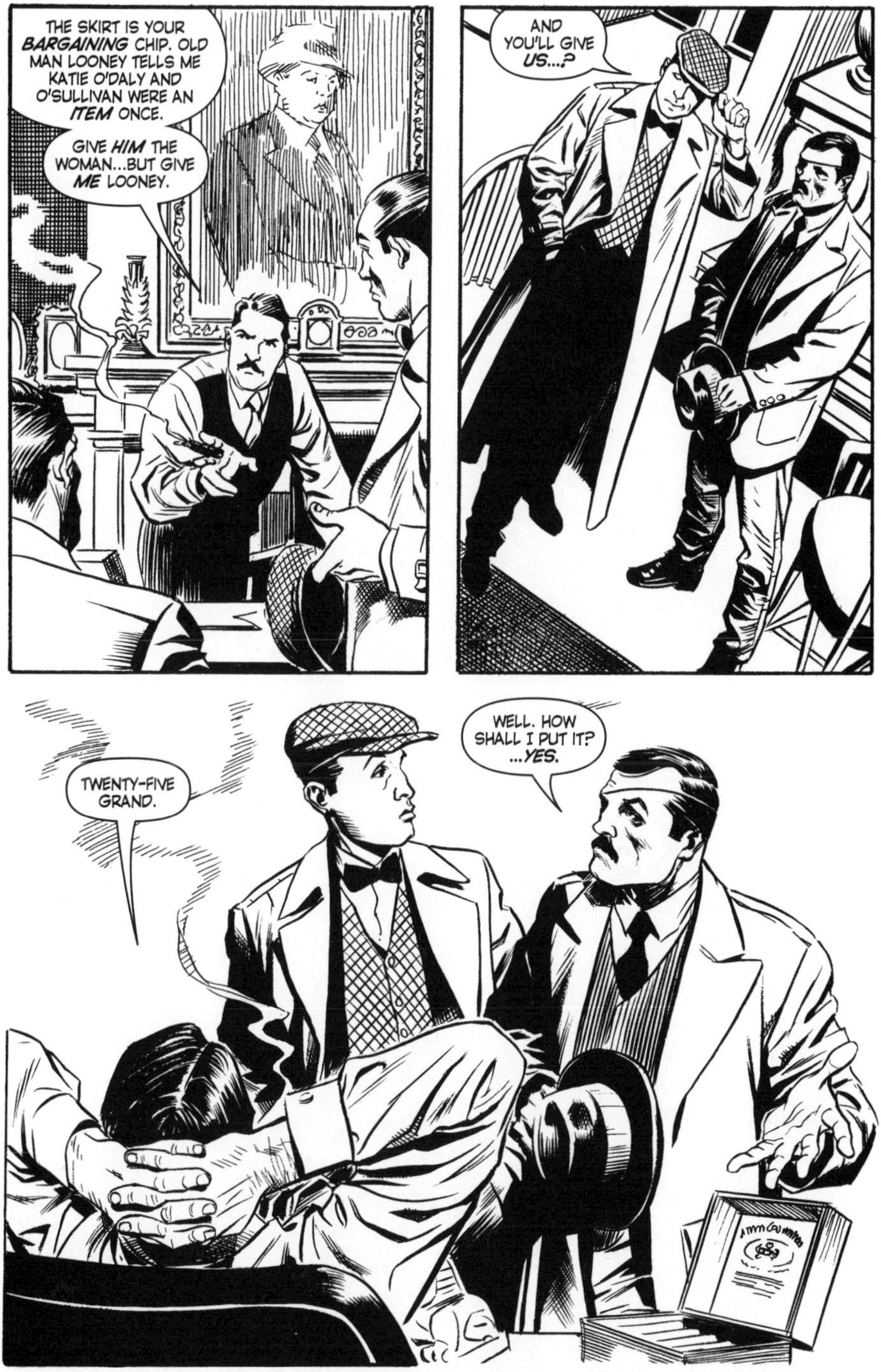
THE SKIRT IS YOUR BARGAINING CHIP. OLD MAN LOONEY TELLS ME KATIE O'DALY AND O'SULLIVAN WERE AN ITEM ONCE.
GIVE HIM THE WOMAN...BUT GIVE ME LOONEY.
AND YOU'LL GIVE US...?
TWENTY-FIVE GRAND.
WELL. HOW SHALL I PUT IT? ...YES.

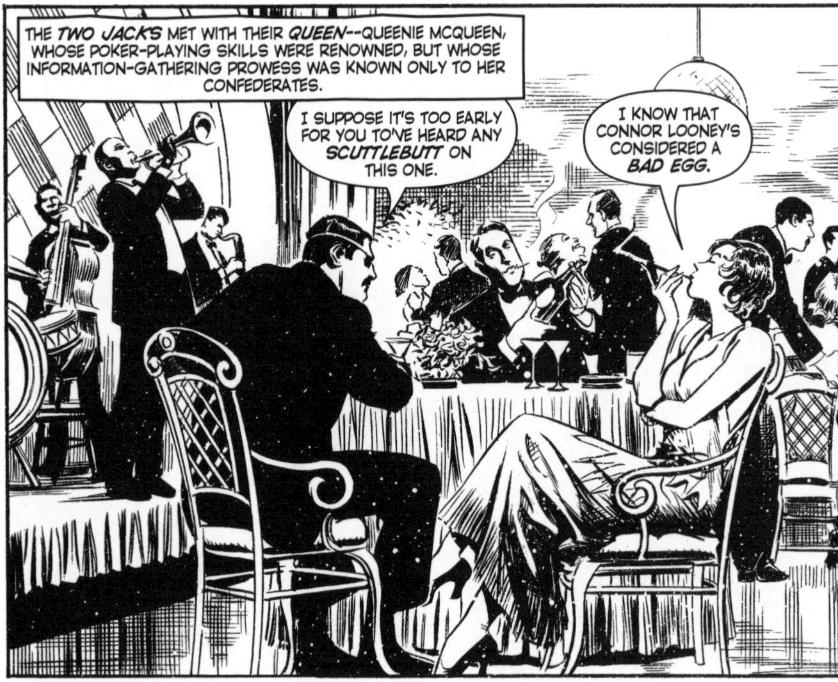
THE TWO JACKS MET WITH THEIR QUEEN--QUEENIE MCQUEEN, WHOSE POKER-PLAYING SKILLS WERE RENOWNED, BUT WHOSE INFORMATION-GATHERING PROWESS WAS KNOWN ONLY TO HER CONFEDERATES.
I SUPPOSE IT'S TOO EARLY FOR YOU TO'VE HEARD ANY SCUTTLEBUTT ON THIS ONE.
I KNOW THAT CONNOR LOONEY'S CONSIDERED A BAD EGG.

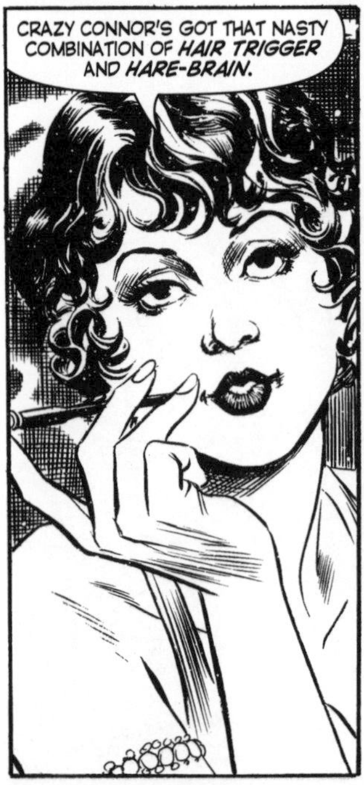
CRAZY CONNOR'S GOT THAT NASTY COMBINATION OF HAIR TRIGGER AND HARE-BRAIN.

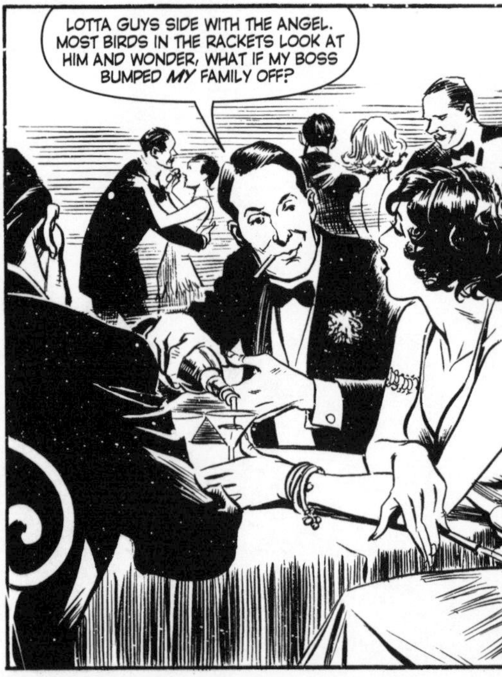
LOTTA GUYS SIDE WITH THE ANGEL. MOST BIRDS IN THE RACKETS LOOK AT HIM AND WONDER, WHAT IF MY BOSS BUMPED MY FAMILY OFF?

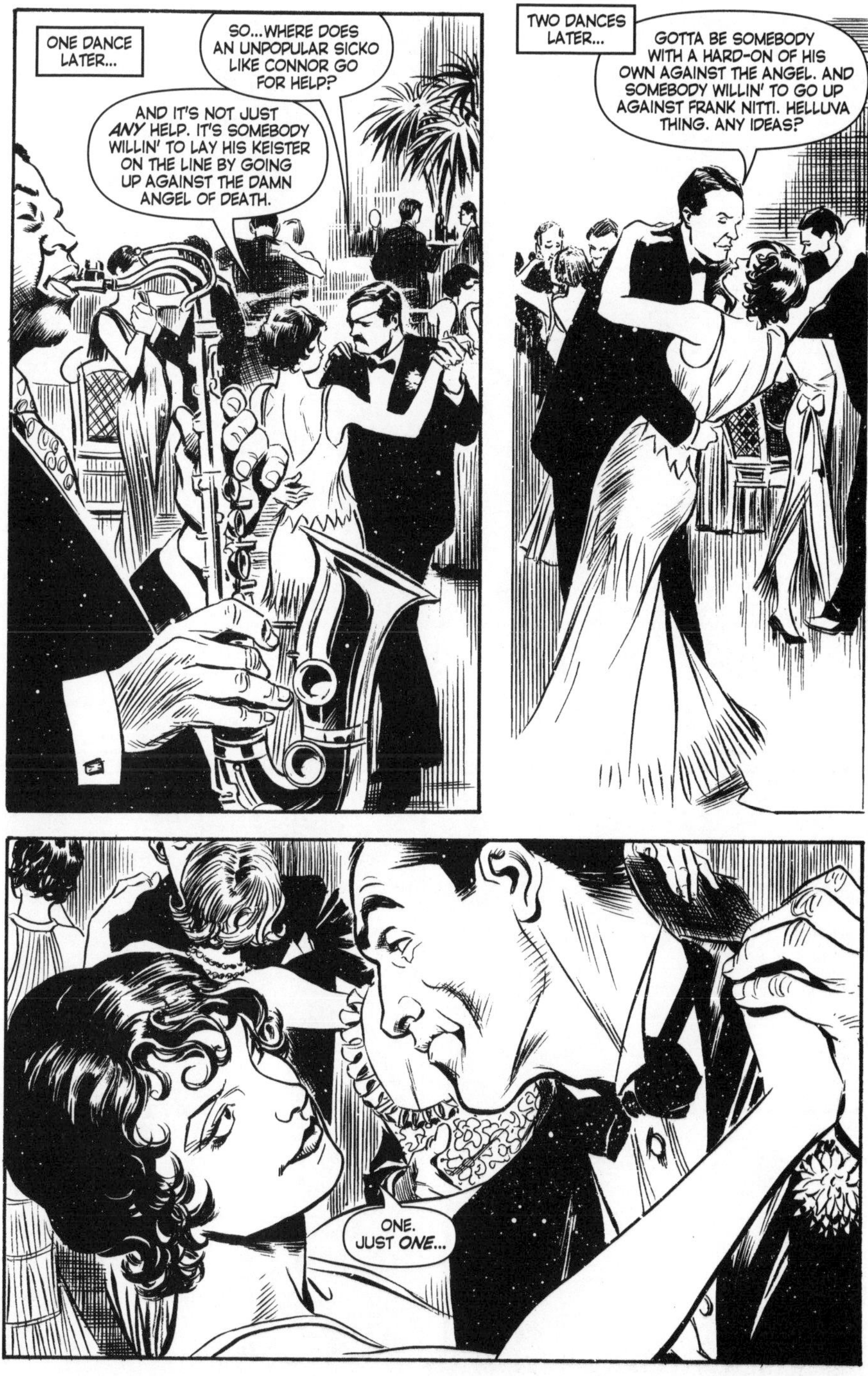

ONE DANCE LATER...
SO...WHERE DOES AN UNPOPULAR SICKO LIKE CONNOR GO FOR HELP?
AND IT'S NOT JUST *ANY* HELP. IT'S SOMEBODY WILLIN' TO LAY HIS KEISTER ON THE LINE BY GOING UP AGAINST THE DAMN ANGEL OF DEATH.
TWO DANCES LATER...
GOTTA BE SOMEBODY WITH A HARD-ON OF HIS OWN AGAINST THE ANGEL. AND SOMEBODY WILLIN' TO GO UP AGAINST FRANK NITTI. HELLUVA THING. ANY IDEAS?
ONE. JUST *ONE*...

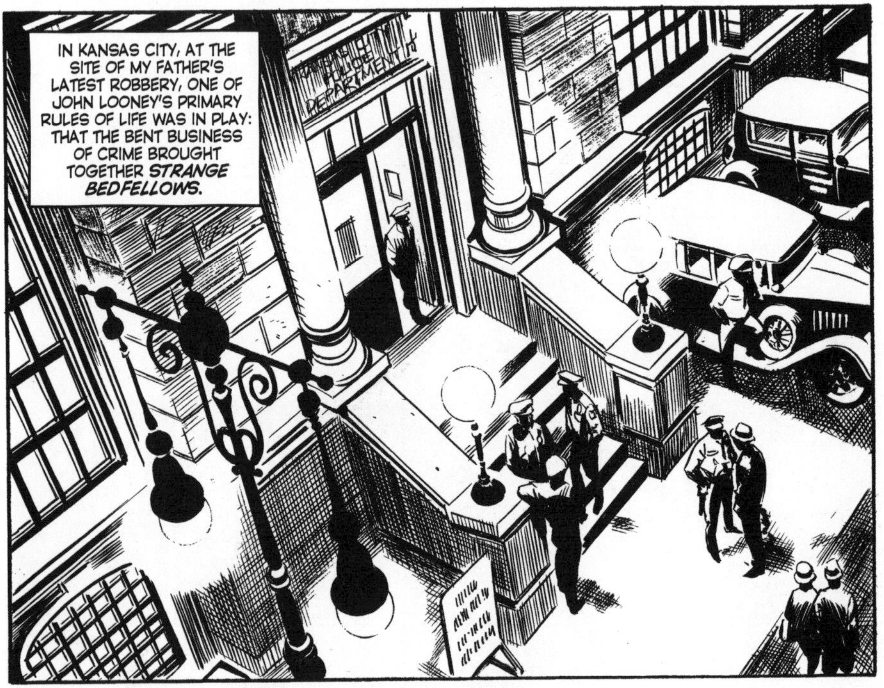
IN KANSAS CITY, AT THE SITE OF MY FATHER'S LATEST ROBBERY, ONE OF JOHN LOONEY'S PRIMARY RULES OF LIFE WAS IN PLAY: THAT THE BENT BUSINESS OF CRIME BROUGHT TOGETHER *STRANGE BEDFELLOWS*.

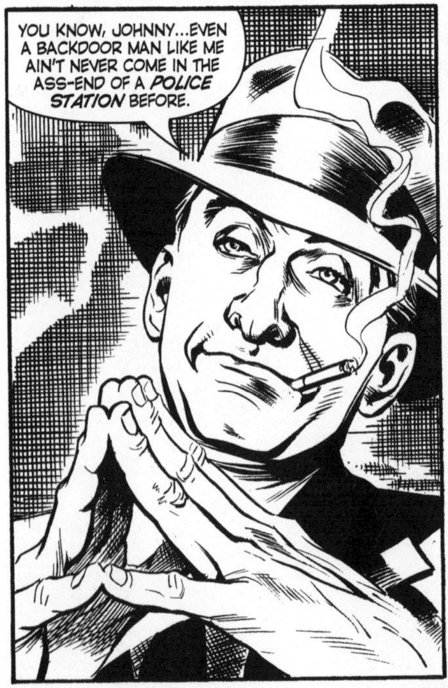
YOU KNOW, JOHNNY...EVEN A BACKDOOR MAN LIKE ME AIN'T NEVER COME IN THE ASS-END OF A *POLICE STATION* BEFORE.

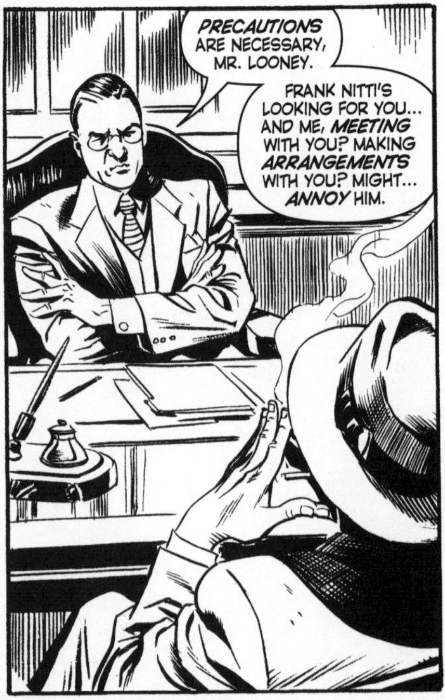
PRECAUTIONS ARE NECESSARY, MR. LOONEY.
FRANK NITTI'S LOOKING FOR YOU... AND ME, *MEETING* WITH YOU? MAKING *ARRANGEMENTS* WITH YOU? MIGHT... *ANNOY* HIM.

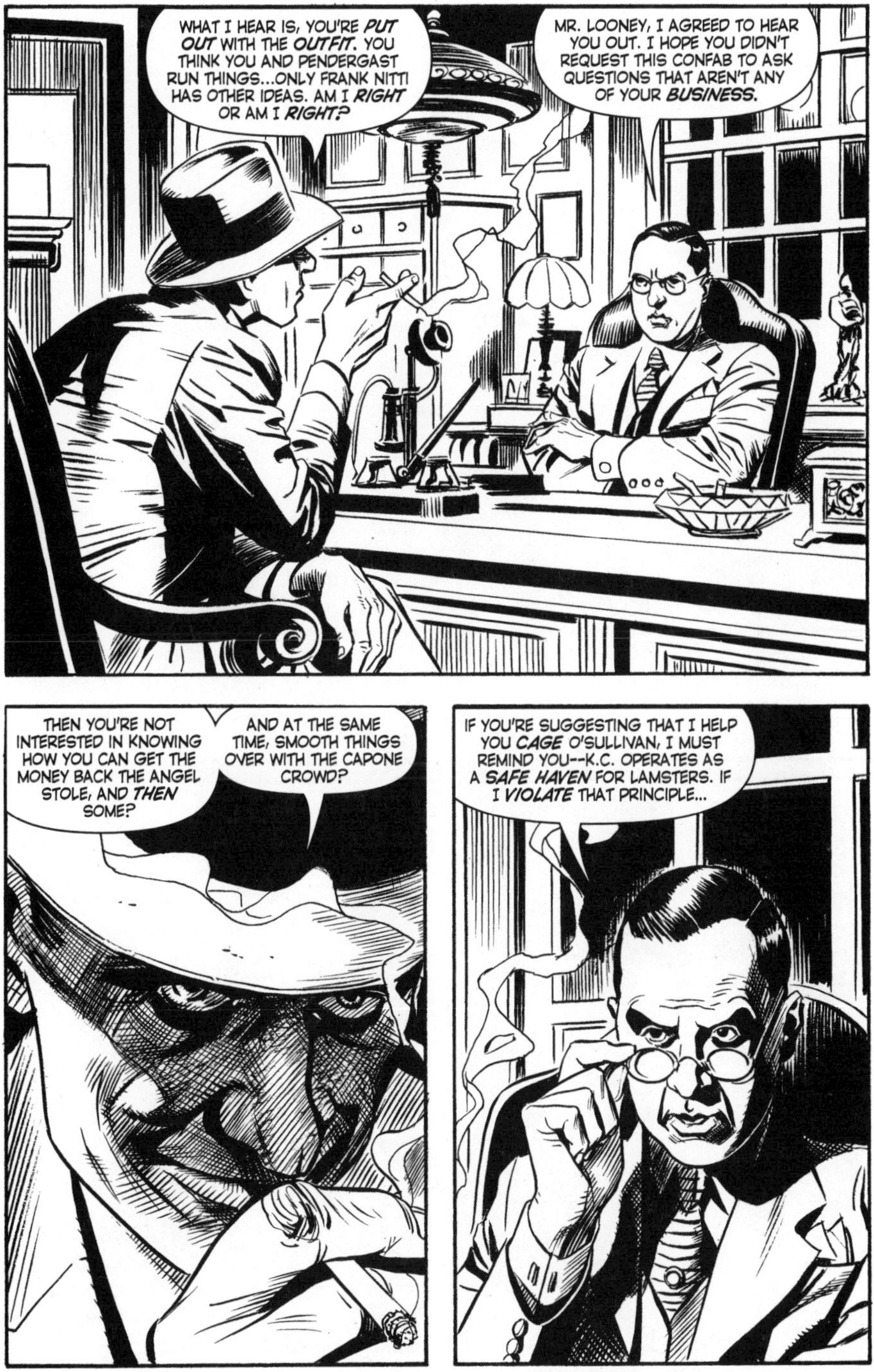

WHAT I HEAR IS, YOU'RE *PUT OUT* WITH THE *OUTFIT*. YOU THINK YOU AND PENDERGAST RUN THINGS...ONLY FRANK NITTI HAS OTHER IDEAS. AM I *RIGHT* OR AM I *RIGHT?*
MR. LOONEY, I AGREED TO HEAR YOU OUT. I HOPE YOU DIDN'T REQUEST THIS CONFAB TO ASK QUESTIONS THAT AREN'T ANY OF YOUR *BUSINESS*.
THEN YOU'RE NOT INTERESTED IN KNOWING HOW YOU CAN GET THE MONEY BACK THE ANGEL STOLE, AND *THEN* SOME?
AND AT THE SAME TIME, SMOOTH THINGS OVER WITH THE CAPONE CROWD?
IF YOU'RE SUGGESTING THAT I HELP YOU *CAGE* O'SULLIVAN, I MUST REMIND YOU--K.C. OPERATES AS A *SAFE HAVEN* FOR LAMSTERS. IF I *VIOLATE* THAT PRINCIPLE...

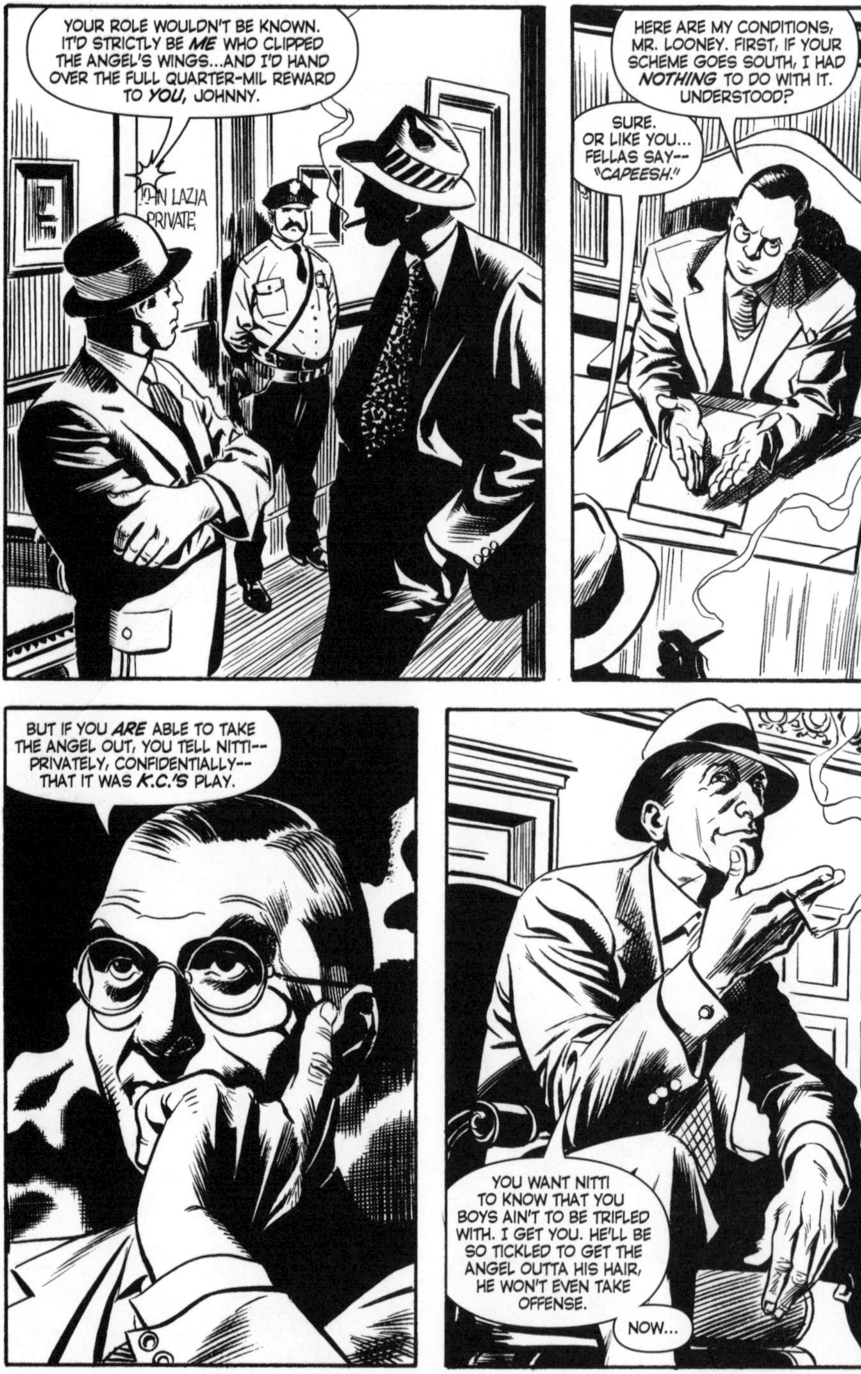
YOUR ROLE WOULDN'T BE KNOWN. IT'D STRICTLY BE *ME* WHO CLIPPED THE ANGEL'S WINGS...AND I'D HAND OVER THE FULL QUARTER-MIL REWARD TO *YOU*, JOHNNY.
JOHN LAZIA
PRIVATE
HERE ARE MY CONDITIONS, MR. LOONEY. FIRST, IF YOUR SCHEME GOES SOUTH, I HAD *NOTHING* TO DO WITH IT. UNDERSTOOD?
SURE. OR LIKE YOU... FELLAS SAY-- "*CAPEESH.*"
BUT IF YOU *ARE* ABLE TO TAKE THE ANGEL OUT, YOU TELL NITTI-- PRIVATELY, CONFIDENTIALLY-- THAT IT WAS *K.C.'S* PLAY.
YOU WANT NITTI TO KNOW THAT YOU BOYS AIN'T TO BE TRIFLED WITH. I GET YOU. HE'LL BE SO TICKLED TO GET THE ANGEL OUTTA HIS HAIR, HE WON'T EVEN TAKE OFFENSE.
NOW...

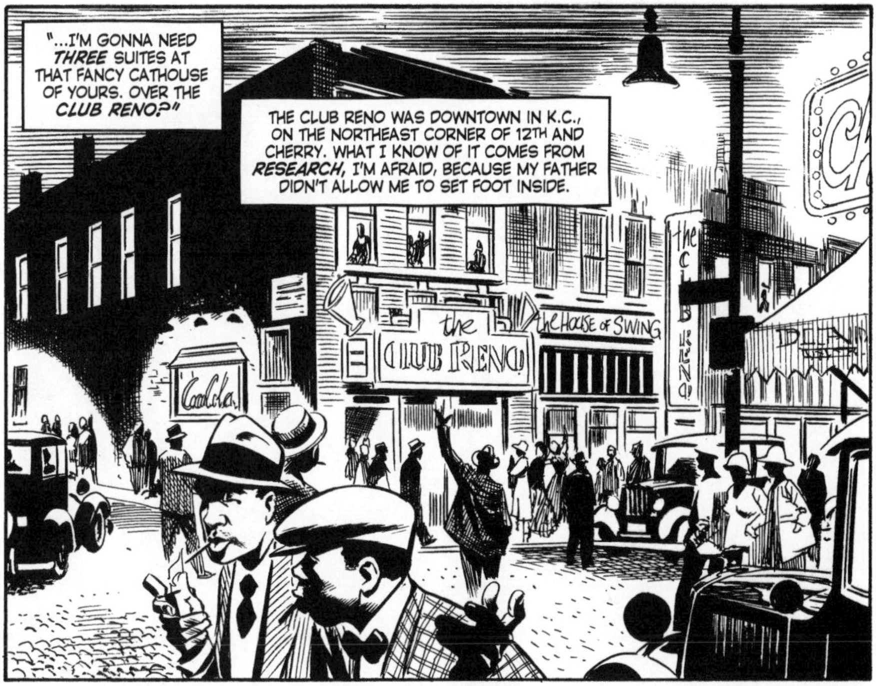
"...I'M GONNA NEED THREE SUITES AT THAT FANCY CATHOUSE OF YOURS. OVER THE CLUB RENO?"
THE CLUB RENO WAS DOWNTOWN IN K.C., ON THE NORTHEAST CORNER OF 12TH AND CHERRY. WHAT I KNOW OF IT COMES FROM RESEARCH, I'M AFRAID, BECAUSE MY FATHER DIDN'T ALLOW ME TO SET FOOT INSIDE.
the CLUB RENO
the HOUSE of SWING

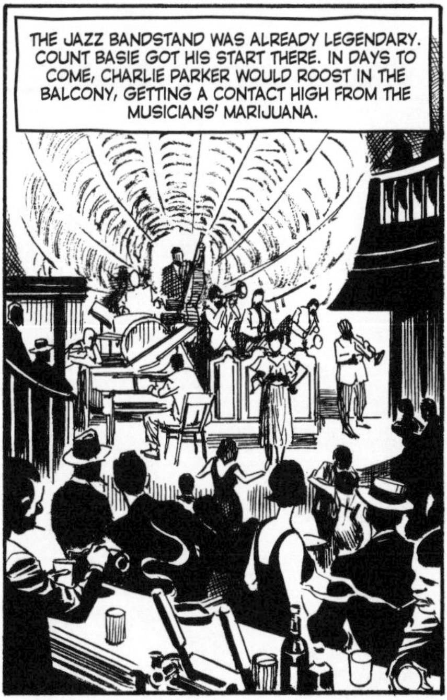
THE JAZZ BANDSTAND WAS ALREADY LEGENDARY. COUNT BASIE GOT HIS START THERE. IN DAYS TO COME, CHARLIE PARKER WOULD ROOST IN THE BALCONY, GETTING A CONTACT HIGH FROM THE MUSICIANS' MARIJUANA.

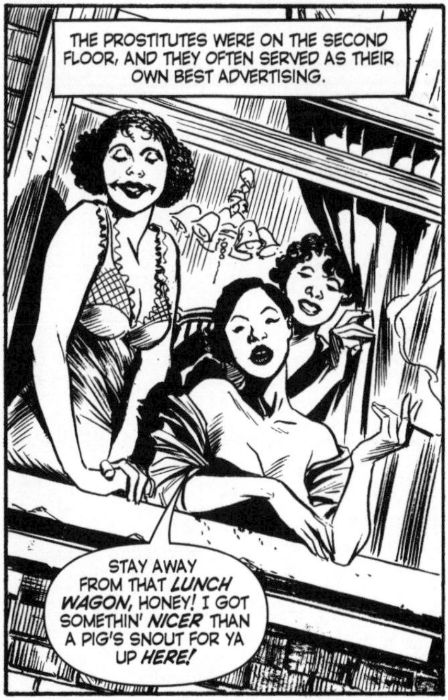
THE PROSTITUTES WERE ON THE SECOND FLOOR, AND THEY OFTEN SERVED AS THEIR OWN BEST ADVERTISING.
STAY AWAY FROM THAT LUNCH WAGON, HONEY! I GOT SOMETHIN' NICER THAN A PIG'S SNOUT FOR YA UP HERE!

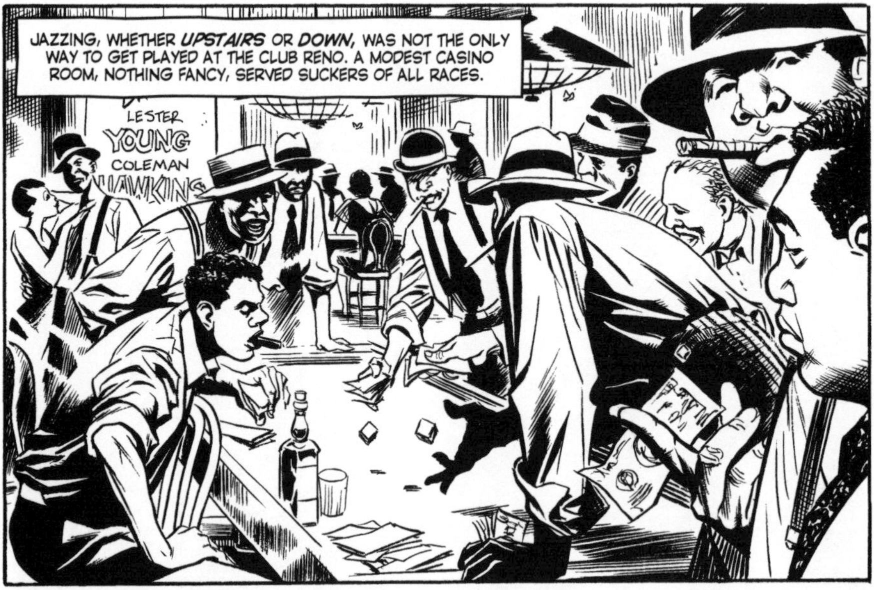
JAZZING, WHETHER UPSTAIRS OR DOWN, WAS NOT THE ONLY WAY TO GET PLAYED AT THE CLUB RENO. A MODEST CASINO ROOM, NOTHING FANCY, SERVED SUCKERS OF ALL RACES.
LESTER
YOUNG
COLEMAN

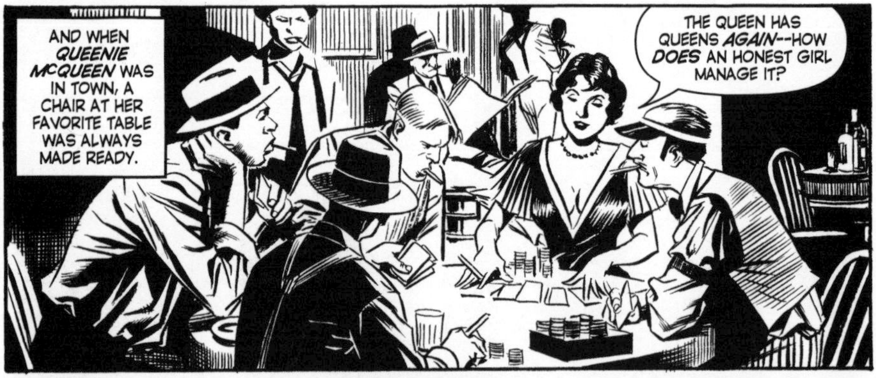
AND WHEN QUEENIE McQUEEN WAS IN TOWN, A CHAIR AT HER FAVORITE TABLE WAS ALWAYS MADE READY.
THE QUEEN HAS QUEENS AGAIN--HOW DOES AN HONEST GIRL MANAGE IT?

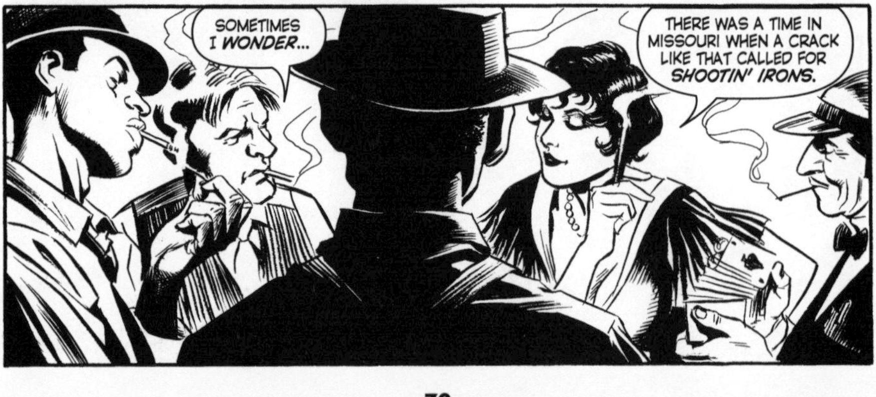
SOMETIMES I WONDER...
THERE WAS A TIME IN MISSOURI WHEN A CRACK LIKE THAT CALLED FOR SHOOTIN' IRONS.

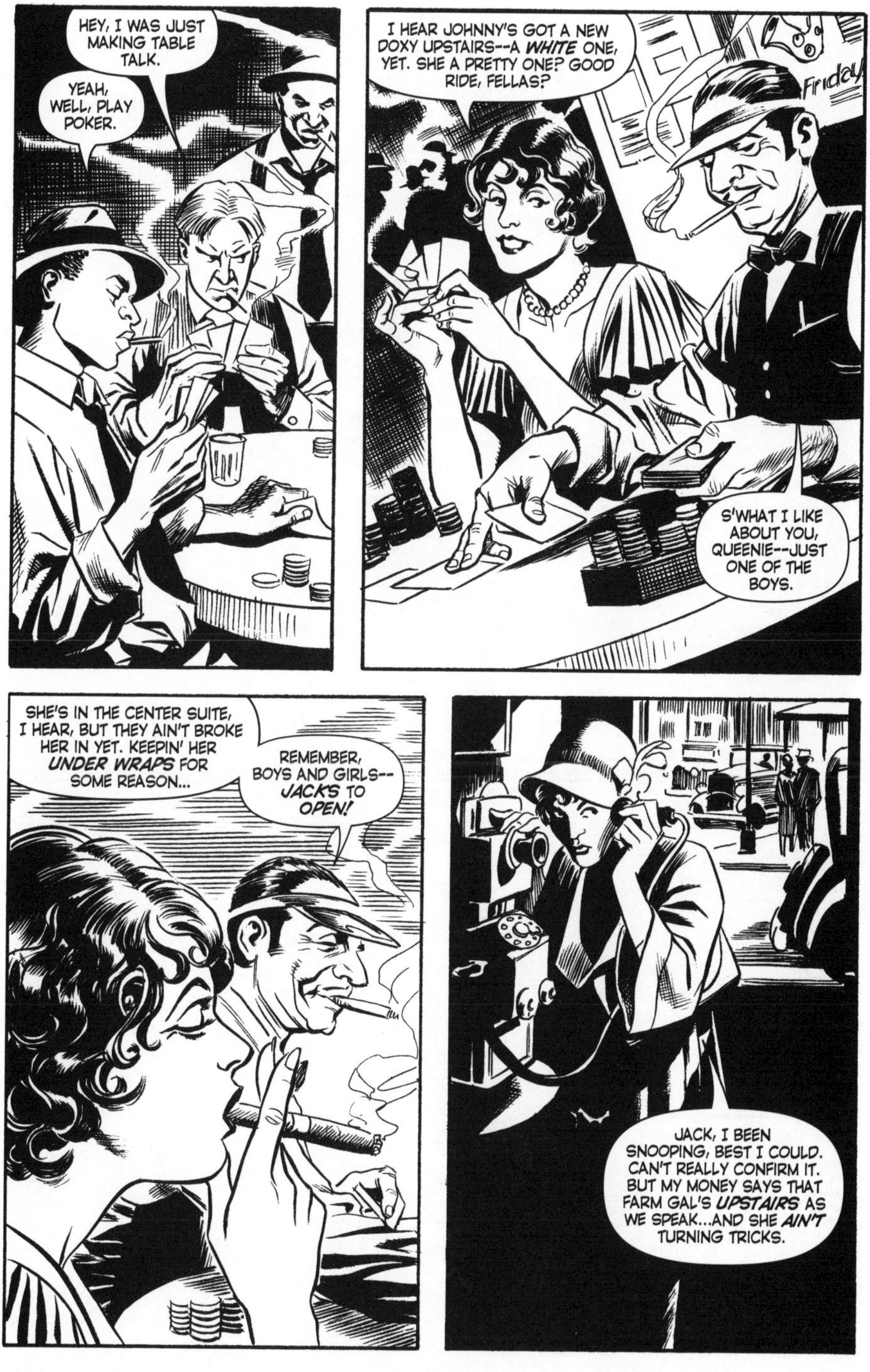
HEY, I WAS JUST MAKING TABLE TALK.
YEAH, WELL, PLAY POKER.
I HEAR JOHNNY'S GOT A NEW DOXY UPSTAIRS--A WHITE ONE, YET. SHE A PRETTY ONE? GOOD RIDE, FELLAS?
Friday
S'WHAT I LIKE ABOUT YOU, QUEENIE--JUST ONE OF THE BOYS.
SHE'S IN THE CENTER SUITE, I HEAR, BUT THEY AIN'T BROKE HER IN YET. KEEPIN' HER UNDER WRAPS FOR SOME REASON...
REMEMBER, BOYS AND GIRLS--JACKS TO OPEN!
JACK, I BEEN SNOOPING, BEST I COULD. CAN'T REALLY CONFIRM IT. BUT MY MONEY SAYS THAT FARM GAL'S UPSTAIRS AS WE SPEAK...AND SHE AIN'T TURNING TRICKS.

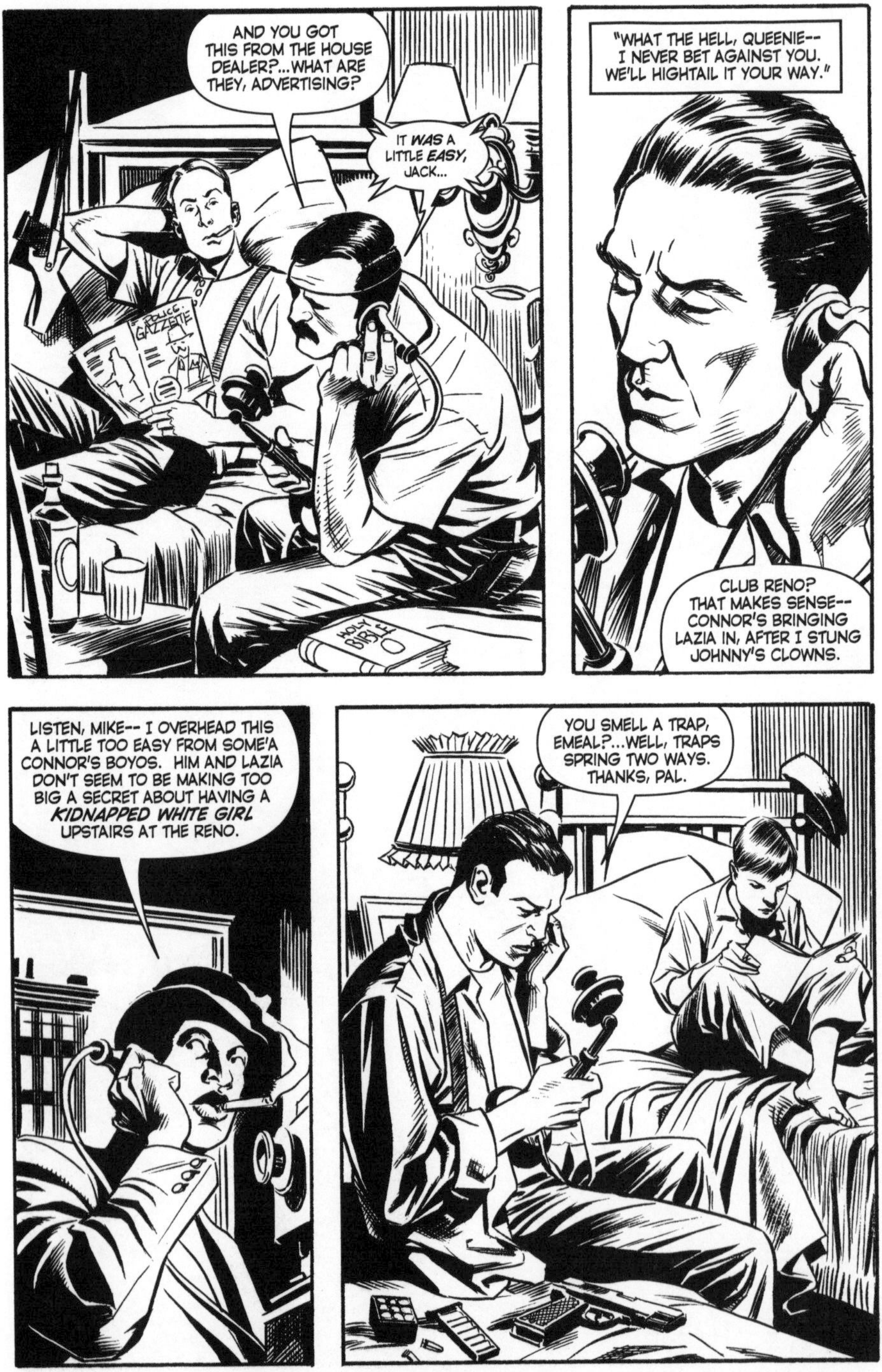
AND YOU GOT THIS FROM THE HOUSE DEALER?...WHAT ARE THEY, ADVERTISING?
IT WAS A LITTLE EASY, JACK...
POLICE GAZZETTE
HOLY BIBLE
"WHAT THE HELL, QUEENIE-- I NEVER BET AGAINST YOU. WE'LL HIGHTAIL IT YOUR WAY."
CLUB RENO? THAT MAKES SENSE-- CONNOR'S BRINGING LAZIA IN, AFTER I STUNG JOHNNY'S CLOWNS.
LISTEN, MIKE-- I OVERHEAD THIS A LITTLE TOO EASY FROM SOME'A CONNOR'S BOYOS. HIM AND LAZIA DON'T SEEM TO BE MAKING TOO BIG A SECRET ABOUT HAVING A KIDNAPPED WHITE GIRL UPSTAIRS AT THE RENO.
YOU SMELL A TRAP, EMEAL?...WELL, TRAPS SPRING TWO WAYS. THANKS, PAL.

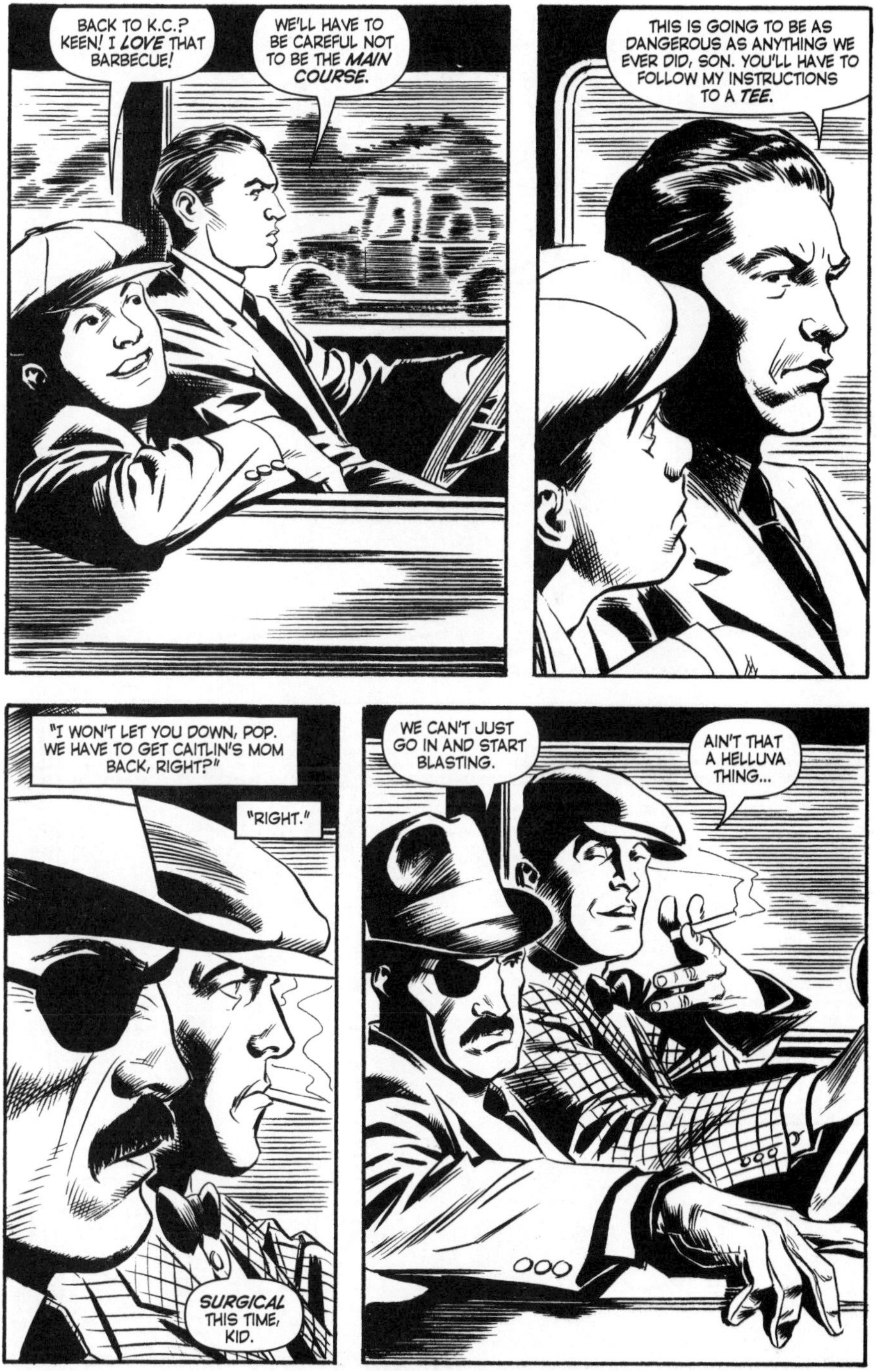
BACK TO K.C.? KEEN! I LOVE THAT BARBECUE!
WE'LL HAVE TO BE CAREFUL NOT TO BE THE MAIN COURSE.
THIS IS GOING TO BE AS DANGEROUS AS ANYTHING WE EVER DID, SON. YOU'LL HAVE TO FOLLOW MY INSTRUCTIONS TO A TEE.
"I WON'T LET YOU DOWN, POP. WE HAVE TO GET CAITLIN'S MOM BACK, RIGHT?"
"RIGHT."
SURGICAL THIS TIME, KID.
WE CAN'T JUST GO IN AND START BLASTING.
AIN'T THAT A HELLUVA THING...

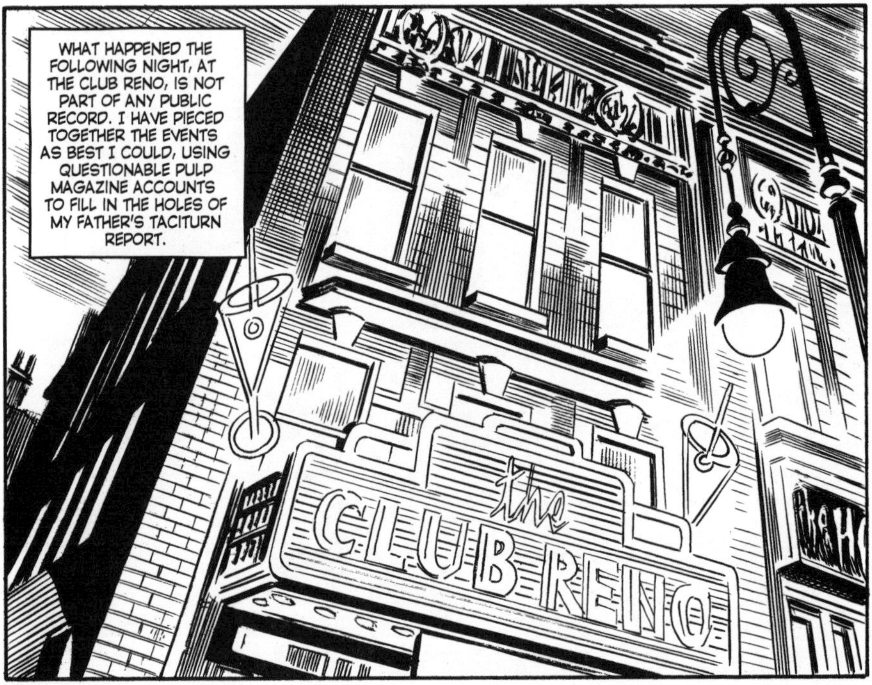
WHAT HAPPENED THE FOLLOWING NIGHT, AT THE CLUB RENO, IS NOT PART OF ANY PUBLIC RECORD. I HAVE PIECED TOGETHER THE EVENTS AS BEST I COULD, USING QUESTIONABLE PULP MAGAZINE ACCOUNTS TO FILL IN THE HOLES OF MY FATHER'S TACITURN REPORT.
the CLUB RENO

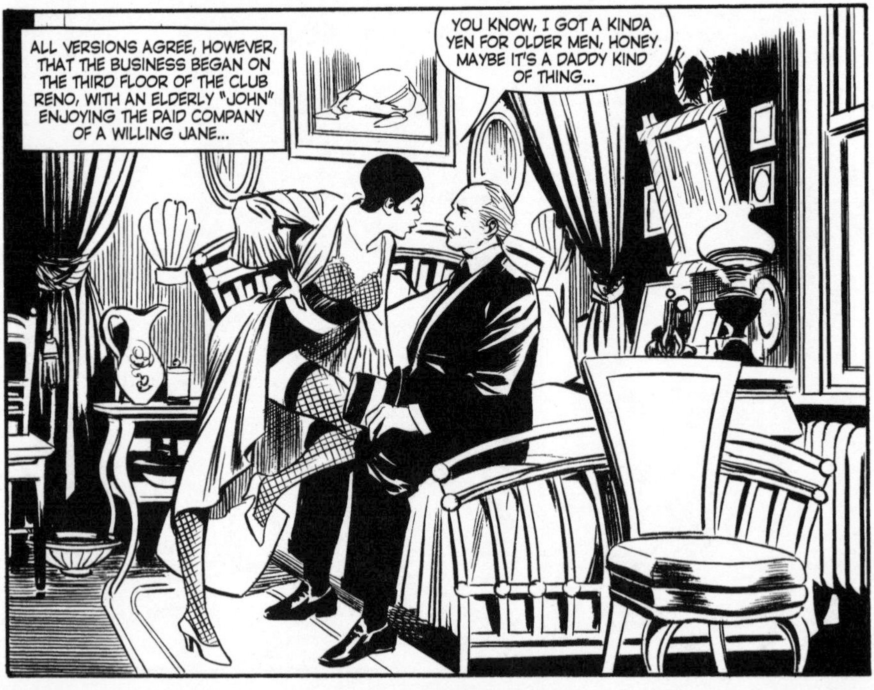
ALL VERSIONS AGREE, HOWEVER, THAT THE BUSINESS BEGAN ON THE THIRD FLOOR OF THE CLUB RENO, WITH AN ELDERLY "JOHN" ENJOYING THE PAID COMPANY OF A WILLING JANE...
YOU KNOW, I GOT A KINDA YEN FOR OLDER MEN, HONEY. MAYBE IT'S A DADDY KIND OF THING...

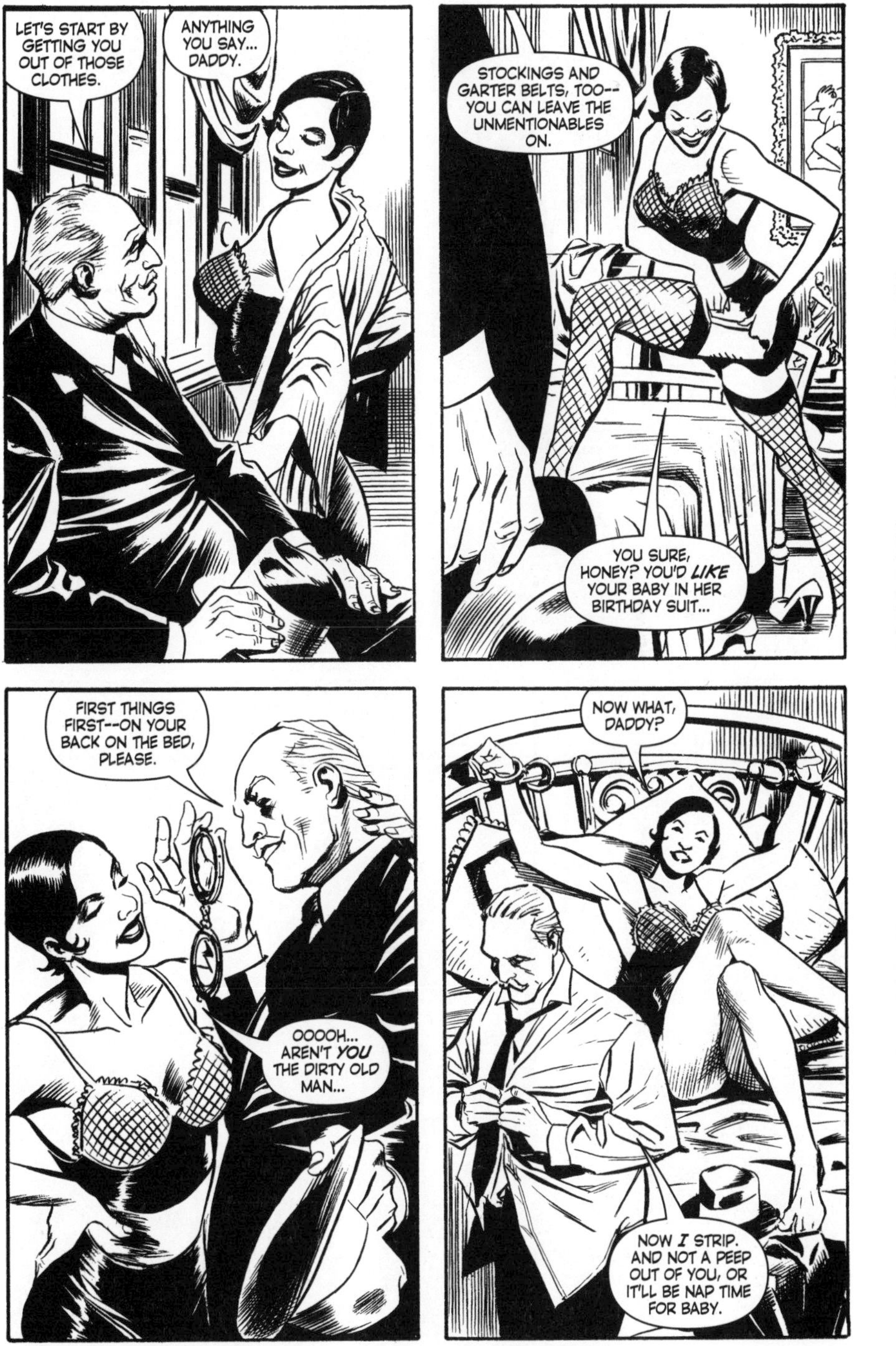
LET'S START BY GETTING YOU OUT OF THOSE CLOTHES.
ANYTHING YOU SAY... DADDY.
STOCKINGS AND GARTER BELTS, TOO-- YOU CAN LEAVE THE UNMENTIONABLES ON.
YOU SURE, HONEY? YOU'D LIKE YOUR BABY IN HER BIRTHDAY SUIT...
FIRST THINGS FIRST--ON YOUR BACK ON THE BED, PLEASE.
OOOOH... AREN'T YOU THE DIRTY OLD MAN...
NOW WHAT, DADDY?
NOW I STRIP. AND NOT A PEEP OUT OF YOU, OR IT'LL BE NAP TIME FOR BABY.

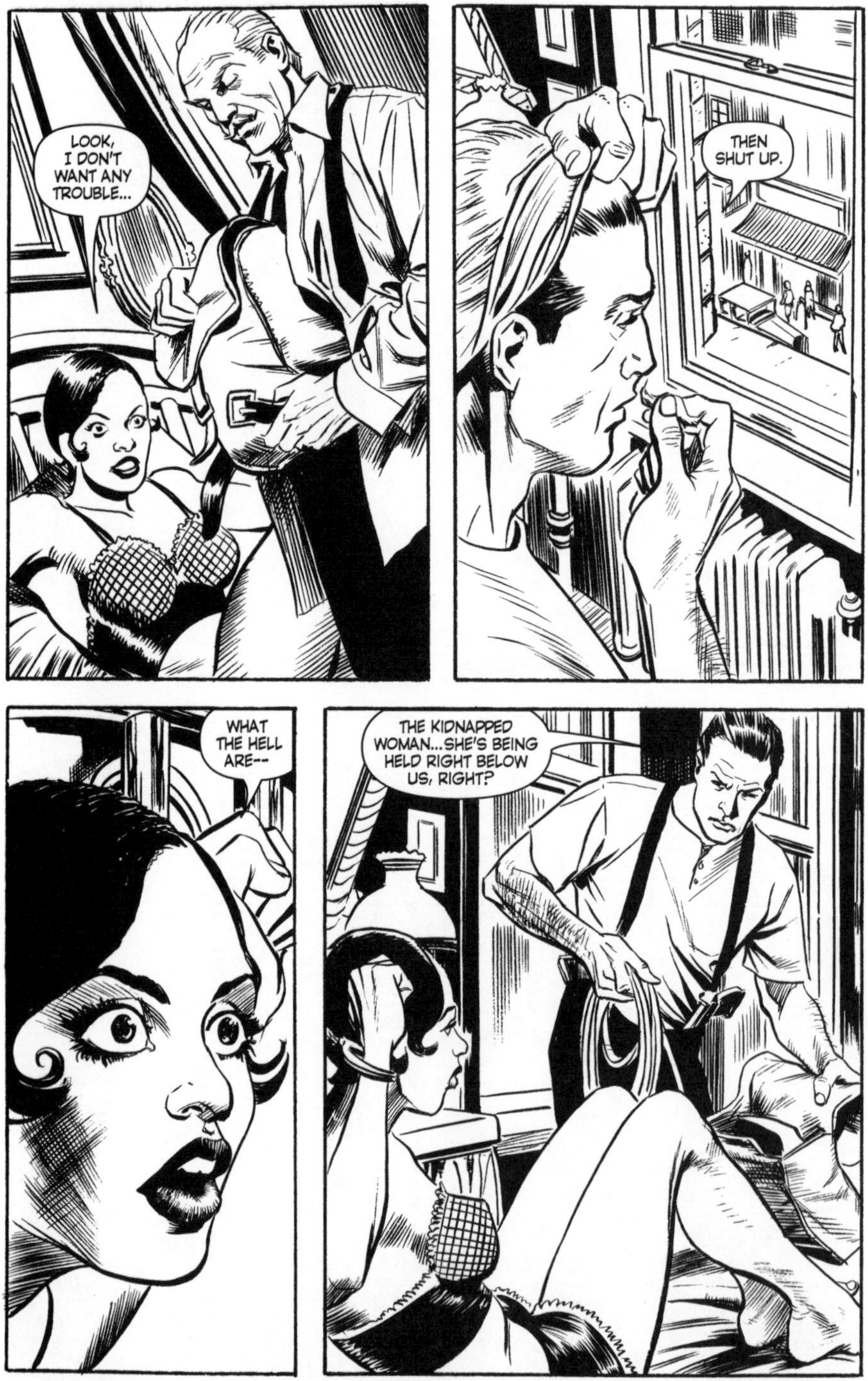
LOOK, I DON'T WANT ANY TROUBLE...
THEN SHUT UP.
WHAT THE HELL ARE--
THE KIDNAPPED WOMAN...SHE'S BEING HELD RIGHT BELOW US, RIGHT?

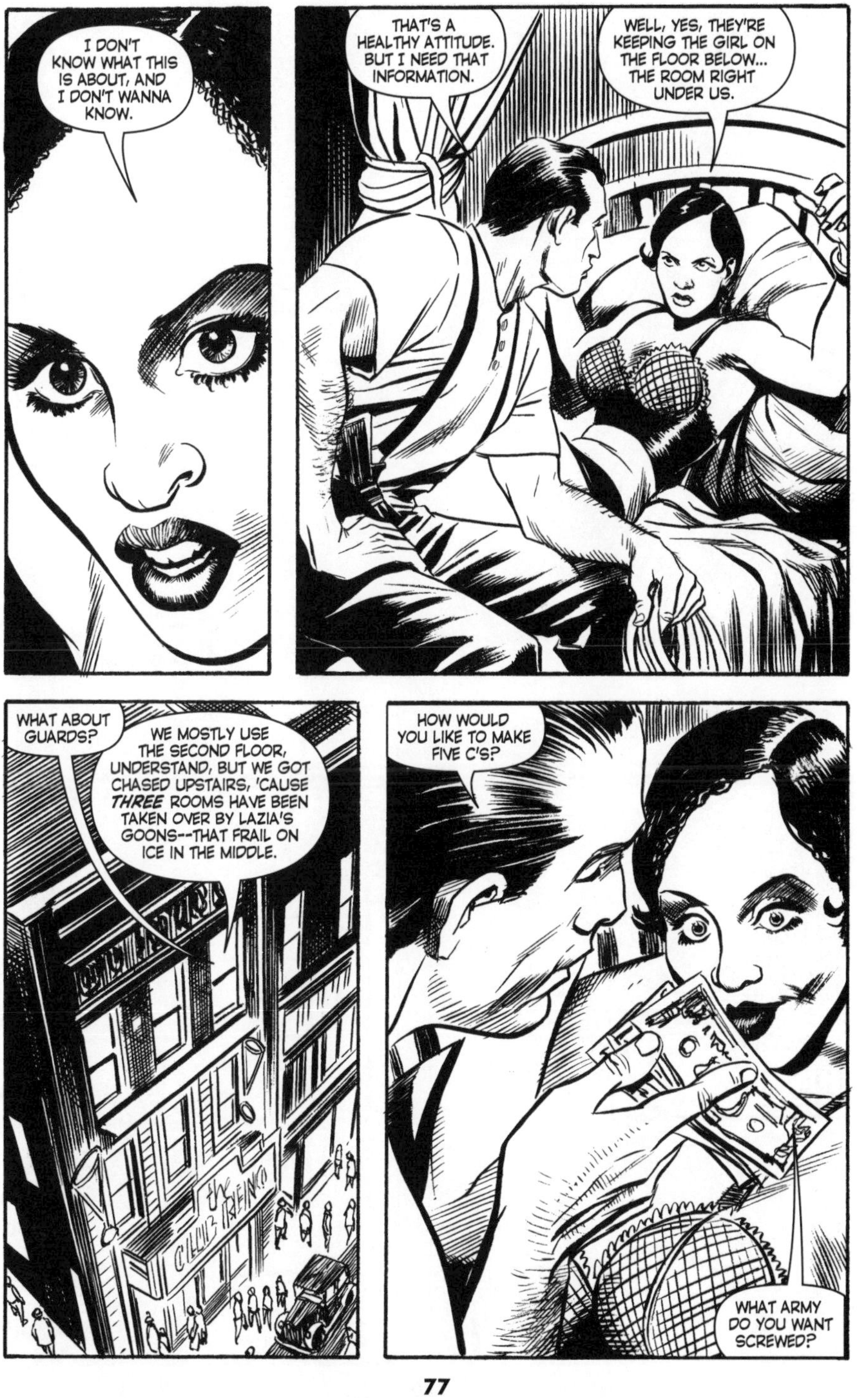
I DON'T KNOW WHAT THIS IS ABOUT, AND I DON'T WANNA KNOW.
THAT'S A HEALTHY ATTITUDE. BUT I NEED THAT INFORMATION.
WELL, YES, THEY'RE KEEPING THE GIRL ON THE FLOOR BELOW... THE ROOM RIGHT UNDER US.
WHAT ABOUT GUARDS?
WE MOSTLY USE THE SECOND FLOOR, UNDERSTAND, BUT WE GOT CHASED UPSTAIRS, 'CAUSE *THREE* ROOMS HAVE BEEN TAKEN OVER BY LAZIA'S GOONS--THAT FRAIL ON ICE IN THE MIDDLE.
the CLUB REINO
HOW WOULD YOU LIKE TO MAKE FIVE C'S?
WHAT ARMY DO YOU WANT SCREWED?

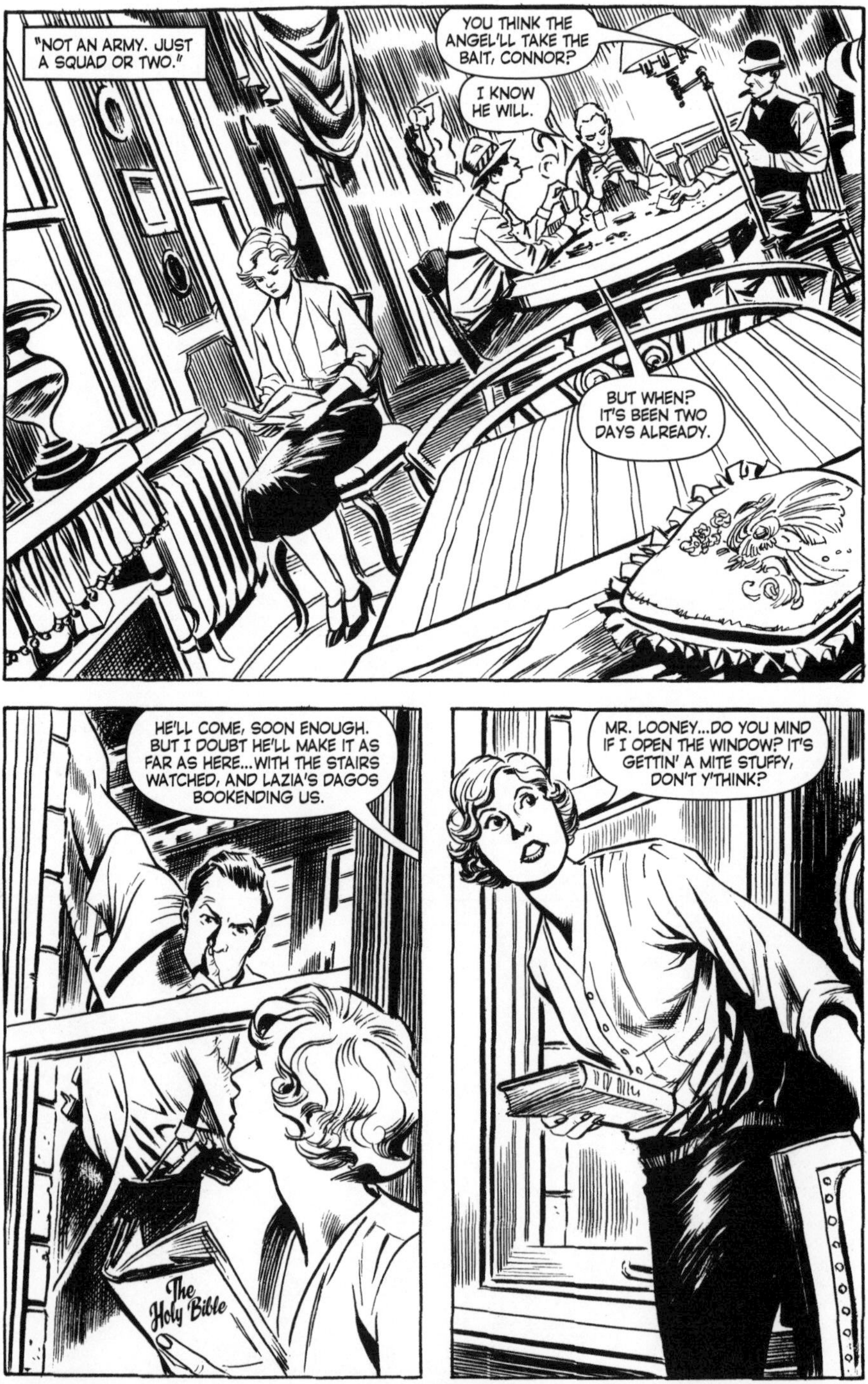
"NOT AN ARMY. JUST A SQUAD OR TWO."
YOU THINK THE ANGEL'LL TAKE THE BAIT, CONNOR?
I KNOW HE WILL.
BUT WHEN? IT'S BEEN TWO DAYS ALREADY.
HE'LL COME, SOON ENOUGH. BUT I DOUBT HE'LL MAKE IT AS FAR AS HERE...WITH THE STAIRS WATCHED, AND LAZIA'S DAGOS BOOKENDING US.
The Holy Bible
MR. LOONEY...DO YOU MIND IF I OPEN THE WINDOW? IT'S GETTIN' A MITE STUFFY, DON'T Y'THINK?

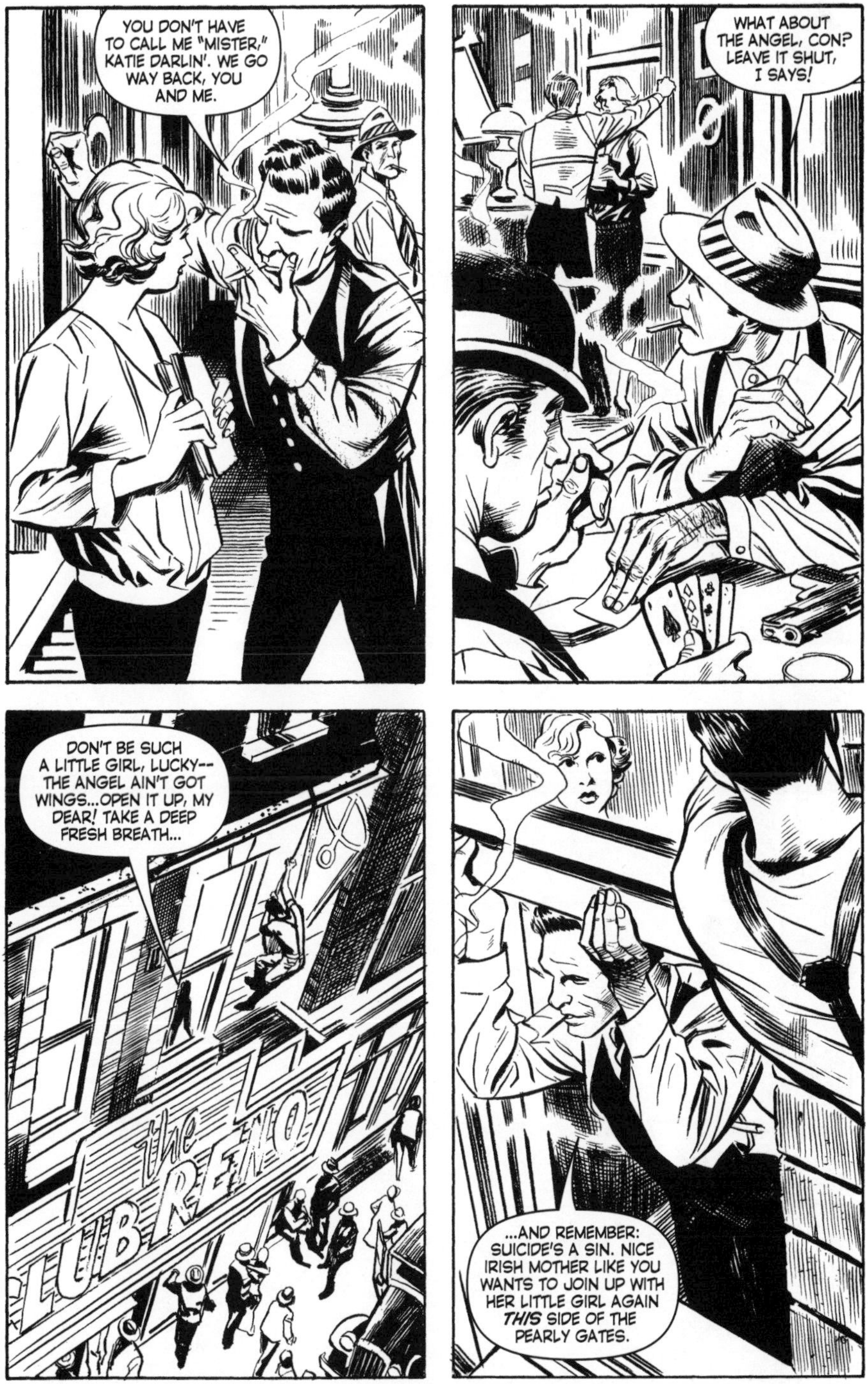
YOU DON'T HAVE TO CALL ME "MISTER," KATIE DARLIN'. WE GO WAY BACK, YOU AND ME.
WHAT ABOUT THE ANGEL, CON? LEAVE IT SHUT, I SAYS!
DON'T BE SUCH A LITTLE GIRL, LUCKY-- THE ANGEL AIN'T GOT WINGS...OPEN IT UP, MY DEAR! TAKE A DEEP FRESH BREATH...
the CLUB RENO
...AND REMEMBER: SUICIDE'S A SIN. NICE IRISH MOTHER LIKE YOU WANTS TO JOIN UP WITH HER LITTLE GIRL AGAIN *THIS* SIDE OF THE PEARLY GATES.

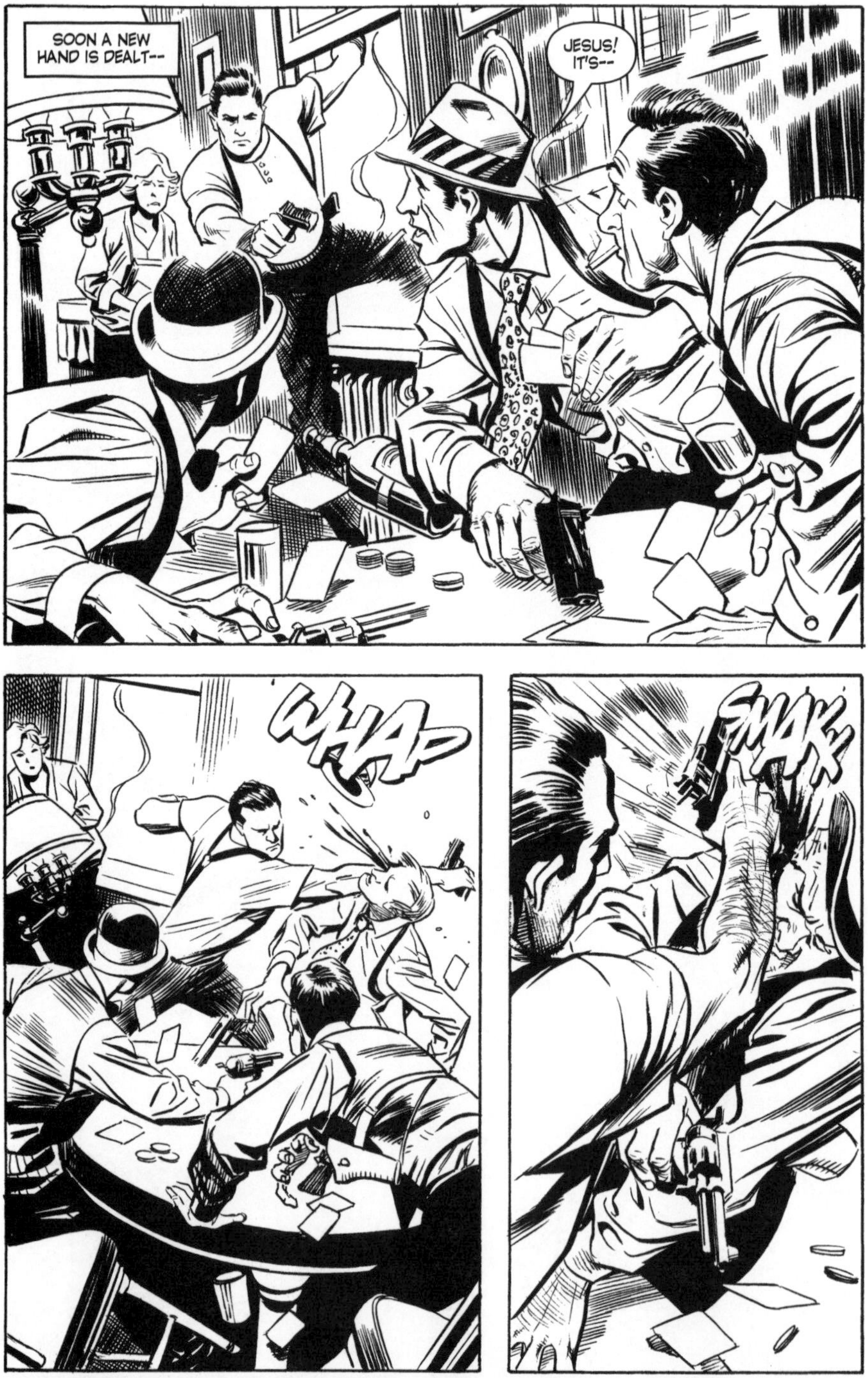
SOON A NEW HAND IS DEALT--
JESUS! IT'S--
WHAP
SMAK

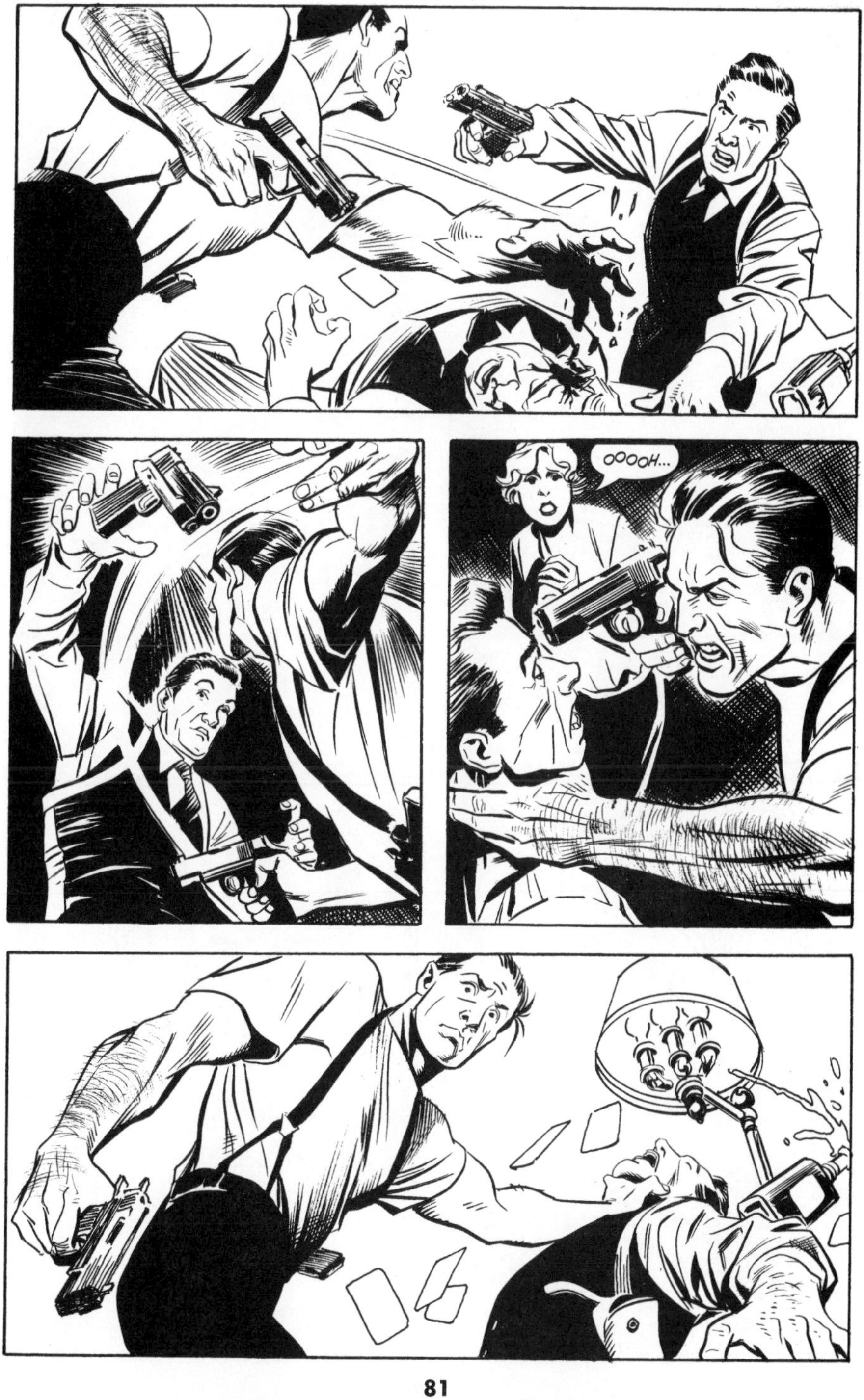
OOOOH...

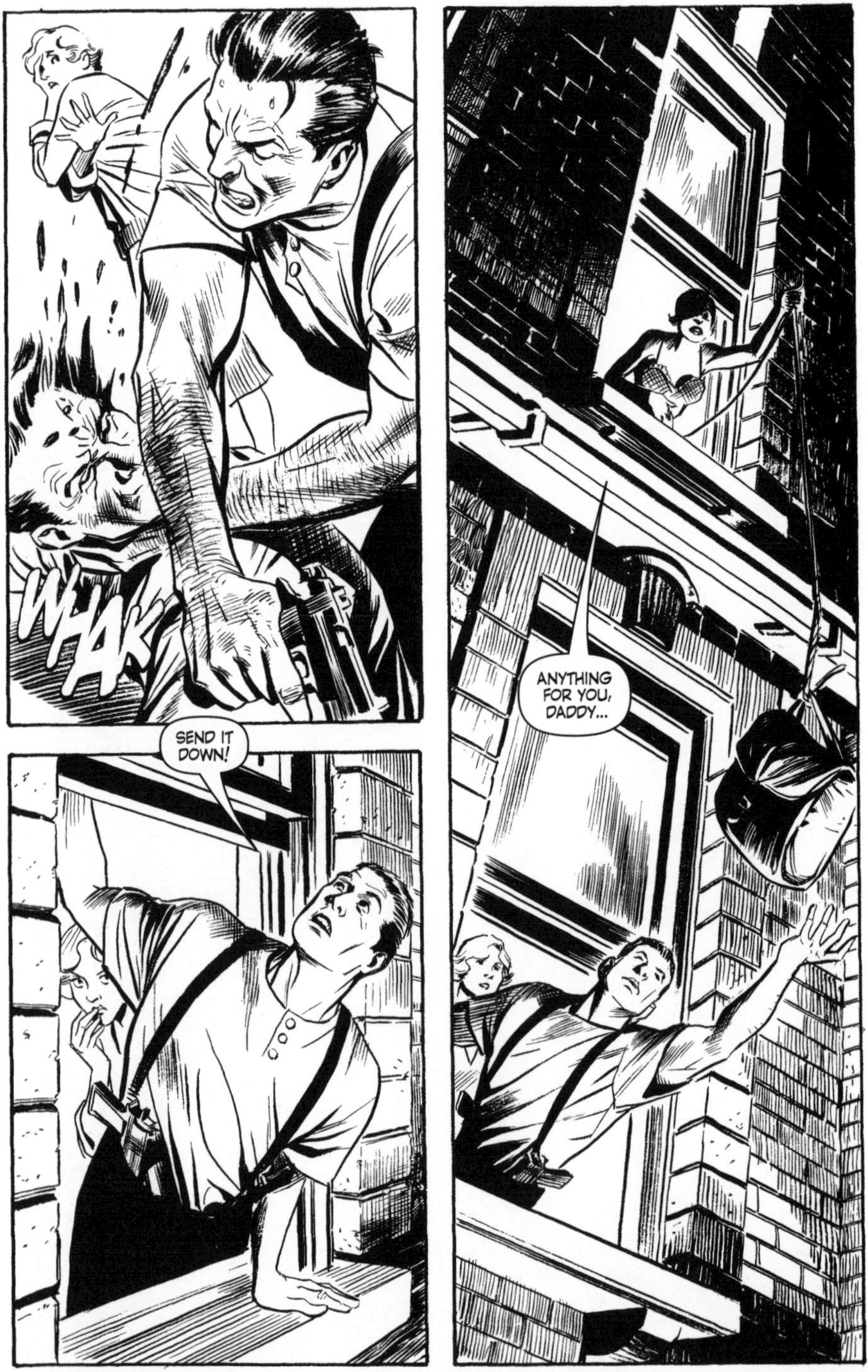
WHAK
SEND IT DOWN!
ANYTHING FOR YOU, DADDY...

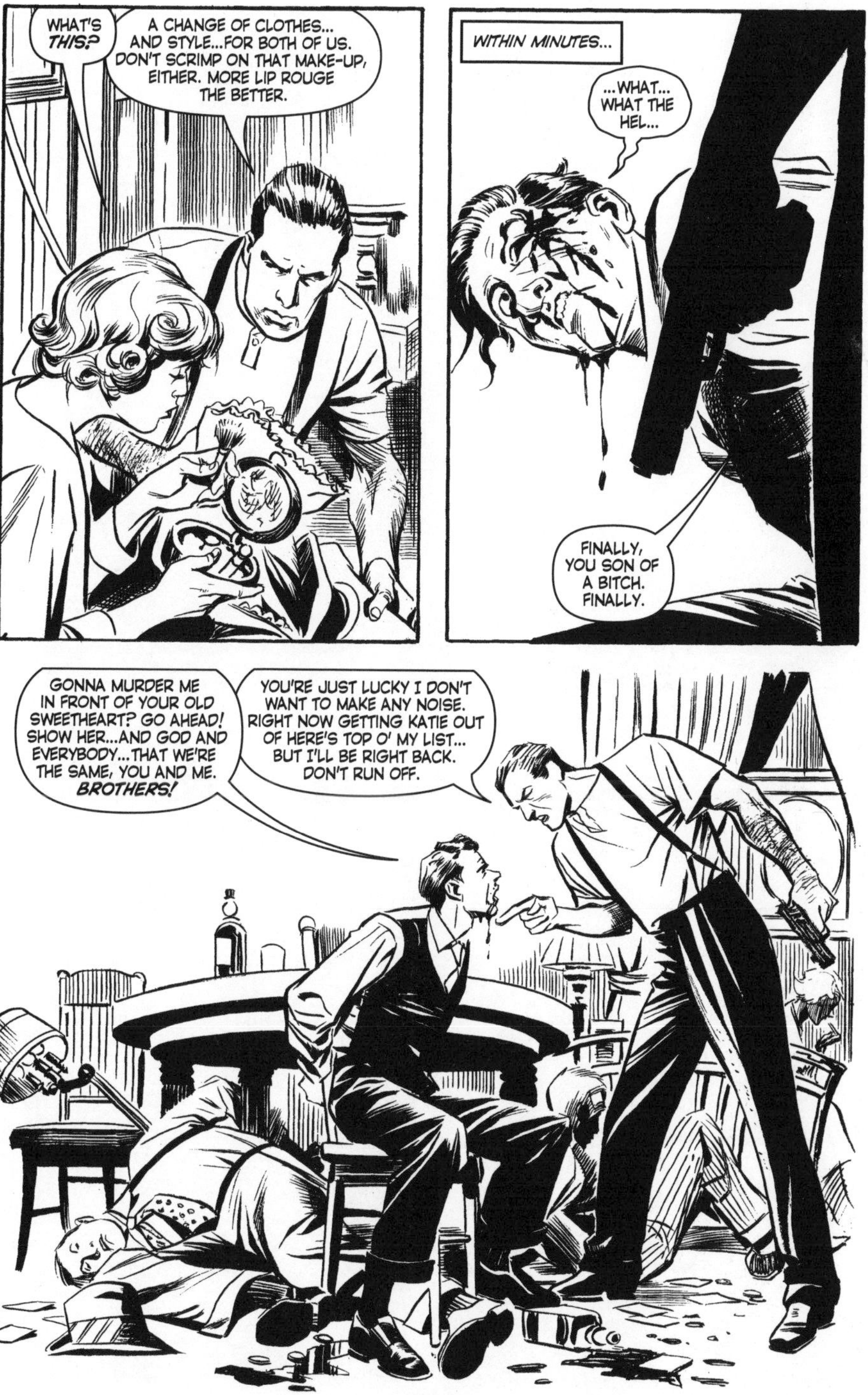
WHAT'S *THIS?*
A CHANGE OF CLOTHES... AND STYLE...FOR BOTH OF US. DON'T SCRIMP ON THAT MAKE-UP, EITHER. MORE LIP ROUGE THE BETTER.
WITHIN MINUTES...
...WHAT... WHAT THE HEL...
FINALLY, YOU SON OF A BITCH. FINALLY.
GONNA MURDER ME IN FRONT OF YOUR OLD SWEETHEART? GO AHEAD! SHOW HER...AND GOD AND EVERYBODY...THAT WE'RE THE SAME, YOU AND ME. ***BROTHERS!***
YOU'RE JUST LUCKY I DON'T WANT TO MAKE ANY NOISE. RIGHT NOW GETTING KATIE OUT OF HERE'S TOP O' MY LIST... BUT I'LL BE RIGHT BACK. DON'T RUN OFF.

I'LL SEE YOU IN HELL.
NO DOUBT OF THAT...HAVE ANOTHER TASTE.
WHAAP
HOW DO I LOOK?
NEVER MORE BEAUTIFUL. AND ME?
NEVER MORE HANDSOME.
WHEN WE WALK DOWN THAT HALLWAY, IF A DOOR OPENS WIDE, YOU DROP TO THE FLOOR. WIDE--UNDERSTAND?

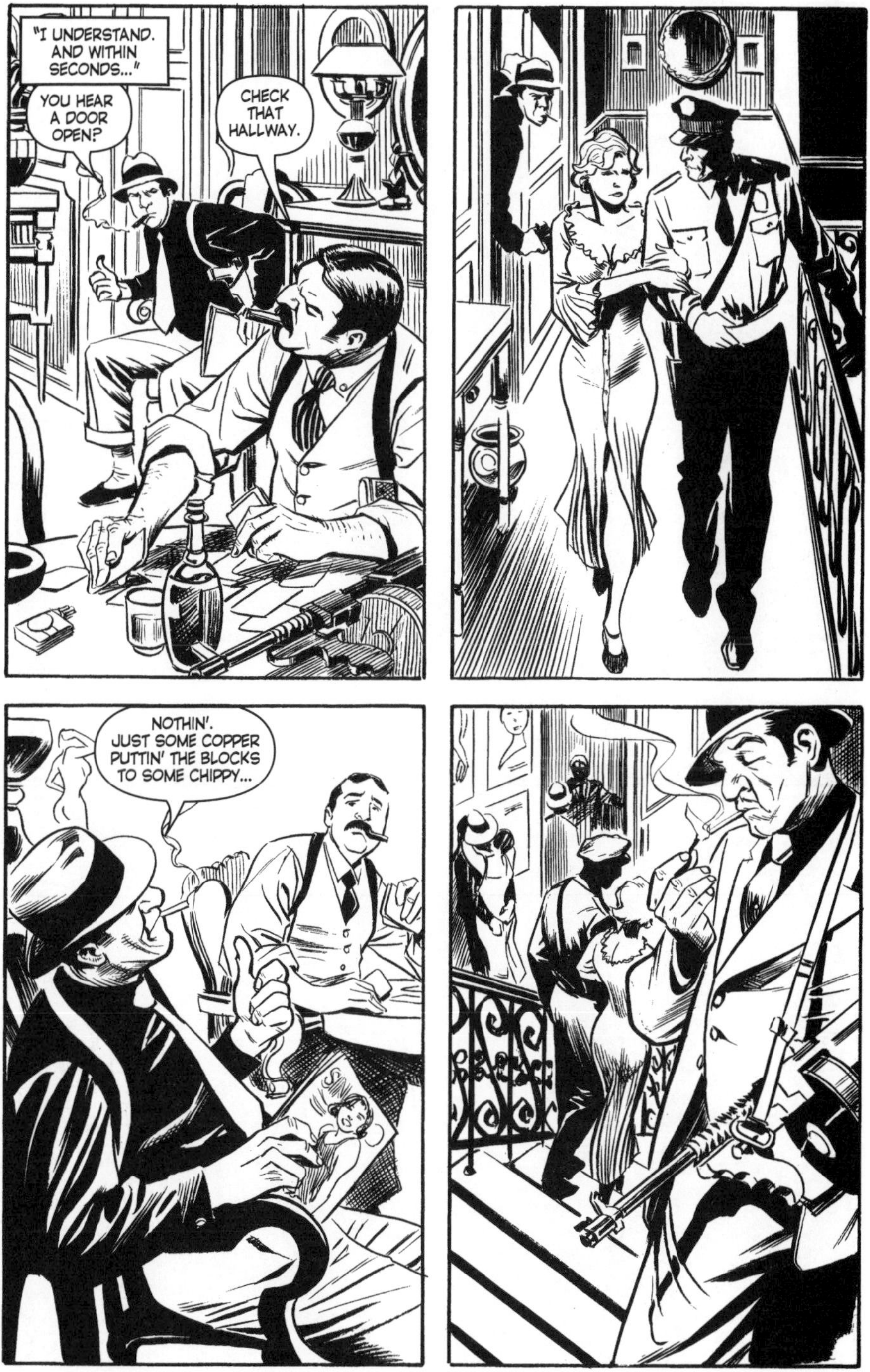
"I UNDERSTAND. AND WITHIN SECONDS..."
YOU HEAR A DOOR OPEN?
CHECK THAT HALLWAY.
NOTHIN'. JUST SOME COPPER PUTTIN' THE BLOCKS TO SOME CHIPPY...

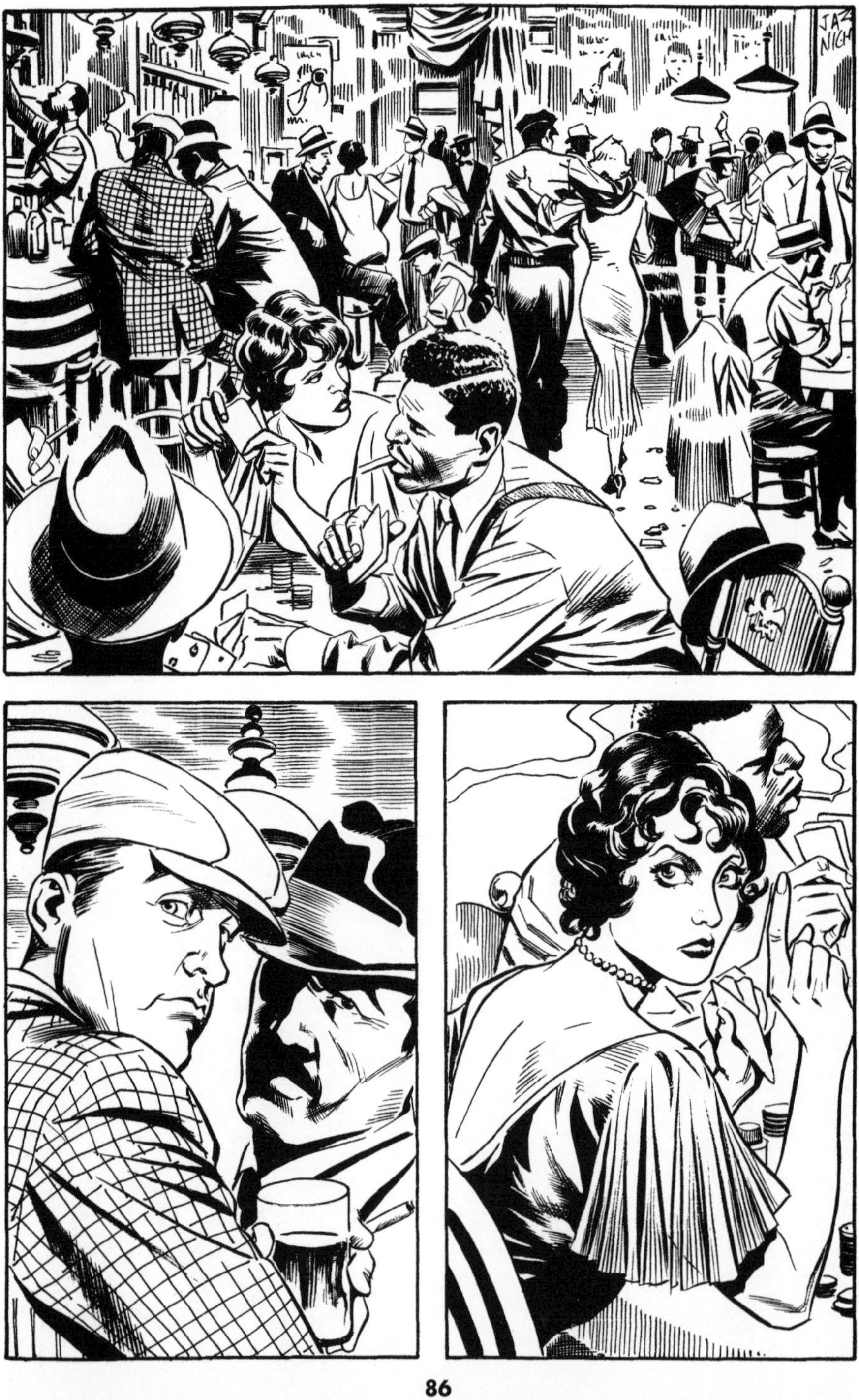

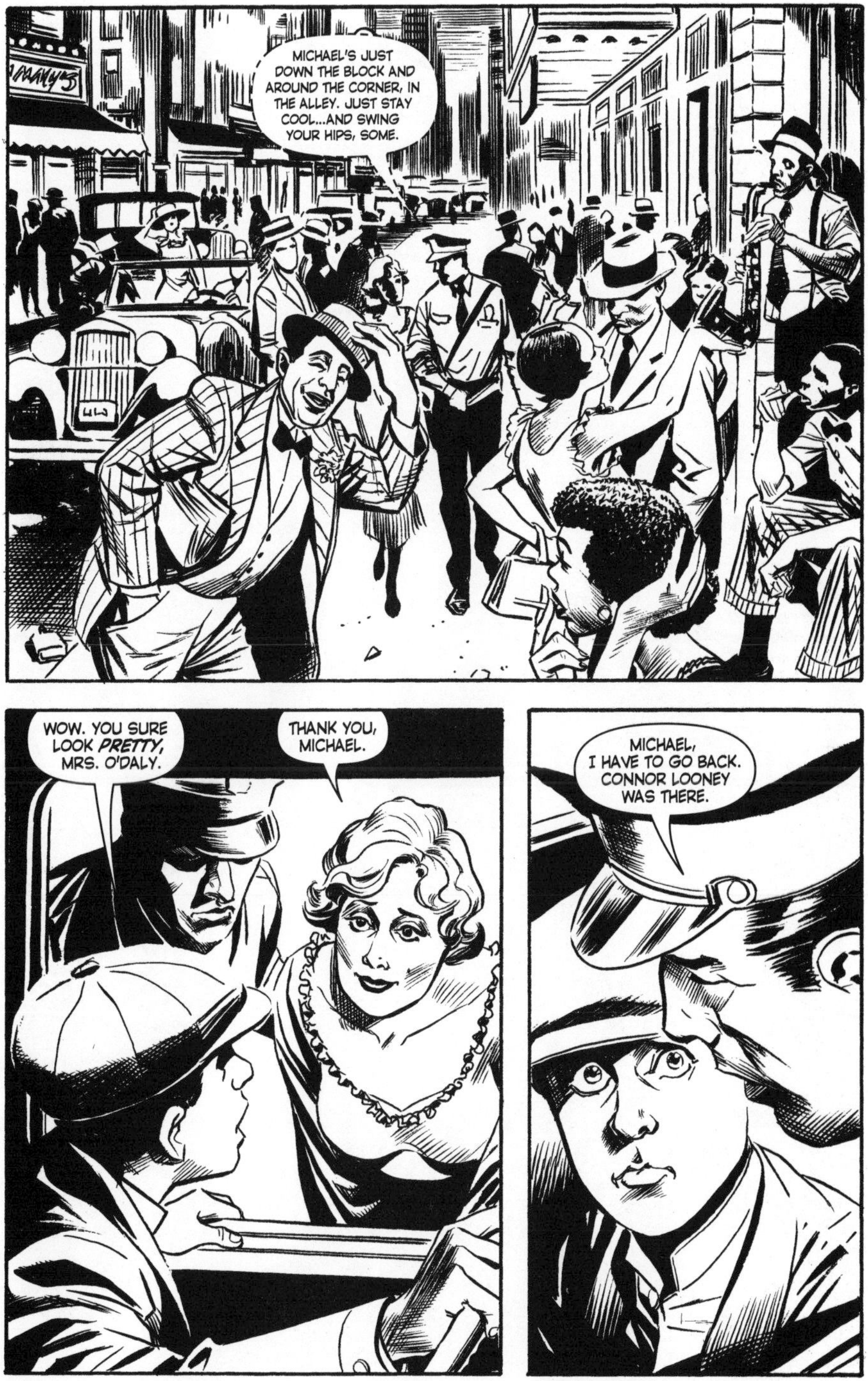
MICHAEL'S JUST DOWN THE BLOCK AND AROUND THE CORNER, IN THE ALLEY. JUST STAY COOL...AND SWING YOUR HIPS, SOME.
WOW. YOU SURE LOOK *PRETTY*, MRS. O'DALY.
THANK YOU, MICHAEL.
MICHAEL, I HAVE TO GO BACK. CONNOR LOONEY WAS THERE.

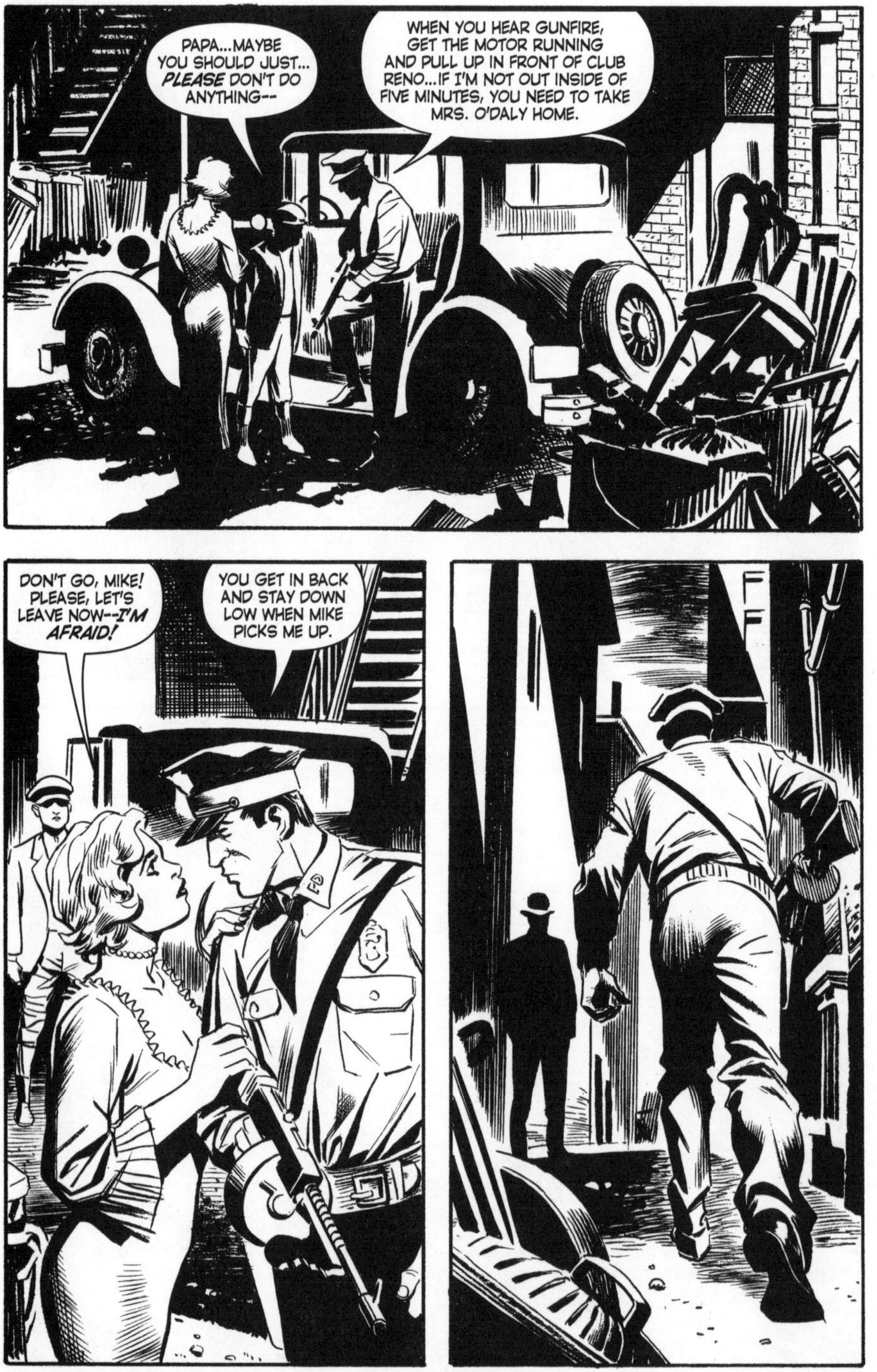
PAPA...MAYBE YOU SHOULD JUST... PLEASE DON'T DO ANYTHING--
WHEN YOU HEAR GUNFIRE, GET THE MOTOR RUNNING AND PULL UP IN FRONT OF CLUB RENO...IF I'M NOT OUT INSIDE OF FIVE MINUTES, YOU NEED TO TAKE MRS. O'DALY HOME.
DON'T GO, MIKE! PLEASE, LET'S LEAVE NOW--I'M AFRAID!
YOU GET IN BACK AND STAY DOWN LOW WHEN MIKE PICKS ME UP.

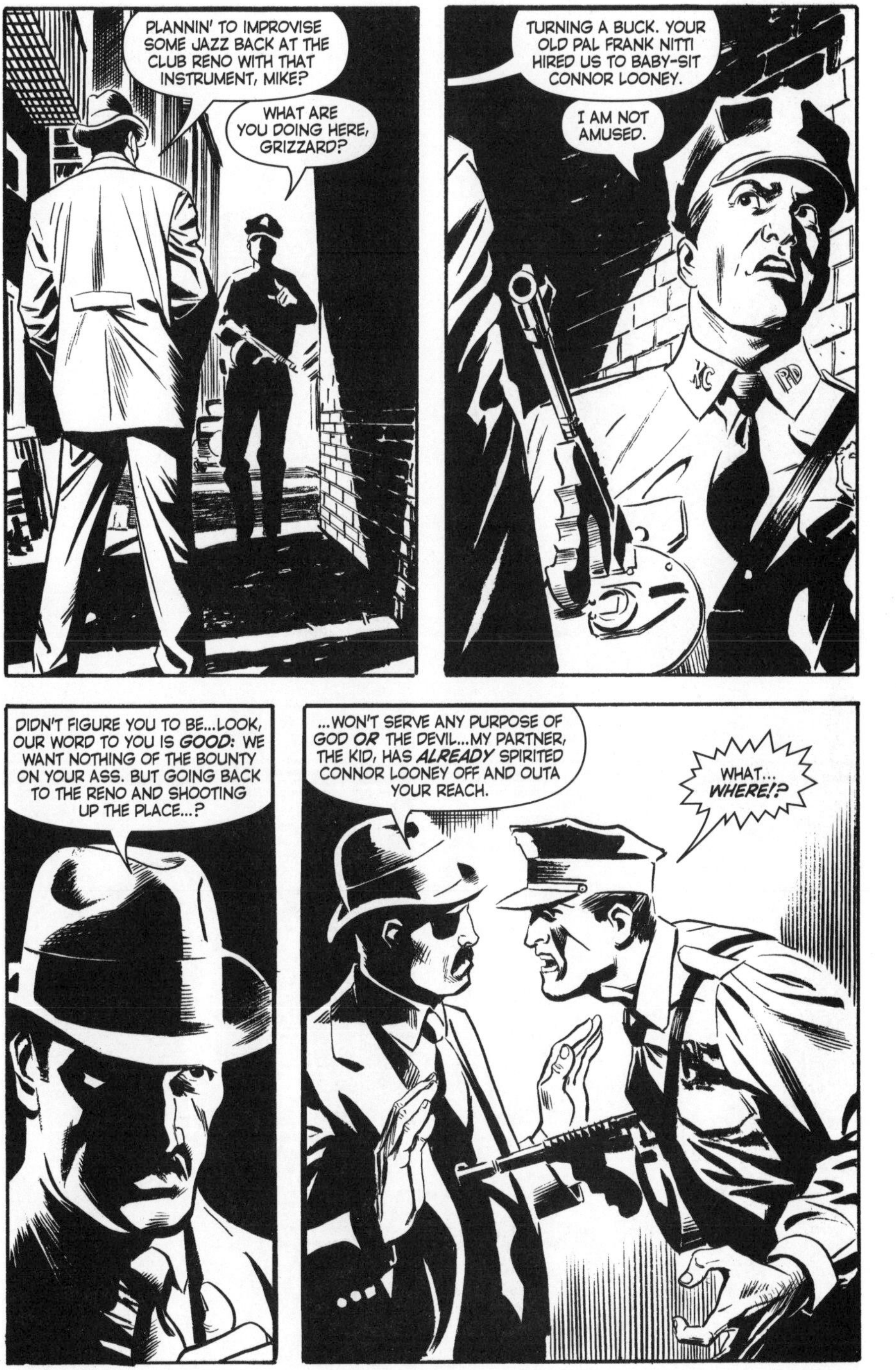
PLANNIN' TO IMPROVISE SOME JAZZ BACK AT THE CLUB RENO WITH THAT INSTRUMENT, MIKE?
WHAT ARE YOU DOING HERE, GRIZZARD?
TURNING A BUCK. YOUR OLD PAL FRANK NITTI HIRED US TO BABY-SIT CONNOR LOONEY.
I AM NOT AMUSED.
KC
PD
DIDN'T FIGURE YOU TO BE...LOOK, OUR WORD TO YOU IS *GOOD:* WE WANT NOTHING OF THE BOUNTY ON YOUR ASS. BUT GOING BACK TO THE RENO AND SHOOTING UP THE PLACE...?
...WON'T SERVE ANY PURPOSE OF GOD *OR* THE DEVIL...MY PARTNER, THE KID, HAS *ALREADY* SPIRITED CONNOR LOONEY OFF AND OUTA YOUR REACH.
WHAT... *WHERE!?*

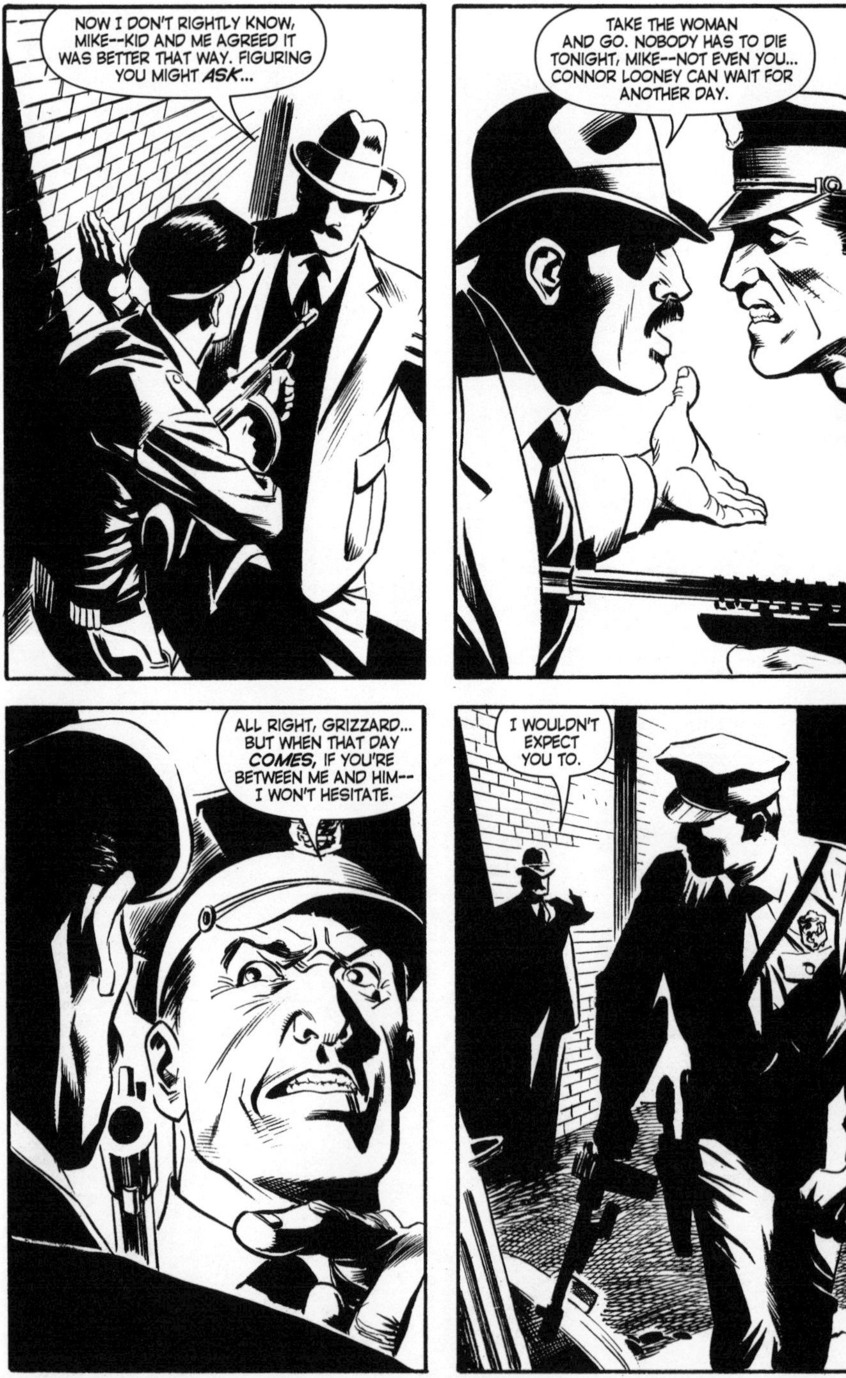
NOW I DON'T RIGHTLY KNOW, MIKE--KID AND ME AGREED IT WAS BETTER THAT WAY. FIGURING YOU MIGHT ASK...
TAKE THE WOMAN AND GO. NOBODY HAS TO DIE TONIGHT, MIKE--NOT EVEN YOU... CONNOR LOONEY CAN WAIT FOR ANOTHER DAY.
ALL RIGHT, GRIZZARD... BUT WHEN THAT DAY COMES, IF YOU'RE BETWEEN ME AND HIM-- I WON'T HESITATE.
I WOULDN'T EXPECT YOU TO.

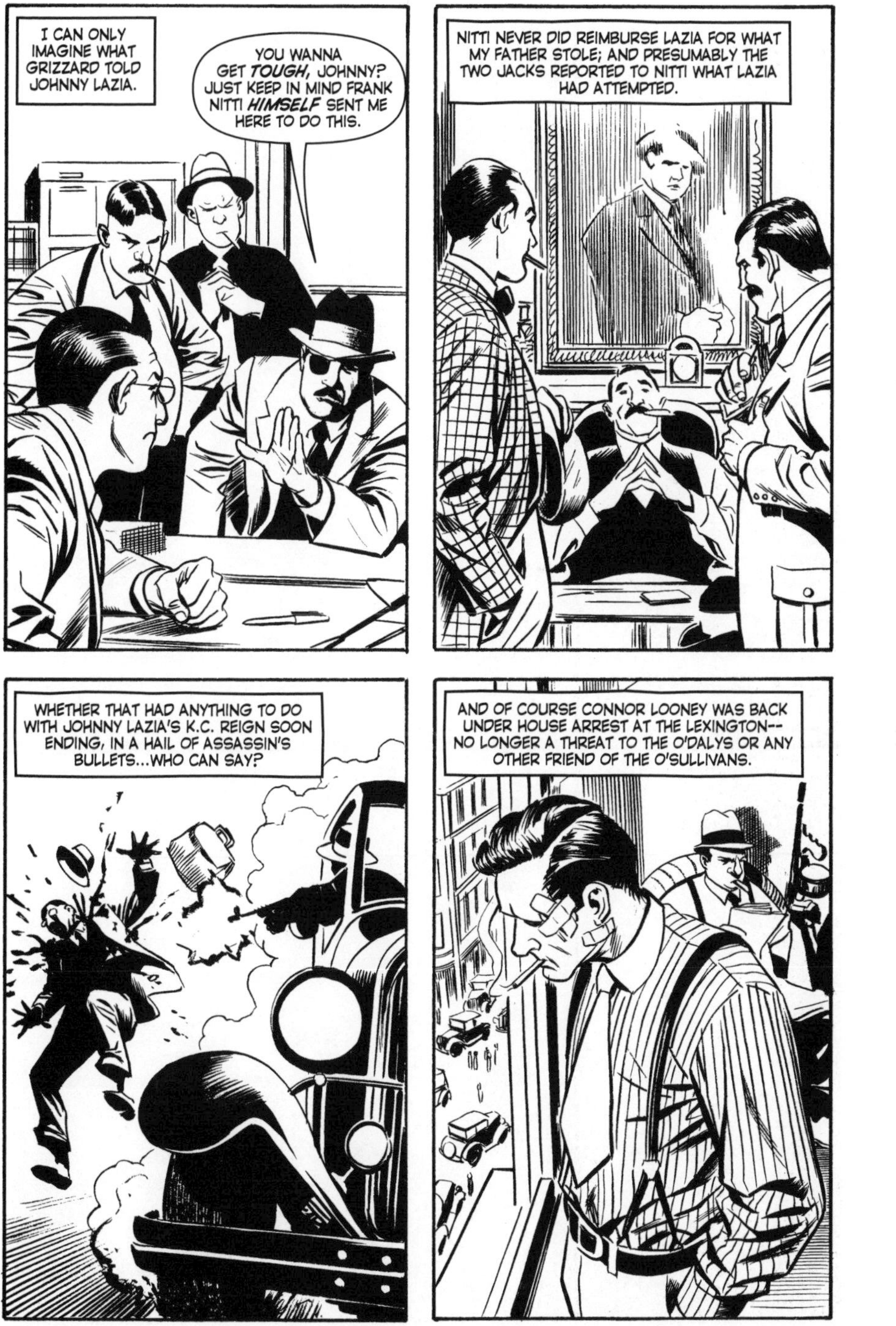
I CAN ONLY IMAGINE WHAT GRIZZARD TOLD JOHNNY LAZIA.
YOU WANNA GET *TOUGH,* JOHNNY? JUST KEEP IN MIND FRANK NITTI *HIMSELF* SENT ME HERE TO DO THIS.
NITTI NEVER DID REIMBURSE LAZIA FOR WHAT MY FATHER STOLE; AND PRESUMABLY THE TWO JACKS REPORTED TO NITTI WHAT LAZIA HAD ATTEMPTED.
WHETHER THAT HAD ANYTHING TO DO WITH JOHNNY LAZIA'S K.C. REIGN SOON ENDING, IN A HAIL OF ASSASSIN'S BULLETS...WHO CAN SAY?
AND OF COURSE CONNOR LOONEY WAS BACK UNDER HOUSE ARREST AT THE LEXINGTON-- NO LONGER A THREAT TO THE O'DALYS OR ANY OTHER FRIEND OF THE O'SULLIVANS.

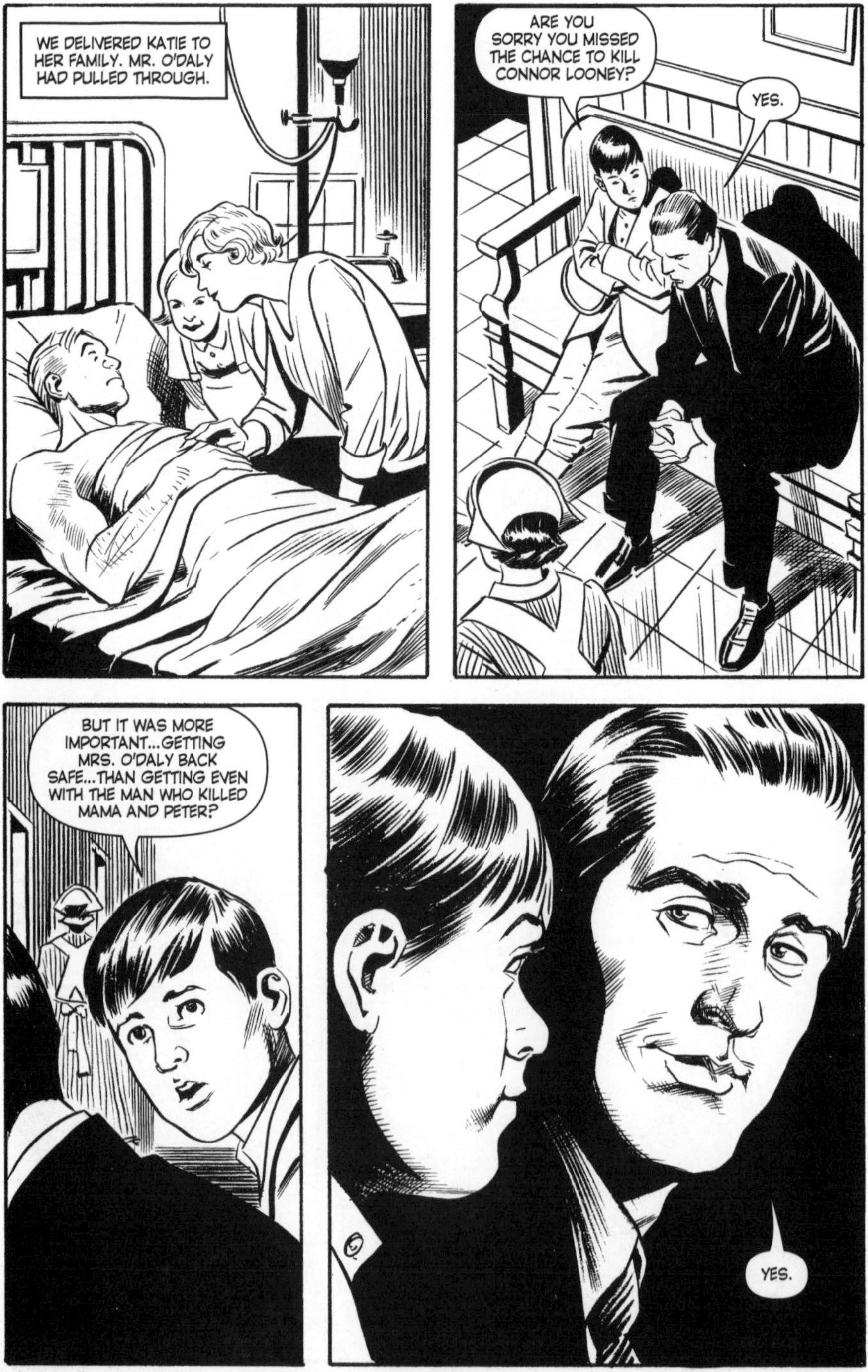
WE DELIVERED KATIE TO HER FAMILY. MR. O'DALY HAD PULLED THROUGH.
ARE YOU SORRY YOU MISSED THE CHANCE TO KILL CONNOR LOONEY?
YES.
BUT IT WAS MORE IMPORTANT...GETTING MRS. O'DALY BACK SAFE...THAN GETTING EVEN WITH THE MAN WHO KILLED MAMA AND PETER?
YES.

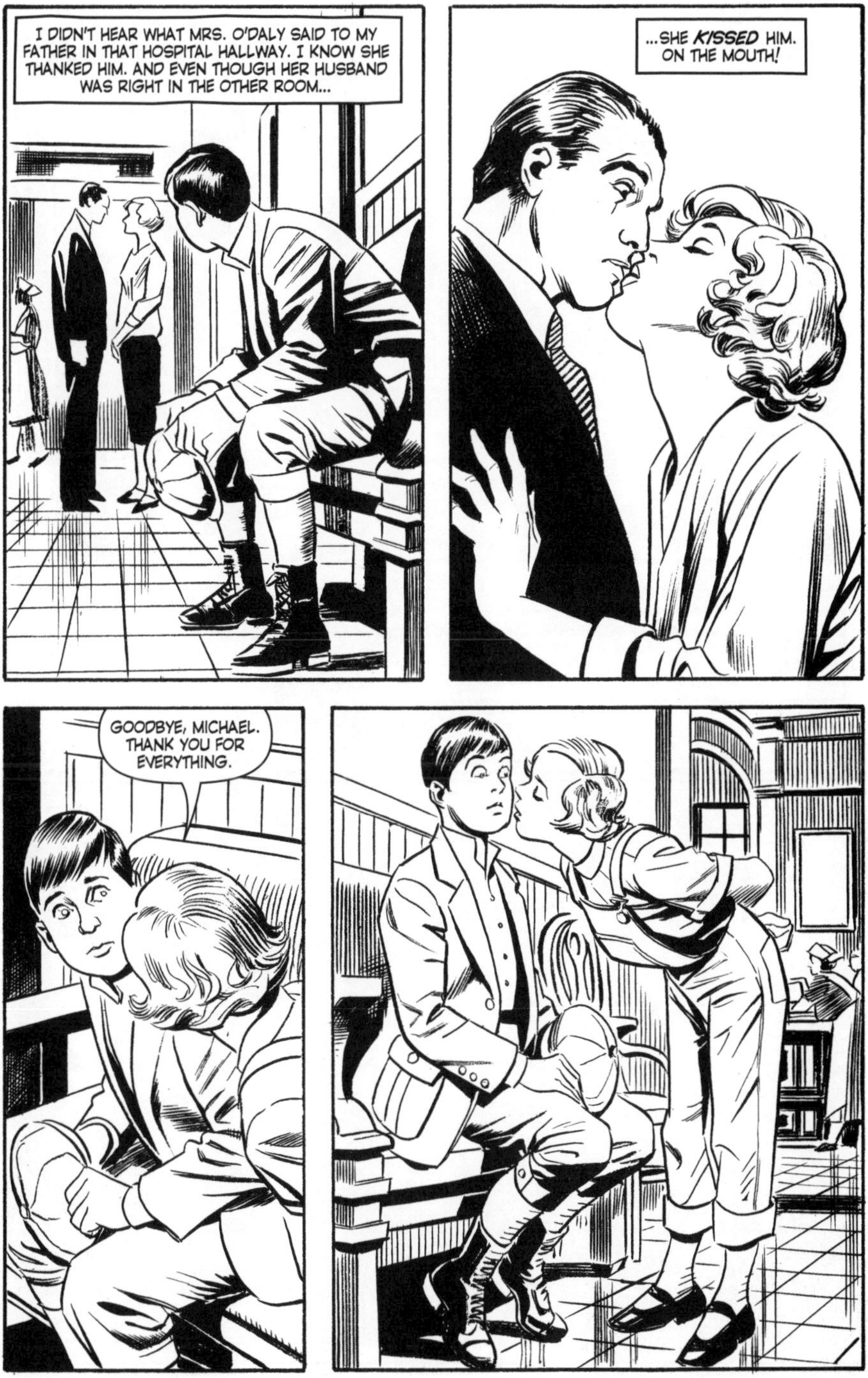
I DIDN'T HEAR WHAT MRS. O'DALY SAID TO MY FATHER IN THAT HOSPITAL HALLWAY. I KNOW SHE THANKED HIM. AND EVEN THOUGH HER HUSBAND WAS RIGHT IN THE OTHER ROOM...
...SHE KISSED HIM. ON THE MOUTH!
GOODBYE, MICHAEL. THANK YOU FOR EVERYTHING.

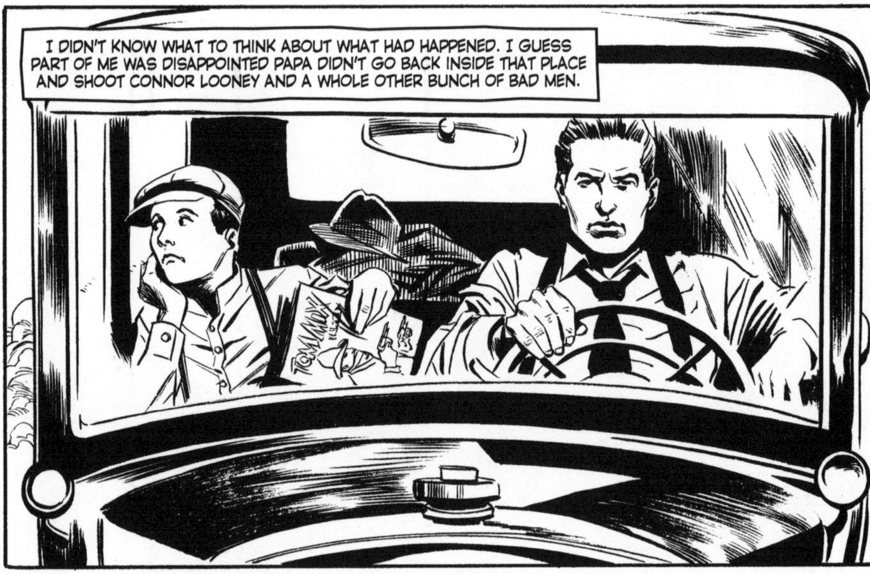
I DIDN'T KNOW WHAT TO THINK ABOUT WHAT HAD HAPPENED. I GUESS PART OF ME WAS DISAPPOINTED PAPA DIDN'T GO BACK INSIDE THAT PLACE AND SHOOT CONNOR LOONEY AND A WHOLE OTHER BUNCH OF BAD MEN.

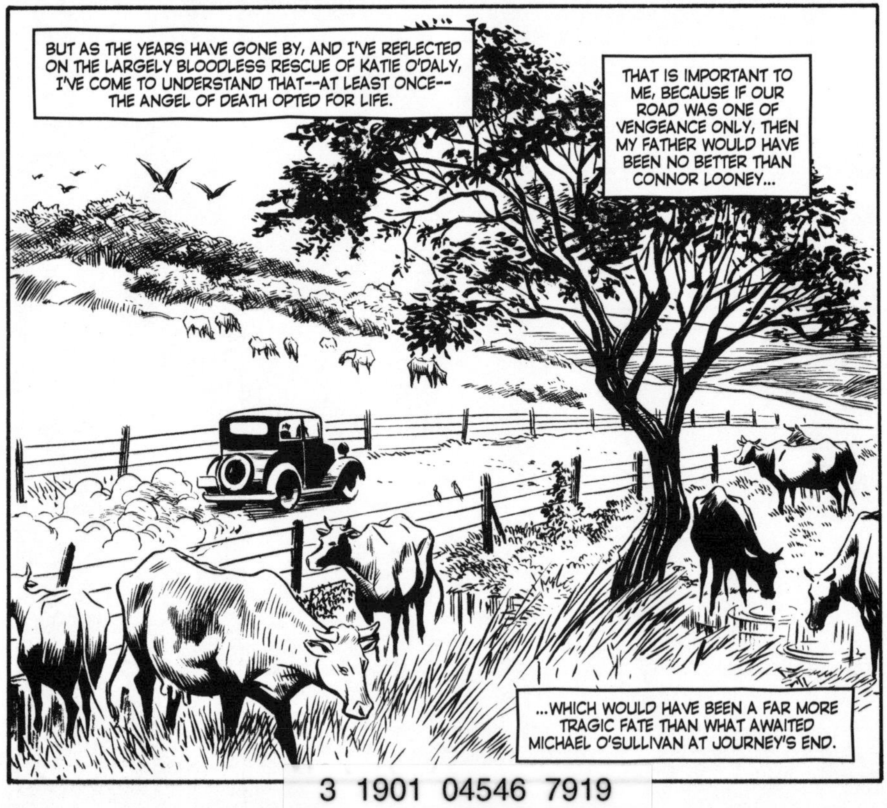
BUT AS THE YEARS HAVE GONE BY, AND I'VE REFLECTED ON THE LARGELY BLOODLESS RESCUE OF KATIE O'DALY, I'VE COME TO UNDERSTAND THAT--AT LEAST ONCE--THE ANGEL OF DEATH OPTED FOR LIFE.
THAT IS IMPORTANT TO ME, BECAUSE IF OUR ROAD WAS ONE OF VENGEANCE ONLY, THEN MY FATHER WOULD HAVE BEEN NO BETTER THAN CONNOR LOONEY...
...WHICH WOULD HAVE BEEN A FAR MORE TRAGIC FATE THAN WHAT AWAITED MICHAEL O'SULLIVAN AT JOURNEY'S END.